Religious Studies and Comparative Methodology

Religious Studies and Comparative Methodology

The Case for Reciprocal Illumination

Arvind Sharma

State University of New York Press

Published by
State University of New York Press, Albany

Printed in the United States of America

For information, address State University of New York Press
194 Washington Avenue, Suite 305, Albany, NY 12210-2384

Production by Diane Ganeles
Marketing by Susan Petrie

Library of Congress Cataloging-in-Publication Data

Sharma, Arvind.
Religious studies and comparative methodology : the case for reciprocal illumination / Arvind Sharma.
p. cm.
Includes bibliographical references and index.
ISBN 0-7914-6455-5 (hardcover: alk. paper) — ISBN 0-7914-6456-3 (pbk.: alk. paper)
1. Religion—Study and teaching. 2. Religions. I. Title.

BL41.S49 2005
200—dc22 2004016063

10 9 8 7 6 5 4 3 2 1

For John Braisted Carman

and

In Memory of

Ineke Carman

Contents

Introduction

Sometimes a throwaway line can enshrine a lot of wisdom, as when we ask a friend: "How are you," and he or she says, "Compared to what?"

Such a witticism smacks of cynicism in the course of daily life, but a fact of academic life contradicts its triviality—the enormously significant role comparison plays in the study of religion. It was central to the emergence of the study of religion as an academic discipline, and has remained a key ingredient of the discipline since its inception.

That comparable data shed light on one another is a well-known phenomenon. This book undertakes a closer examination of the phenomenon by identifying one aspect of it, referred to as "reciprocal illumination." The expression requires a word of explanation.

The academic study of religion, as it is pursued today, is a multitraditional and polymethodic discipline. That is to say, it comprises the study of such religions as Hinduism, Buddhism, Confucianism, Taoism, Judaism, Christianity, Islam, the Primal religions, and so on. Moreover, it also consists of various methods utilized in the course of such study, such as the historical, the phenomenological, the sociological, the psychological, and so on. Such a schematic presentation generates two kinds of possibilities in terms of reciprocal illumination: that of one tradition shedding light on another and that of one method doing the same in relation to another (the latter possibility being less intuitively obvious than the former).

This book focuses on such reciprocal illumination as results among the religious traditions when they are viewed in the light of one another. This is to be expected. It, however, also goes on to focus on a related phenomenon, which would initially appear less promising in this respect—namely, the reciprocal illumination that might result from studying a religious tradition alongside a methodological tradition of studying religion.

The reciprocal illumination that might result from comparing one method with another, however, is left unexamined in this book, for fear of far exceeding the limit the author has set for it in terms of size.

The typical unit for comparison used in this book is a religious tradition: say, Hinduism or Buddhism (or a component thereof); or a method, such as the historical or the phenomenological. The first part of the book is devoted to a discussion of the principle of reciprocal illumination in general, and tries to locate it in the broader framework of the academic study of religion. It serves as a propaedeutic to the two parts that follow: part 2, in which religious traditions are compared with one another; and part 3, in which religious traditions are compared with the methodological traditions that have evolved for studying them.

Part I

1

Does One Religious Tradition Help Us Understand Another?

A Wide Lens Approach

This chapter makes the claim that one religious tradition helps in understanding another, that a knowledge of tradition A helps us understand tradition B better, and that the resulting phenomenon of enhanced understanding may be described as one of "reciprocal illumination." One is tempted to wonder whether this approach by itself can constitute a vector of "dominant theorizing" in the field of the study of religion, but it is rather early in the day to raise such a question.[1] In the rest of the chapter I shall proceed, more modestly, to substantiate the claim regarding the possibility of reciprocal illumination, with examples drawn from Hinduism, Buddhism, Confucianism, Taoism, Judaism, Christianity, and Islam.

Hinduism

An understanding of the doctrine of karma is central to an understanding of the Hindu religious tradition.[2] This doctrine is variously formulated in the Hindu tradition; it reflects virtually all the intervening shades of opinion between the two polar extremes of complete free will, on the one hand,[3] and complete predeterminism on the other.[4] The standard presentation of the doctrine steers a course almost midway between these two extremes and classifies karma as consisting of three types: *āgāmi* (forthcoming karma); *sañcita* (accumulated karma); and *prārabdha* (fate). A correct grasp of the interrelationships among this cluster of concepts may hold the key to the proper understanding of the standard version of the doctrine. The following general statement about it must suffice for the time being:

> Hindu thinkers distinguish three kinds of karma: *sañcita, prārabdha* and *āgāmi. Sañcita* is all the accumulated karma of the past. Part of it is seen in the inclinations and desires, etc. *Prārabdha* is that portion of the past karma, which is responsible for the present body. *Āgāmi* is the coming karma, which includes also the karma that is being gathered at present. An apt analogy is usually given to bring home to our minds the element of freedom that karma involves. Imagine a bowman, with a quiver of arrows, taking aim at a target. He has already sent a shaft; and another arrow he is about to shoot. The bundle of arrows in the quiver on his back is the *sañcita;* the arrow he has shot is *prārabdha;* and the one, which he is about to send forth from his bow, is *āgāmi.* Of these, he has perfect control over the *sañcita* and *āgāmi;* it is only the *prārabdha* that cannot but take effect. Man has the freedom to reform his character and alter his ways. Only the past, which has begun to take effect, he has to suffer.[5]

A student of the Hindu religious tradition is likely to be familiar with this trichotomy of karma. It could be suggested, however, that these three categories seem to become clear as never before, and their experiential content explicit as never before, when one considers them in the light of the following Serenity Prayer used by Alcoholics Anonymous: "God grant me the serenity to accept the things I cannot change, courage to change the things I can, and the wisdom to know the difference."[6] The serenity to accept the things one cannot change is obviously the proper mental attitude toward *prārabdha* karma; the courage to change the things one can seems to reflect the proper attitude toward *sañcita* karma, which is in the process of becoming but has not yet become *prārabdha;* and the wisdom to know the difference between the two is the domain of *āgāmi,* or forthcoming karma.

Buddhism

One of the distinguishing features of the Mahāyāna Buddhist religious tradition is the bodhisattva ideal.[7] This ideal is typically contrasted with the Hīnayāna ideal of the arhat, who seeks nirvana only for himself, while the bodhisattva, by contrast, seeks and even postpones his own salvation for the sake of others.[8] This explanation of the difference, though popular, doesn't quite click. For the greatest gift conceived of in Buddhism is that of dharma; but how could one who had himself not realized nirvana presume to guide others to it? Such doubts about the above-mentioned description of the bodhisattva are only aggravated by the answer given by Milarepa, the eleventh/twelfth-century Tibetan mystic, to the question: could the disciples "engage in worldly duties, in a small way, for the benefit of others." Milarepa said:

> If there be not the least self-interest attached to such duties, it is permissible. But such detachment is indeed rare; and works performed for the good of others seldom succeed, if not wholly freed from self-interest. Even without seeking to benefit others, it is with difficulty that works done even in one's own interest are successful. It is as if a man helplessly drowning were to try to save another man in the same predicament. One should not be over-anxious and hasty in setting out to serve others before one has oneself realized the Truth in its fullness; to do so, would be like the blind leading the blind. As long as the sky endures, so long will there be no end of sentient beings for one to serve; and to every one comes the opportunity for such service. Till the opportunity comes, I exhort each of you to have but the one resolve, namely to attain Buddhahood for the good of all living beings.[9]

Yet both the aspects of the situation—that of the bodhisattva seeking salvation for himself and seeking it for the sake of others—seem to fall into place when the situation is viewed in the light of the following statement by Hillel:

> He used to say: If I am not for myself who is for me? And being for mine own self what am I? and if not now, when? (M. Aboth, 1.14)

Confucianism

The example from Confucianism requires some initial textual and conceptual explanation. The text involved is the 36th verse of the fourteenth book of Lun Yü, a verse that is translated by Arthur Waley as follows:

> Someone said, What about the saying "Meet resentment with inner power (*te*)"? The Master said, In that case, how is one to meet inner power? Rather, meet resentment with upright dealing and meet inner power with inner power.[10]

This translation is literal to the point of being opaque, so one may turn to another, which runs as follows:

> Someone inquired: "What do you think of 'requiting injury with kindness?' " Confucius said: "How will you then requite kindness? Requite injury with justice, and kindness with kindness." [14:36][11]

This brings the verse more within one's reach but not quite within one's grasp. The full force of the statement, however, seems to hit home when the verse is placed in the context of the Christian ethic of returning evil with good. It is when Confucius's statement is paraphrased in these terms, one may venture to suggest, that its full impact is felt, for then it would read thus: Confucius is asked, "What would you say concerning the principle that one should return evil with good?" Confucius replies, "If you return evil with good, what will you return good with? Therefore return evil with justice and good with good."

A lofty pragmatism thus replaces the unilateral altruism of the Christian teaching. One may now proceed to explore further the pragmatism generally regarded as characteristic of Confucius's teaching. The statement and its logic are clear—but its intentionality may still prove elusive. Another verse from the Analects, which possesses a similar flavor, might help:

> Tzu-kung asked, saying, what would you feel about a man who was loved by all his fellow-villagers? The Master said, that is not enough.
>
> What would you feel about a man who was hated by all his fellow-villagers? The Master said, that is not enough. Best of all would be that the good people in his village loved him and the bad hated him.[12]

These statements are not made as directly applying to the "true gentleman" but the context leaves little doubt that they are meant to.

These contours of the character of the true gentleman might appear only like outlines waiting to be filled in. Perhaps the Bhagavadgītā could help make their full import clear. The Mahābhārata war itself represents a case of returning evil with justice. The Pāṇḍavas are portrayed therein as suffering the evils perpetrated on them by the Kauravas, until they finally decide to fight back in the interest of justice. The case of the true gentleman being loved by the good and being hated by the wicked is also instructive here. I think the key point to note is that although the wicked hate the true gentleman, the true gentleman does not hate the wicked. He chastises them. In the Bhagavadgītā, Arjuna is rarely shown as hating the Kauravas; in the early chapters he is shown as pitying them, and himself, but not hating them. In the portrayal of the realized man in the Bhagavadgītā, whether as the *stithaprajña* (2.55–72), or as one who has attained *brahmanirvāṇa* (5.17–28), or as the devotee or *bhakta* (12.13–20), or as the *guṇātīta* (14), equanimity and absence of enmity are emphasized. Actually, absence of enmity is emphasized repeatedly (11.55, 18, 54), which on the face of it seems rather strange for a text in which Arjuna is exhorted to engage in combat.

This suggests the perspective that the frame of mind with which an act is performed is as important an aspect of the situation as the act itself. It may be said that Kṛṣṇa and Confucius care as much for the adverb as for the verb.

Taoism

The profoundly enigmatic Tao Te Ching sometimes leaves the reader in a state of sublime stupefaction. One senses that something profound has been said, but one is not quite sure as to what it is. Consider, for instance, the following selection from the twenty-seventh chapter:

> 27. 1. The skilful traveller leaves no traces of his wheels or footsteps; the skilful speaker says nothing that can be found fault with or blamed; the skilful reckoner uses no tallies; the skilful closer needs no bolts or bars, while to open what he has shut will be impossible; the skilful binder uses no string or knots, while to unloose what he has bound will be impossible. In the same way the sage is always skilful at saving men, and so he does not cast away any man; he is always skilful at saving things, and so he does not cast away anything. This is called "Hiding the light of his procedure."[13]

The passage is formidable; let us consider only the first line, which may be paraphrased as "One may move so well that a footprint never shows."

Lines such as these could linger on the horizon of noncomprehension for years. A few flashes of understanding may be produced by such Upanishadic statements as those that claim that the realized being moves in the world like a bird through the air or the fish through water—without leaving a trace. But moving on terra firma is a different matter. How could one move without leaving a footprint?

A parable, encountered in the context of Kāśmīra Śaivism,[14] may help provide some illumination here, although the parable itself may have found its way into Kāśmīra Śaivism from elsewhere. It goes as follows. God and devotee are walking on the seashore engaged in conversation. The devotee says to God: "As I look back upon my life I can see two sets of footprints on the shore stretching out into the past. One of them is mine and the other yours—walking beside me. But what baffles me is that there are spots where I see only one set of footprints." And God responds by saying: "That was when *I* was carrying *you*."

There could, of course, be Taoist explanations of what it means to move without leaving a footprint behind—one way of doing so would perhaps be to step into the footprints left by the previous traveler! But that an illustration from theism should seem to shed light on Taoism is not without its element of serendipitous synchronicity.

Judaism

The destruction of the Temple by the Romans in AD 70 is widely acknowledged as a turning point in the history of Judaism. For one trying to understand its significance, it is perhaps useful to distinguish between what may be called the Masada syndrome and the Jamnia syndrome.[15] As the tragic events surrounding the fall of Masada amply illustrate, military resistance to the Romans was doomed to failure. It was the rise of Rabbinic Judaism, with its beginnings in the school set up by Johanan ben Zakkai at Jamnia, which ultimately "saved" Judaism.

There is something perplexing in this course of events when, for a defeated people, peace, or rather submission, produces a victory greater than that of war. Then one day, while scouting Ḥadīth literature in preparation for a class on Islam, the following saying of the Prophet Muḥammad arrested attention—actually a well-known saying, as I soon discovered. It runs: "The ink of the scholar is more sacred that the blood of the martyr."[16] As one reads it, the events of the history of Judaism in the first century AD can be seen in a flash with all the intensity and clarity of the proverbial drowning man.

Christianity

Christianity can be puzzling to the non-Christian. Although, of course, "no concept in Christendom has enjoyed greater reputation for obscurity"[17] than the doctrine of the Trinity, for the moment the doctrine of virgin birth may be examined (Luke 1.26–31; Matthew 1.18–21). The traditional explanation that the original sin of Adam is transmitted through carnal conception and that virgin birth ensured Jesus's freedom therefrom may still seem too ingrown, that is, until insights from Islam come into play. One may begin with the recognition that the virgin birth of Jesus is accepted in the Qur'ān (3.47; 4.171). This is an interesting bit of information but by itself contributes little further to an understanding of virgin birth. It does, however, orient the mind toward Islam, wherein the doctrine of the illiteracy of the Prophet[18] had been somewhat of a puzzle, given the celebration of learning in the Qur'ān itself, which is enshrined in the very first verse revealed to the Prophet according to tradition.[19] Could the resolution of this point finally lead one back to virgin birth?

Once the fact that the Qur'ān is literally the word of God according to Islam is accepted, then the insistence by tradition on the illiteracy of the Prophet begins to make sense in the following way: the Prophet did not contaminate God's words with his own. He had need only of being a true mouthpiece. The purity of the verbal revelation of the Qur'ān is thereby ensured. The point has often been made that the proper comparison in the context of Christianity and Islam is not so much between Muḥammad and Jesus, as between the Qur'ān and Jesus. Just as the Qur'ān represents revelation in Islam, Jesus represents the revelation in Christianity—the word becoming flesh.[20] If such indeed were the case, then it is easy to see how conception by a virgin in the case of Jesus would correspond to the reception of the Qur'ān by an illiterate Prophet. In both cases the stake seems to be the same—that of safeguarding the purity of the revelation by ensuring that it was not contaminated by the channel through which it was received.

Islam

The issue of the relationship between God's will and man's will, or the issue of *qadar*, has been acknowledged as one of the subtler ones in *kalām* or Islamic theology.[21] Various points have been made in this connection: that the Qur'ān leaves the question of divine omnipotence and individual moral responsibility unreconciled, asserting both; or that in Islam, while the general supremacy of God's will is asserted theoretically, in practice men are regarded as morally responsible for their own actions. For those to whom none of these reconciliations seem quite satisfactory,[22] the study of Buddhist philosophy may provide a turning point.

Mahāyāna Buddhism developed the doctrine of the two levels of truth—the conventional and the ultimate.[23] One need not delve into the philosophical subtleties of the Mahāyāna schools to recognize the wider applicability of this distinction. We encounter it in the course of daily life all the time. In daily life we know that a currency note is really paper, but we treat it as if it were money! We know that the surface of the earth is spherical, but we move about on it as if it is flat. We do not worry about rolling off it, nor do we take its curvature into account as we go around Chicago. The idea of two levels of truth is not a mere philosophical construct; it is a given of daily existence.

If we now approach the question of God's will and man's will in Islam—equipped with this insight—the dilemma seems more amenable to resolution. Thus, ontologically everything could depend on God—could be God's will—but morally human beings could still be responsible for their own actions. The fact of gravity makes both falling and walking possible. If we trip by walking too fast, the responsibility is ours and not gravity's—though the activity of walking or falling itself remains dependent on the force of gravity.

Conclusion

We have now considered seven instances of reciprocal illumination, cases in which our understanding of a Hindu doctrine was arguably furthered by a Christian prayer; of a Buddhist ideal by a rabbinic saying; of a statement of Confucius by a Hindu text; of a line from the Tao Te Ching by Hindu theism; of a turning point in the history of Judaism by a Ḥadīth; of virgin birth by an Islamic parallel and of a theological issue in Islam by a distinction drawn from Buddhist philosophy. It does not, therefore, seem too far-fetched to maintain that one religious tradition may indeed at times help understand another, that one tradition may shed light on another, and that the horizon of the comparative study of religion may, at least occasionally, be lit up by a phenomenon we may choose to describe as reciprocal illumination.

2

Does One Religious Tradition Help Us Understand Another?

A Zoom Lens Approach

I would like to pursue this phenomenon of reciprocal illumination, identified in the preceding chapter, further in this chapter and, if possible, move in a new direction. I used the expression "reciprocal illumination" in the previous chapter to refer to occasions when our knowledge of another tradition enables us to gain a better understanding of some aspect of our *own* tradition and vice versa. And I presented seven such occasions on which this might be said to have occurred. These examples were drawn from seven so-called major world religions. The skeptical reader, however, might be inclined to consider them as no better than flashes. I shall, therefore, endeavor to offer a more sustained illustration of the phenomenon in this chapter.

I

Anyone who gains even a passing acquaintance with Buddhism soon becomes familiar with the concept of *upāyakauśalya* or skill in means. The doctrine gains greater prominence in Mahāyāna Buddhism but is not entirely absent in Theravāda Buddhism. One must distinguish here between *upāya* and *upāyakauśalya.* The full term is sometimes shortened to *upāya,* which is handy but carries with it two dangers.

The first is that it can be confused with an aspect of *karuṇā* as understood in Prajñāpāramitā literature.[1] The second is that it can be paired with *prajñā* in Buddhist Tantra.[2] In this chapter I am only concerned with *upāyakauśalya*, or skill in means as practiced by the Buddha, as one of the ten *pāramitās* to be attained by the bodhisattva in the course of his career to Buddhahood, and as an element in monastic instruction to the laity. Even when used in this context, especially in the context of the bodhisattva perfecting "skill in means" as a *pāramitā*, there is the danger of a misunderstanding, which must be avoided. I shall not be using the term to indicate the skill the bodhisattva employs in relation to his *own* means to salvation. The term has been understood in this sense at least in the Aṣṭasāhasrikaprajñāpāramitā,[3] in the sense of the skill with which the bodhisattva perfects his *own* virtues. In this chapter the term is used exclusively in the context of imparting knowledge of the highest religious insights, especially as understood within Buddhism, to others. One must proceed with the clear recognition that although the concept of *upāyakauśalya* is more self-consciously elaborated in Mahāyāna Buddhism, especially in the Saddharmapuṇḍarīka Sūtra, it is also already clearly identifiable in Theravāda Buddhism.

> In spite of the paucity of references in Pali writings, it is remarkable that *upāya* here assumes a double aspect, referring to the activities both of aspiring monk and good teacher, skilled in the ways of helping others across the spiritual threshold. Variously emphasized, this double usage is frequently found in early Mahāyāna, although no direct textual lineage should be assumed. Other Pali usage is either non-technical or late and incidental. This relative inattention to the term in Pali texts does not mean, however, that the way of thinking assumed in this terminology is foreign either to Theravāda Buddhism in its fully developed form or to the earliest Buddhists in general. Admittedly, there is no direct evidence that the Buddha himself made use of this specific term to explain the way his teaching was to be understood. Nevertheless, there are many indications that his message was presented with conscious, pragmatic skill. In support of this, one need only think of such well known scriptural similes as the raft, the poisoned arrow, the pith, and the water snake, in which the provisional and practical nature of the Buddha's teachings is made clear.[4]

I will not abuse the patience of the reader by alluding to the references to it in Mahāyāna Buddhism but will now proceed to fix the sense in which it has largely been understood within Buddhism and in which I employ it here. Suffice it to say then that

> UPĀYA is a Sanskrit and Pali term meaning "device, stratagem," or "means." The term has a technical function in Buddhism, most especially in the Mahāyāna, where it is also frequently used in the compound *upāyakauśalya* ("skill in means"). In Buddhist usage, it refers to certain manners of teaching or forms of practice that may be employed along the path to final release, and in which a Buddha or *bodhisattva* is especially skilled. Often, these involve the skilful evaluation of the spiritual capacities of beings on the part of a Buddha or *bodhisattva,* and a concomitant revelation of just that degree of truth that is most beneficial to the specific religious needs of the devotee.[5]

The point I wish to emphasize here is that the "skill in means" pertains to the teacher; it is a quality of the instructor, the teacher, the monk, the guide, the Buddha, and the bodhisattva.

II

If we now turned our attention to Hinduism we will find that no such term is applied to the guru. When the qualifications of a guru are discussed in Hinduism, they are said to be twofold according to the Muṇḍakopaniṣad (1.2.12).

> For the sake of this knowledge, let him only approach, with sacrificial fuel in hand, a teacher who is learned in the scriptures and established in Brahman.[6]

The key terms here are (1) *śrotriya,* one who knows the *śruti* or the revealed scriptures and (2) *brahma-niṣṭha,* one who is firmly established in the experiential realization of Brahman or the ultimate reality.

This would then lead one to discount the Hindu tradition in terms of the doctrine of skill in means. If, however, the gaze is shifted from the master to the disciple, one does come across a doctrine as popular within Hinduism as *upāyakauśalya* is within Buddhism, namely, the doctrine of *adhikāra-bheda,* sometimes referred to only as *adhikāra*. The following passage constitutes a useful introduction to the concept:

> There are various cults in Hinduism and a variety of creeds. But conflict among them is avoided by the twin doctrines of *adhikāra* and *iṣṭa*. *Adhikāra* means eligibility. A person's faith is determined by the kind of man he is. There is no use, for instance, in putting a boy in the Honours Class, if he is fit only for the Pass Course. What is meat for one may be poison for another. A man's creed depends upon his *adhikāra*. And it is his eligibility that determines his *iṣṭa* or ideal. Hinduism prescribes to each according to his needs. Hence it is not to be considered as a single creed or cult, but as a league of religions, a fellowship of faiths.[7]

Adhikāra-bheda thus refers to difference in eligibility. Individuals differ with regard to the kind and nature of spiritual teaching appropriate for them, or, to put it in other terms, the path they are eligible for, the path to which they have a right, or to the path that is right. A little reflection will suggest that this is the Hindu counterpart to the Buddhist "skill in means." The apparent difference arises from a difference in perspective. This will become clearer after the following exposition of the doctrine—perhaps as lucid as any:

> The doctrine of *adhikāri-bheda* is an application of this epistemological notion of absolute relativity to the specifically religious sphere. The difference of *adhikāra* or spiritual status is not necessarily a gradation; and so far as it is a gradation it does not suggest any relation of higher and lower that implies contempt or envy. The notion of *adhikāra* in fact means in the first instance just an acceptance of fact or realism in the spiritual sphere. It is a question of duty rather than of rights in this sphere; and a person should be anxious to discover his actual status in order that he may set before himself just such duties as he can efficiently perform in spirit. It is a far greater misfortune here to over-estimate one's status than to underestimate it. A higher status does not mean greater opportunity for spiritual work, since work here means not outward achievement, but an "inwardizing" or deepening of the spirit. Again, from the standpoint of toleration, one not only respects the inner achievement of a person admitting an inferior status, but can whole-heartedly identify oneself with it; the highest *adhikārin* should feel it a privilege to join in the worship of the humblest. There is aristocracy in the spiritual polity; spiritual value is achieved by the strong and is much too sacred a thing

to be pooled. At the same time every individual has his sacred *svadharma* and has equal opportunity with everyone else to realize or "inwardize" it.[8]

III

What is common to both the approaches, though known by different names, is "the skilful evaluation of the spiritual capacities of beings" and "a concomitant revelation of just that degree of truth which is most beneficial to the specific spiritual needs of the devotee." Two examples of its actual operation, one drawn from Buddhism and the other from Hinduism, will perhaps help to further the comparison.

Let us examine the classic story of Kisā Gotamī in this connection:

> She came from a poor family in Sāvatthi. Gotamī was her name—she was called Kisā because of her thinness. She was married into a rich family, by whom she was disdainfully treated; but as soon as she bore a son she was shown respect. The boy, however, died when just old enough to run about; his mother, distraught with grief, fearful lest the dead child should be taken from her, went about with him on her hip, seeking medicine to revive his life. People laughed at her, until one wise man, realizing her condition, directed her to the Buddha. The Buddha asked her to bring him a mustard seed from a house where no one had yet died. In the course of her search for the impossible her frenzy left her, and having grasped the truth, she laid the child in the charnel field, and returning to the Master begged admission to the Order. She became a *sotāpanna*, and soon after, when her insight was developed, the Buddha appeared before her in a blaze of radiance and, listening to his words, she became an arahant.[9]

It should be noted that the Buddha practised "deception" in this case; sublime deception maybe, salvific deception maybe, but still deception. Nevertheless,

> While the means used to ensure deliverance may thus seem to involve an element of deception, or at least, of withholding the full truth, the discrepancy between the forms in which the message is couched and its ultimate meaning is understood to arise owing to the restive ignorance of the living beings that

> receive it. The sincerity and the consistency of the Dharma regarded from the point of view of the Buddha are considered to be unimpeached.[10]

We may now turn to the following dialogue between a master and a disciple in the late medieval Advaita digest, called the Advaita-Bodha-Dīpikā.

> 115. D.: Master, not only I but also all others directly experience this world of sentient beings and insentient things and take it as proven and real. How is it said to be unreal?
>
> 116. M.: The world with all its contents is only superimposed upon the Ether of Consciousness.
>
> D.: By what is it superimposed?
>
> M.: By Ignorance of the Self.
>
> D.: How is it superimposed?
>
> M.: As a painting of sentient beings and insentient things presents a scene upon a background.
>
> 117. D.: Whereas the scriptures declare that this entire universe was created by the will of Iswara, you say it is by one's own ignorance. How can these two statements be reconciled?
>
> 118. M.: There is no contradiction. What the scriptures say that Iswara by means of Maya, created the five elements and mixed them up in diverse ways to make the diversities of the universe, is all false.
>
> D.: How can the scriptures say what is false?
>
> M.: They are guides to the Ignorant and do not mean what appears on the surface.
>
> D.: How is that?
>
> M.: Man, having forgotten his true nature of being the all-perfect Ether of Consciousness, is deluded by Ignorance into identifying himself with a body, etc. and re-

> garding himself as an insignificant individual of mean capacity. If to him it is told that he is the creator of the whole universe, he will flout the idea and refuse to be guided. So coming down to his level the scriptures posit an Iswara as the creator of the universe. But it is not the truth to the competent seeker. You are now mistaking the nursery tale for metaphysical truth.[11]

One shouldn't be surprised if later on the same text avers that the scriptures never lie! What light have these two concepts shed on each other? Can it be said to be the case that they have? In a nutshell, it is *adhikārabheda* that necessitates *upāyakauśalya*. It is because people stand at different levels on the path of spiritual progress and because they occupy different rungs on the spiritual ladder that the teachings have to be adjusted to their level. And the skill in means consists precisely in presenting the insights to them in such a way that they become meaningful to them at their own level. The Hindu version of the doctrine focuses on the differences among the aspirants; the Buddhist version on the skill of the teacher in adapting the teaching to the needs of the spiritual aspirants. The two doctrines, when placed in apposition, clarify each other. They are reciprocally illuminating.

But the point I wish to make cuts deeper. The concept of reciprocal illumination, as I see it, is not confined to merely stimulating such a realization. It will be recalled that I defined it in terms of our encounter with another tradition deepening our understanding of our *own* tradition, (although a similar deepening of our understanding of another tradition is not ruled out by any means). How has the above illustration advanced a Hindu's understanding of Hinduism and a Buddhist's understanding of Buddhism?

IV

Hinduism is known and distinguished by the acceptance of the Vedas as its foundational scriptures. It calls itself *vaidika*, based on the Vedas, and the Hindu schools of philosophy are considered orthodox on account of at least their nominal acceptance of Vedic authority. The two schools of Hindu thought that are allied most closely to the Vedas set even greater store by Vedic authority or *śrutiprāmaṇya*. One would therefore expect the Hindu tradition to be quite dogmatic in the matter of Vedic authority. But as every student of Hinduism knows, although Hinduism can be fairly dogmatic about *asserting* Vedic authority, it is not equally dogmatic about *applying* it. It is, in this sense, dogmatic in *theory*—in upholding Vedic authority—but not dogmatic in *practice*, on account of the principle of *adhikāra-bheda*, or *upāya*.

How is our understanding of Buddhism advanced through reciprocal illumination? Buddhism has often been considered universalistic in contrast to Hinduism, which has at times been considered ethnic. Indeed, Buddhism has often been applauded for its universalistic ethic. This is especially significant, as the term *svadharma* was used in expounding the concept of *adhikāra-bheda* and some scholars of Buddhism have commented that "Buddhists do not even have the term *svadharma*—behaving in the manner appropriate to one's station. Their values are universalistic; what is right for one will be right for all."[12] However, to be universalistic means to be capable of being applied to all, but everyone is different; so, if people differ in their spiritual capacities, can what is right for one invariably be right for all—an assumption inherent in the concept of *upāyakauśalya*? The pieces do not seem to fit, and this forces us to take a closer look at the tradition. Such a search leads one to identify a passage such as the following:

> "Is a Tathagata compassionate towards all living breathing creatures?"
>
> "Yes, headman," answered the Lord.
>
> "*But does the Lord teach Dhamma in full to some, but not likewise to others?*
>
> "Now, what do you think, headman? Suppose a farmer had three fields, one excellent, one mediocre, and one poor with bad soil. When he wanted to sow the seed, which field would he sow first?"
>
> "He would sow the excellent one, then the mediocre one. When he had done that, he might or might not sow the poor one with the bad soil. And why? Because it might do if only for cattle fodder."
>
> "In the same way, headman, my monks and nuns are like the excellent field. . . ." "Then my men and women lay followers are like the mediocre field. To these too I teach Dhamma. . . ." "Then recluses, Brahmins and wanderers of other sects than mine are like the poor field with the bad soil. To these too I teach Dhamma. . . ."[13]

V

In this chapter I have tried to develop the suggestion further that the study of religion may now be ripe for moving in a new direction. Living as we do in an age of religious pluralism, we are all aware of the existence of other religious traditions. At the same time, attempts to deprive these traditions of their autonomy through various forms of attempted universalization—ecumenical, irenic, or academic—have not succeeded in destroying their boundaries. Most serious students of comparative religion emerge from their study with a deeper appreciation of both the differences and the similarities among these traditions. Reciprocal illumination, as a method, respects the integrity of each tradition. It allows it to speak for itself, and the other tradition to hear for itself. It allows each tradition to be studied on its own terms, yet at the same time it renders such a respectful study of one tradition meaningful for another, in terms of the other tradition.

The point can be pressed even further. An appreciation of reciprocal illumination reveals that while in some respects the two traditions may seem asymmetrical in form, they may turn out to be symmetrical in content; and though they may seem symmetrical in form, they may in fact be asymmetrical in content.

Hinduism has no single founder. In that sense, it is not a historical religion. Buddhism possesses a historical founder—namely, in the form of Gautama, the Buddha. Thus, they are asymmetrical in form, yet in terms of their teachings both the traditions are ahistorical. The point may be substantiated with the help of two citations. The first deals with Hinduism and constitutes the opening remarks of D. S. Sarma's *Hinduism Through the Ages*.

> One of the characteristics of ancient Hindu thought is its indifference to history. In discussing the contents of a book, for instance, ancient and even mediaeval Indian writers care very little for the date or the life of the author. They care more for the truth of experience or the soundness of doctrine than for the circumstances that gave it birth. What Sir Charles Eliot says of the religious mind in general is particularly applicable to them. "The true religious mind does not care for the history of religion, just as, among us, the scientific mind does not dwell on the history of science." But there is no doubt that the Hindu writers went to one extreme in ignoring history altogether while modern Western writers go to the other extreme in making too much of the historical treatment of thought and

> art and digging at the roots of a tree instead of enjoying its flower and fruit.[14]

The second is drawn from the Pali canon, and it emphasizes the ahistorical character, not of the Buddha, but of his insights.

> Whether Buddhas arise, O priests, or whether Buddhas do not arise, it remains a fact and the fixed and necessary constitution of being, that all its constituents are transitory. This fact a Buddha discovers and masters, and when he has discovered and mastered it, he announces, teaches, publishes, proclaims, discloses, minutely explains, and makes it clear, that all the constituents of being are transitory.
>
> Whether Buddhas arise, O priests, or whether Buddhas do not arise, it remains a fact and the fixed and necessary constitution of being, that all its constituents are misery. This fact a Buddha discovers and masters, and when he has discovered and mastered it, he announces, teaches, publishes, proclaims, discloses, minutely explains, and makes it clear, that all the constituents of being are misery.
>
> Whether Buddhas arise, O priests, or whether Buddhas do not arise, it remains a fact and the fixed and necessary constitution of being, that all its elements are lacking in an Ego. This fact a Buddha discovers and masters, and when he has discovered and mastered it, he announces, teaches, publishes, proclaims, discloses, minutely explains, and makes it clear, that all the elements of being are lacking in an Ego.[15]

Now the next point. In both Mahāyāna Buddhism and Advaita Vedānta the process of liberation is ultimately illusory. There is a certain symmetry here, as illustrated by the following passages. Edward Conze remarks, after describing the Indian rope trick in some detail:

> The whole process of salvation is of the same nature as this conjuring trick. Witness this dialogue between the Lord Buddha and Subhuti. "Lord: *'Just as if, Subhuti, a clever magician, or magician's apprentice, would conjure up at the cross roads a great crowd of people; and, after he had conjured them up, he would make that great crowd of people vanish again. What do you think, Subhuti, has there anyone been killed by anyone, or murdered, or destroyed, or made to vanish?'* Subhuti: *'No, indeed, Lord!'* Lord: *'Even so a Bodhisattva, a great being, leads innumerable and incalculable be-*

> *ings to Nirvana, and yet there is not any being that has been led to Nirvana, nor anyone who has led one. If a Bodhisattva hears this, and does not tremble, is not frightened, nor terrified, then he is to be known as 'armed with the great armour.'* "[16]

And in Advaita Vedānta:

> The duality of teacher and pupil is also included in this list of dualities, which are not ultimately real. Yes; even these and why, the teaching that is imparted belong to the region of mitthyā. The guru, the siśya and the upadeśa, all belong to the vyāvahārika world, which will all be sublated on the dawn of jñāna. Even the śrutis, the Vedic texts teaching the ultimate truth pertain to the predicament of duality and are annulled in the last resort in the unitary experience of transcendental aloneness. The Vedas too cease to be Vedas in that stage (*yatra vedā avedāh*).[17]

The asymmetry lies in the fact that while *śruti* is *śruti*-annulling, Buddhahood is not Buddha-annulling. Since the *śruti* is impersonal, realization can be impersonalized in Hinduism in a way it is harder to do in Buddhism, as its founder the Buddha was a person, the doctrine of *anatta* (no soul) notwithstanding.

VI

These are interesting points and could be pursued further. My point in introducing them has been to illustrate the thesis that it is possible to impart a new direction to religious studies; that this can be done by recognizing the phenomenon that can be called "reciprocal illumination"; that from its recognition one can move a step toward to its application as a method in a study of religion; and that this method may help overcome the current impasse in the study of religion in which one is either encouraged to contemplate a religious tradition only in its phenomenological virginity, or invited to molest it by subjecting it to an array of reductionistic methodologies abhorrent to its followers.[18]

3

Reciprocal Illumination as a Formal Concept

Comparative religion—or, more properly, the comparative study of religion—has antecedents in the ancient world[1] but is usually believed to have come into its own in its modern sense around the middle of the nineteenth century.[2] The decade from 1859 to 1869 saw the transformation of Max Müller's celebrated statement "he who knows one, knows none" from an epigram into a method.

> The method that resulted can be characterized as scientific, critical, historical and comparative: scientific because of its inductive pattern and its belief in universal laws of cause and effect, and because of its distrust of obvious a priori arguments; critical because of its fundamental attitude to evidence; historical because of the new sense of continuity between the past and the present to which it gave rise; comparative because it claimed comparison to be the basis of all knowledge. It compared the known with the unknown, it compared phenomena in apparent temporal sequence, it compared phenomena belonging to different areas but having features in common. In all this, in true scientific spirit, it set out to determine, with regard to religion, the genus "religion" which underlay the species "the religions."[3]

I would like to focus here on the comparative dimension of the method, which indeed was so prominent as to lend its name to the enterprise of comparative religion itself.

I

It is so obvious as to be banal to state that only the commensurable may be properly compared. Folklore no less than scholarship questions the wisdom of comparing apples and oranges. But while it is obvious that the similar should be compared, it is not equally obvious as to what items may be considered similar. This point will, I hope, gain in clarity as we proceed. It is enough that it be recognized at this point. I shall revert to it later.

Comparative religion, as it has been practiced virtually to this day, arranges comparable material according to topic, that is, thematically. Mircea Eliade's book *From Primitives to Zen: A Thematic Sourcebook of the History of Religions* exemplifies this approach;[4] the works of G. van der Leeuw[5] and W. B. Kristensen,[6] which come somewhat earlier, are also good examples. Eliade arranges the contents according to themes such as Gods, Goddesses, and Supernatural Beings; Myths of Creation and Origin; and so on. Within these major themes he mentions subsidiary themes. Thus, the chapter "Man and the Sacred" lists themes such as types of sacrifice, prayers and hymns, patterns of initiation, and so on. This same approach is represented in its more rudimentary form in elementary textbooks that speak of "founders,"[7] "sacred writings," and so forth, of various religions. What is important to bear in mind is the fact that the difference between the thematic approach of an elementary textbook and that of the more sophisticated texts such as Eliade's is one of scale rather than of principle: the principle is that of classification of comparables.

What are obviously comparable phenomena, however, may on inspection turn out to be otherwise. To begin with a simple terminological example, the word *dharma* is used in modern India to translate the English word "religion." Hence, in any comparative study, the words would be put alongside one another. A little reflection will suggest, however, that the comparability may be deceptive. This is revealed in an anecdote referred to by Radhakrishnan:

> It is related of an Indian Christian convert who attended the church on Sunday and the Kali temple on Friday, that when the missionary gentleman asked him whether he was not a Christian, he replied, "Yes, I am, but does it mean that I have changed my religion?"[8]

In the version of the anecdote I heard, the convert says: "Yes, but does it mean that I have changed my *dharma*?" and this serves to illustrate the point that *dharma* may at times properly mean culture rather than religion. More generally then, one might distinguish between a literal and a cultural translation. What is called Hindu polytheism is really polymorphism, and a word had to be coined in Hindi to translate the word "polytheism."

I would like to suggest that comparisons can be of two kinds—homonymous and synonymous. Homonymous comparisons are between phenomena, which appear similar but are really different, just as homonyms are words with similar sounds but with different meanings. Synonymous comparisons are between phenomena that appear different but possess similar significance in each tradition, just as synonyms are words that have different sounds but are similar in meaning. Old comparative religion has been oriented toward making homonymous comparisons, but new comparative religion —at least, the kind I would like to practice—will be oriented toward making synonymous comparisons. Now, when synonymous comparisons are made between two traditions, they often result in what I like to call reciprocal illumination. That is to say, one tradition sheds light on the other. But here we must draw a distinction between goal and method.

II

A distinction between homonymous and synonymous comparisons was proposed in the previous section. In this section I shall now proceed to offer some examples of what I, until shown the error of my ways, regard as synonymous comparisons constitutive of the new comparative religion. Then I shall try to demonstrate how such comparisons may result in reciprocal illumination.

For my first example I would like to take up the claim to or the conferment of divinity on the Brahmins within the Hindu tradition. As Professor A. L. Basham states, "[T]he Brāhmaṇ was a great divinity in human form."[9] To stop here, however, in the context of Hindu culture would be to stop short. For Brahmins were not the only ones who claimed divinity; it was also claimed by kings who took on such titles as *deva* or God.[10] Indeed, the various questions put by the *yakṣa* to Yudhiṣṭhira in the famous episode in the third book of the Mahābhārata includes two analogous questions: (1) wherein does the divinity of the Brahmins lie? and (2) wherein does the divinity (*devatvam*) of the Kṣatriyas lie?[11]

Thus divinity was claimed by both the Brahmins and the Kṣatriyas. A little investigation yields the finding that the divinity claimed by the Brahmins was on the basis of birth, but the divinity claimed by the kings was on the basis of functions. Thus it is said: Because the king is like the lord of men he was like Indra, because he ordered the execution of criminals, he was like Yama, and so on. It may be argued that royalty was also meant to be by birth as well. This may be true in theory; but in practice one hears of Śūdra dynasties (the Nandas), Vaiśya dynasties (Guptas), degraded Kṣatriya dynasties (Maurayas), and Brāhmaṇa dynasties (Śuṅgas). One even hears of Niṣāda kings, who were sometimes considered "Untouchables." Thus the *political* reality of ancient India may have been such that it was difficult to always lay claim to royalty by right of birth, but the *social* reality of ancient India may have been such that priesthood was preeminently based on birth.

This suggests that the proper parallel to the claim to divine right by the Brahmins in India is *not* to be found in similar claims, if any, made by Christian priests, but rather in the divine right of kings—a claim with which the history of medieval Europe has made us familiar and which makes the Brahmanical claim look less absurd. For in the West, unlike India, the priestly vocation could be adopted by choice and was not conferred by birth, whereas in India the priestly vocation was by birth, or at least far more often by birth than by choice.[12] But although the claim to royalty may also have rested on birth, the claim became hard to sustain. Thus, once a synonymous comparison between the divine right of Brahmins in India and the divine right of kings in the West is instituted, it is reciprocally illuminating. It becomes easier to see how the Brahmins came to claim the same privilege in the Hindu milieu as the kings did in the medieval West, and it is easier to see in the Western case how the issue of the privileges of birth had a more political color to it, while in India it had and continues to have a religious color.[13]

My next example is a more elaborate one and pertains to resurrection. Most historians, at least most Christian historians, claim that the resurrection of Jesus was a unique event. This is not to say that there are no previous accounts of the dying and rising gods—but these are considered myths by Christian historians. Nor is it to say that there are no accounts, prior to Jesus, of the dead coming back to life. However, it is argued that although this is remarkable, such people were human and not divine—unlike Jesus, who did not merely rise from the dead but was raised from the dead by God.

There is, however, a detail from the last days of the life of the famous Tibetan saint Milarepa (11th/12th century) that provides an interesting point of comparison with that of Jesus. Milarepa's story is not a myth in the usual sense, as his biography is a famous text of Tibetan Buddhism. Nor is he an ordinary human being; the Buddhist tradition would accord him the status of a saint, or even a bodhisattva.

The facts regarding the resurrected body of Jesus are well known and may be briefly recapitulated. The resurrected body of Jesus could perform certain physiological functions; it could eat (Luke 24:41f.) but it could also perform parapsychological feats like passing through walls (John 20:26). Despite this, it could be witnessed by others (1 Cor. 15:6) and even touched, as by Thomas (John 20:27). It bore the signs of crucifixion (John 20:27), but these could be disguised (John 20:15, Luke 24:15f.). It appeared to Paul (Act 9, 1 Cor. 15:8) and to the apostles (John 21:7ff.; Matthew 28:16), and it ascended (Luke 24:51, Mark 16:19, Acts 1:9), inducing the belief that God had raised it (1 Cor. 15:15). As the sheets were beheld lying there by John (John 20:6), it obviously had a physical dimension to it, even though sometimes Jesus would prevent people from touching it (John 20:17, Luke 24:39). But it is equally clear that it possessed an ethereal aspect to it as well. If we are psychophysical organisms, Jesus was a parapsychophysical organism after his resurrection.

Let us now turn to the life of Milarepa. It appears that toward the end of his life Milarepa was poisoned by a learned rival. The biography refers to his death quite explicitly: "Thus did Jetsun pass away at the age of eighty-four years, on the fourteenth day of the last of the three winter months of the wood-hare year (A.D. 1135), at dawn."[14]

But the account does not end here. It so happened that Milarepa's favorite disciple Rechung, was not around when Milarepa passed away. Rechung, however, had had a strong premonition about the event and rushed to see Milarepa. By the time he arrived, Milarepa had passed away. However, he was prevented from approaching the body of Milarepa by some of the "most recently accepted disciples" who "did not know Rechung." Greatly grieved at this, Rechung in his agony offered a hymn to his guru. It is called the "Seven Branches of Offering"[15] in the biography.

The narrative proceeds to cite the hymn, and states that even when those "brethren in the faith, as well as female lay-disciples" who knew Rechung, "came to welcome him . . . he felt so deeply hurt at having been prevented from approaching Jetsun's body by those disciples who did not know him that he would not move until he had finished his hymn of prayer."[16] Now follows the crucial part of the account:

> So great was the force and earnestness of Rechung's faith that Jetsun, who had already sunk into the state of the Clear Light,

> reanimated his corpse and addressed these words to the most recently accepted disciples: "O ye younger disciples, act not thus; one lion is far more to be preferred than a hundred tigers. Such [a lion] is my son Rechung. Permit him to approach me." Then to Rechung he said, "And thou, my son Rechung, take it not so much to heart, but come near to thy Father."
>
> At first every one present was startled and filled with wonder; then this feeling gave way to one of gladness. Rechung himself caught hold of Jetsun, and burst forth in a flood of tears; and so overcome was he with excess of alternate joy and sorrow that for a while he swooned. When Rechung had regained consciousness, he found all the disciples and followers seated round about the front of the cremation-house. Meanwhile, Jetsun had risen in the Indestructible Body, into which are merged both the spiritual body and the phenomenal body. The flames of the funeral pyre assumed the shape of an eight-petalled lotus, and from the midst of this, like the stamens of the blossom, Jetsun sat up, one of his knees half raised and his right hand extended in the preaching attitude pressing down the flames. "Listen," he said, "Unto this old man's last testament." Then, both as a reply to Rechung's prayer and as his final teachings to his disciples, with his left hand placed against his cheek, he sang this final hymn concerning the Six Essential Commandments from the midst of the funeral pyre, in a divine voice issuing from the Indestructible Body:[17]

"Having uttered these words," the text tells us, Jetsun sank "in a trance into the Clear Light."[18]

Then some hymns were chanted by *ḍākinīs*. "When the chanting of the hymns was finished, evening had set in, and the funeral fire had burnt itself out, so that the cremation-house was empty again."[19] The account continues:

> The disciples then opened the door of the cremation-house [that the ashes might cool quickly]; and, being in high expectation of precious reliques of wonderful shapes and virtue, all slept [that night] with their heads pointed towards the cremation-house. Early in the morning, Rechung dreamt that five *Dakinis*, dressed like celestial *Yoginis*, in robes of silk and adorned with bone and precious ornaments, surrounded by many attendants of various colours, fair, yellow, red, green, and blue, were worshipping at the funeral pyre and making

> various offerings. The five chief *Dakinis* were taking out a sphere of Light from within the cremation-house. For a while he was fascinated with the sight. Then it suddenly occurred to him that the *Dakinis* might actually be removing the reliques and ashes. So he went to see; and the *Dakinis* all flew away. Calling his brethren in the Faith, he went inside the cremation-house; and then it was seen that the ashes and bones had been completely swept away. They saw not even a particle of dust or ash. Rechung became very sad; and, addressing the *Dakinis*, he demanded of them a portion of the reliques, for the benefit of human beings. The *Dakinis*, in reply, said, "As for you, the chief disciples, ye have obtained the best of all reliques; for ye have obtained the Truths, by which ye have found the *Dharma-Kaya* in your own minds. If that be insufficient, and ye must have something more, ye had better pray earnestly to Jetsun, and he may possibly grant you something. As regardeth the rest of mankind, why, they have not valued Jetsun as much as a firefly, although he was like the Sun and the Moon. They do not deserve any of his reliques at all; these are our own special property." After saying this, the *Dakinis* remained stationary in the sky above.[20]

What follows is essentially an account of Jetsun's ascension to the realm of happiness wherein the Bhagavān Akṣobhya reigns—namely, the Eastern Paradise (as distinguished from the Western Paradise of Amitābha).

The parallels between the two accounts are striking, and, at the *homonymous level*, a comparison reveals the following points. First of all, there is no recorded case of Jesus appearing simultaneously to people at different places, sometimes referred to as bilocation or multiple location, either prior to his death and resurrection or with his resurrected body. The case of Milarepa is different. When Milarepa was ill he asked to be carried to a particular place where he wanted to die.

> Thereupon, some of the younger disciples went on ahead, but they found that Jetsun had already reached the Cave of Brilche (Cow-Yak's Tongue). The elder disciples, who followed later, escorted and attended another Jetsun. Another Jetsun was at the "Poison-to-Touch Rock," manifesting the phenomena of illness. While the one Jetsun was being escorted and served by the devout followers on the journey to Chubar, another was

> preaching to those who had assembled for a final sermon at the Red Rock. And, again, to every one who remained at home and made religious offering in farewell to Jetsun, a Jetsun appeared.[21]

After his resurrection, nobody mistook Jesus for anyone else, nor did anyone mistake the identity of Milarepa. But when Milarepa de-animated himself after meeting Rechung, it is said that "although the disciples assembled there beheld the same funeral pyre, the corpse itself appeared to one as Gaypa-Dorje, to another as Demchog, to a third as Sang-Do, and to a fourth as Dorje-Pa-Mo."[22] There was similar speculation about Jesus but *before* resurrection.

The various points of comparison may be presented as follows.

1. Although Jesus' body was para-physical, it couldn't precipitate itself simultaneously at many places, nor did it appear as other than Jesus to the onlookers, unlike Milarepa. It is clear, however, that in their *resurrected form* the identities of both Jesus and Milarepa were clearly distinguishable.
2. Jesus is believed to have preached *after* resurrection (Luke 24:45), so did Milarepa.
3. Both Jesus and Milarepa ascended to another world.
4. Both parted with their garments, Jesus with his tunic (John 19:23) and Milarepa with his cotton mantle, which the disciples were to divide among themselves in strips.[23]
5. Both made forecasts about the behaviour of their disciples; Jesus about how he will be betrayed by Judas and disowned by Peter, Milarepa about how Rechung will soon arrive.[24]
6. Both Judas, who betrayed Jesus, and the Geshe, who poisoned Milarepa, repent. Judas threw away the bribe and hanged himself (Matthew 27:3) and the Geshe "placing Jetsun's feet upon his head and shedding tears profusely . . . wailed . . . in repentance."[25]
7. It was in the power of both Jesus and Milarepa to avoid the suffering in a sense, but both accepted it—Jesus did not wish to act contrary to the will of God (Matthew 26:42). Milarepa could have transferred his karma but did not.[26]
8. Both felt before dying that their work was finished. Jesus says so (John 19:30), so does Milarepa.[27]

9. Jesus helped feed people after his resurrection (John 21:614); so did Milarepa though in a different way.[28]

10. Both Jesus and Milarepa had difficulty in dealing with the karma, so to say, of those involved in their "death." In one gospel account Judas alone gets the bread and Jesus commands him to go and do what he must (John 13:21–30). In the same account Satan is described as entering Judas, which again highlights the problematic nature of the question. When the Geshe asks to be forgiven for poisoning Milarepa, Milarepa could only say: "With respect to thy present transgression, earnestly will I pray that no evil *karma* may overtake thee and that thou mayst not suffer because of it."[29] No definite promise is made.

I have chosen the resurrection account of Jesus and Milarepa for homonymous comparison to demonstrate how remarkably similar they are, despite some differences. Yet, although Christianity could not exist without Christ's resurrection, it would make little difference to the history of Buddhism if Milarepa had not resurrected himself. However, there would have been no Buddhism if the Buddha had not *taught*. Hence the synonymous correspondence is between the rising of Jesus and the salvific potential of the teaching of the Buddha. For, after his resurrection Jesus says: "Follow me." After his resurrection Milarepa says, "Follow my teaching."

Combine these in a single whole, and worship that;
The goal of aspiration, the meditation, and the
practice—
Combine these in a single whole, and gain Experimental
Knowledge;
This life, the next life, and the life between [in the *Bar
do]*—
Regard these all as one, and make thyself accustomed to
them [thus as one].
This is the last of my Selected Precepts,
And of my Testament the end;
Than that, no more of Truth is there, O Rechung;
Acquire from it Practical Knowledge, O my son.[30]

Now that we have graduated from a homonymous to a synonymous comparison, the question may be asked: what kind of reciprocal illumination does this synonymous comparison provide?

Before this question is answered, it may be pointed out that even the homonymous comparison has not been without significance in the context of the old comparative religion. It has demonstrated that the typology of a dying and rising god not only has its natural and historical versions, as in the case of the "vegetation" deities and Jesus, but that these two categories may be combined as *"theistic"* interpretations of the same core event of death and resurrection of which Buddhism may be said to offer a *nontheistic* interpretation! This carries the discussion of the savior figure beyond the point reached in van der Leeuw.[31] But as we are more concerned here with the illuminating properties of synonymous comparisons, let me revert to the main theme.

In order to see how a synonymous comparison may be illuminating, it would help to recognize that the central fact corresponding to resurrection in Christianity is enlightenment in Buddhism, and that the "person" of Jesus stands in same relation to the former as the teaching of the Buddha does to the latter.

With this in mind let us turn to some episodes in the life of Jesus and the life of Buddha with the renewed realization that the central fact of the Christian religious tradition is resurrection, and the central fact of the Buddhist religious tradition is enlightenment. Thus, doubts expressed regarding resurrection would correspond to doubts expressed regarding the Buddha's enlightenment. Doubts regarding the resurrection are associated with the followers of Jesus (Mark 16:12, Luke 24:11, John 20:24–29) and doubts regarding Buddha's enlightenment were initially expressed by the five ascetics whom he approached after the enlightenment in the famous Deer Park near Banaras. Gotama Buddha first proclaimed his achievement of enlightenment:

> When this had been said, the group of five monks spoke thus to the Lord: "But you, reverend Gotama, did not come to a state of further-men, to the eminence of truly ariyan vision of knowledge, by this conduct, by this course, by this practice of austerities. So how can you now come to a state of further-men, to the eminence of the truly ariyan vision of knowledge, when you live in abundance, are wavering in striving, and have reverted to a life of abundance?"
>
> When this had been said, the Lord spoke thus to the group of five monks: "A Truthfinder, monks, does not live in abundance, he does not waver in striving, he does not revert to a life of abundance. A Truthfinder, monks, is a perfected one, a fully awakened one. Give ear, monks, the deathless has been found; I instruct, I teach *dhamma*. Going alone in accor-

> dance with what has been enjoined, having soon realised here and now by your own super-knowledge that supreme goal of the Brahma-faring for the sake of which young men of family rightly go forth from home into homelessness, you will abide in it."
>
> And a second time did the group of five monks speak thus to the Lord. . . . And a second time did the Lord speak thus to the group of five monks. . . . And a third time did the group of five monks speak thus to the Lord: "But you, reverend Gotama, did not come to a state of further-men . . . by this practice of austerities . . . to a life of abundance?"
>
> When this had been said, the Lord spoke thus to the group of five monks: "Do you allow, monks, that I have never spoken to you like this before?"
>
> "You have not, Lord."
>
> "A Truthfinder, monks, is a perfected one, a fully awakened one. Give ear . . . you will abide in it." And the Lord was able to convince the group of five monks.[32]

The point to be noted is that Buddha convinced the skeptical five ascetics with the following logic: If earlier on, when I never claimed to be in possession of enlightenment you did not doubt me, then why do you doubt me now when I make the claim?

Thus if it is true, as is being contended, that in Christianity the person of Jesus saves and in Buddhism the teaching of Buddha performs the same role, then doubts about the resurrection of Jesus should be compared to the doubts about Buddha's enlightenment.

The parallel here, then, is not between Thomas and Upaka. The case of Doubting Thomas (John 20:24–29) is too well known to be repeated here. The encounter between Buddha and Upaka is less well known and is now recounted. Upaka was an

> Ājīvaka whom the Buddha met on his way between Gayā and the Bodhi Tree, after he set out from Isipatana for the preaching of the First Sermon. Upaka questioned the Buddha on his attainments, and when the Buddha told him what he had accomplished he asked the Buddha if he were "Anantajina." When the Buddha acknowledged it, Upaka shook his head saying, "It may be so, friend," and went along by another road. It is said that the Buddha walked all the way from the Bodhi Tree to Isipatana—instead of flying through the air, as is the custom of Buddhas—because he wished to meet Upaka.

> After this meeting Upaka went to the Vaṅkahāra country and there, having fallen desperately in love with Cāpā, the daughter of a huntsman who looked after him, starved for seven days and in the end persuaded the huntsman to give her to him in marriage. For a living, Upaka hawked about the flesh brought by the huntsman.
>
> In due course Cāpā bore him a son, Subhadda. When the baby cried, Cāpā sang to him saying, "Upaka's son, ascetic's son, game-dealer's boy, don't cry," thus mocking her husband. In exasperation he told her of his friend Anantajina, but she did not stop teasing him. One day, in spite of her attempts to keep him, he left her and went to the Buddha at Sāvatthi. The Buddha, seeing him coming, gave orders that anyone asking for Anantajina should be brought to him. Having learnt from Upaka his story, the Buddha had him admitted to the Order.[33]

Thomas doubts the resurrection; Upaka does not follow the Buddha until later, but expresses indifference rather than doubt about Buddha's enlightenment at the first meeting. The proper parallel is between Thomas and Purāṇa, who expressly questions Buddha's teachings as they were being recited for subsequent preservation. It is said of Purāṇa that when he visited Rājagaha after the holding of the First Council, he was asked to give his approval to the "findings" of the same. His answer was that he preferred to remember what he himself had heard and learnt from the Buddha,[34] and did not endorse the "official" rendition.

Purāṇa does not have to accept the teaching of the communal gathering, because it is the teaching of the Buddha as he appropriated it that is going to save him. It is also interesting that five hundred arhats are said to have attended the council at Rājagaha at which Buddha's teachings were recited and accepted, and at one point five hundred witnessed the resurrected body of Christ. Conze alludes to the incident of Purāṇa though his name is not mentioned. Conze writes: "It is commonly believed that immediately after the decease of the Buddha a council of 500 Arhats rehearsed the scriptures as Ananda had heard them. But even at that time there was another monk, who said that the sayings of the Lord as he remembered them were quite different, and he was allowed to go in peace."[35] The point is significant because a superficial correspondence between Christianity and Buddhism could have the effect of concealing it.

III

One final comment. Is reciprocal illumination a goal or a method? It is a goal inasmuch as one wishes to understand a religious tradition; it is a method inasmuch as it represents one way in which comparison brings about such an understanding. Of course, if one maintains that goal is method congealed, and method is goal liquefied, then one does not even have to answer the question.

III

4

Reciprocal Illumination in Relation to the Lived Experience of Other Religions

I

The experience of the enlarged knowledge of a religious tradition enhancing the understanding of *that* tradition is not new to students of religion. Similarly, the experience of the enlarged knowledge of *another* tradition enhancing the understanding of our own tradition, though perhaps less frequent, is also not unknown to students of comparative religion—whether in academia or in the world at large. Wilfred Cantwell Smith, for instance, testifies to it from within the confines of the ivied ivory tower when he writes: "In coming to understand the meaning that an alien symbol has had for an alien community, you may discover therein a meaning—of life, of the universe, of man's destiny, or whatever—that was in your own heritage all along but that previously you personally had not seen."[1] An obvious illustration in support of this conclusion is provided by the way the emphasis on mysticism in Eastern religions and its consequent attraction for Westerners has led Christians to a greater recognition of the mystical strand within Christianity.[2]

And far from the reaches of academia, the voice of Mahatma Gandhi is heard above the din of the rough and tumble of Indian politics when he declares, defending his right, as a Hindu among Hindus, to undertake a reverential study of the scriptures of every religion:

> My respectful study of other religions has not abated my reverence for or my faith in the Hindu scriptures. They have indeed left their deep mark upon my understanding of the Hindu scriptures. They have broadened my view of life. They have enabled me to understand more clearly many an obscure passage in the Hindu scriptures.[3]

This experience of discovering the treasures in our own house as a result of having wandered abroad is actually more universal than may be apparent at first glance. It is true that the fundamental supersessionists in all religions may deny this to be the case,[4] but it is equally true that no sober and serious student of religion can deny it altogether and will concede that point grudgingly[5] or wholeheartedly.[6] In fact, the phenomenon may be so universal as to be archetypal, and perhaps for this reason it has even become enshrined in folklore. Heinrich Zimmer, for instance, concludes his well-known book on Hindu myths and symbols, very appropriately it seems, with a parable. He introduces it with this fragment of autobiographical reflection:

> There is a humorous Jewish parable in the tradition of the Hassidim (this is the text on which I wish to close) that brings into an eloquent image the final sense to the individual of a broad-minded, fearless adventure into the worlds of "gentile" faith and life. When I first read this tale, some ten years ago, I realized that I had been living and acting along its lines for over a decade—ever since that moment when the millenary, spiritual, treasure of Hindu myth and symbol had begun to reveal itself to me through my academic studies of Indian sacred diagrams and Mandalas, in conjunction with research in the Tantras and Puranas. It is a brief story, told of the Rabbi Eisik, son of Rabbi Jekel, who lived in the ghetto of Cracow, the capital of Poland. He had remained unbroken in his faith, through years of affliction, and was a pious servant of the Lord his God.[7]

The rest of the story runs as follows:

> One night, as this pious and faithful Rabbi Eisik slept, he had a dream; the dream enjoined him to proceed, afar, to the Bohemian capital, Prague, where he should discover a hidden treasure, buried beneath the principal bridge leading to the castle of the Bohemian kings. The Rabbi was surprised, and

put off his going. But the dream recurred twice again. After the third call, he bravely girded his loins and set forth on the quest.

Arriving at the city of his destiny, Rabbi Eisik discovered sentries at the bridge, and these guarded it day and night; so that he did not venture to dig. He only returned every morning and loitered around until dusk, looking at the bridge, watching the sentries, studying unostentatiously the masonry and the soil. At length, the captain of the guards, struck by the old man's persistence, approached, and gently inquired whether he had lost something or perhaps was waiting for someone to arrive. Rabbi Eisik recounted, simply and confidently, the dream that he had had, and the officer stood back and laughed.

"Really, you poor fellow!" the captain said; "Have you worn you shoes out wandering all this way only because of a dream? What sensible person would trust a dream? Why look, if I had been one to go trusting dreams, I should this very minute be doing just the opposite. I should have made just such a pilgrimage as this silly one of yours, only in the opposite direction, but no doubt with the same result. Let me tell you my dream." He was a sympathetic officer, for all of his fierce moustache, and the Rabbi felt his heart warm to him. "I dreamt of a voice," said the Bohemian, Christian officer of the guard, "and it spoke to me of Cracow, commanding me to go thither and to search there for a great treasure in the house of a Jewish rabbi whose name would be Eisik son of Jekel. The treasure was to have been discovered buried in the dirty corner behind the stove. Eisik son of Jekel!" The captain laughed again, with brilliant eyes. "Fancy going to Cracow and pulling down the walls of every house in the ghetto, where half of the men are called Eisik and the other half Jekel! Eisik son of Jekel, indeed!" And he laughed, and he laughed again at the wonderful joke.

The unostentatious Rabbi listened eagerly, and then, having bowed deeply and thanked his stranger-friend, he hurried straightway back to his distant home, dug in the neglected corner of his house and discovered the treasure which put an end to all his misery. With a portion of the money he erected a prayer house that bears his name to this day.[8]

Zimmer then concludes the felicitous story, the chapter, which contains the story, and the book, which contains the chapter, with the following remarks:

> Now the real treasure, to end our misery and trials, is never far away; it is not to be sought in any distant region; it lies buried in the innermost recess of our own home, that is to say, our own being. And it lies behind the stove, the life-and-warmth giving centre of the structure of our existence, our heart of hearts—if we could only dig. *But there is the odd and persistent fact that it is only after a faithful journey to a distant region, a foreign country, a strange land, that the meaning of the inner voice that is to guide our quest can be revealed to us. And together with this odd and persistent fact there goes another, namely, that the one, who reveals to us the meaning of our cryptic inner message, must be a stranger, of another creed and a foreign race.*
>
> The Bohemian captain at the bridge does not believe in inner voices or in dreams, yet he opens to the stranger from afar the very thing that terminates his troubles and brings to fulfillment his quest. Nor does he do this wonderful thing by intention; on the contrary, quite inadvertently his epochal message is delivered while he is making a special point of his own. Hindu myths and symbols, and other signs of wisdom from afar, in just such a way will speak to us of the treasure, which is our own. And we then must dig it up from the forgotten recesses of our own being. And at last it will end for us our troubles and permit us to erect for the benefit of all around us a temple of the living spirit.[9]

I do not agree with Zimmer, and it pains me to have to disagree with a point in so eloquent a testimony, that the "one who reveals to us the meaning of our own cryptic inner message, must be a stranger of another creed and a foreign race."[10] I don't think a guru, to be a guru, must be a foreign guru, but I do concur with Zimmer that when another tradition guides us (and not necessarily unwittingly, as he maintains) to our own home-truth this "epochal message" is delivered when the other tradition "is making a special point of [its] own."

The hallmark of a good parable is its hermeneutical versatility, and this parable can move one's sensibility in many directions. I would now like to indicate the direction in which I do not wish to move our sensibility and then shall proceed to indicate the one direction in which I do wish to see it moved.

It is easy to connect this story with two aspects of Jungian thought: dreams and archetypes. Jung briefly states his approach to the interpretation of dreams as follows:

> I call every interpretation, which equates the dream images with real objects, an *interpretation on the object level.* In contrast to this is the interpretation, which refers every part of the dream and all the actors in it back to the dreamer himself. This I call *interpretation on the subject level.* Interpretation on the object level is analytic, because it breaks down the dream content into complexes of memory that refer to external situations. Interpretation on the subject level is synthetic, because it detaches the underlying complexes of memory from their external causes, regards them as tendencies or components of the subject, and reunites them with that subject.[11]

On the relative employments of the interpretation at the level of the subject and the object, Jacobi summarizes Jung's position as follows: "Where the dream deals with persons who stand in a vital relation to the dreamer, it is always interpreted on the object level and, according to the individual case, sometimes on the subject level as well, if this yields a satisfactory meaning; otherwise the subject level is regularly applied."[12]

At this point it is possible to argue that the story confirms the following assessment as it redirects the rabbi's psychic energy in the right direction: "Interpretation on the subject level proves particularly fruitful when it is necessary to activate or revive the creative powers of the psyche, for the process in which the ego encounters and comes to terms with the symbols of the unconscious is extremely beneficial in removing and transforming the blockages and obstructions of psychic energy."[13] It is also possible to argue, in keeping with the previous remarks, that the rabbi received a clue from the collective unconscious. However, it is perhaps not an inappropriate suggestion that the whole story be treated as a myth, not in the sense of something factually false but as something psychologically true. Now, myth at the level of community may be said to correspond to dreams at the level of the individual. Myths are collective dreams. The rabbi, according to this view, would qualify as the Grand Old Man[14] (who is himself in need of wisdom?). If now the story—myth—is itself considered as the counterpart of the individual's dream as suggested above, the wisdom of the story becomes apparent. It helps Polish Jewry harken back to itself instead of falling prey to the alien treasures so tempting in their allure.[15]

Thus, the two directions in which an interpretive movement is not helpful for my purposes are to regard the story as indicating that we come to know ourselves only through the other, pace Buber, and to regard it as a representation of the Wise Old Man.

A third direction in which the parable could move our sensibility, apart from the realm of reflexive cultural self-realization as suggested by Zimmer, or the realm of the collective unconscious by an extension of Jungian techniques, is the realm of the idealistic metaphysic of Advaita Vedānta. To identify this possibility one needs to refer again to a statement made by Zimmer after narrating the parable. It runs as follows: "Now the real treasure, to end our misery and trials, is never far away; it is not to be sought in any distant region; it lies buried in the innermost recess of our own home, that is to say, our own being. And it lies behind the stove, the life-and-warmth giving centre of the structure of our existence, our heart of hearts—if we could only dig."[16]

The three key elements here are (1) the treasure being sought is lying within us; (2) it is lying in the heart; and (3) this revelation is mediated in this parable through a dream. In the following passage from Ramana Maharshi, the major representative of existential Advaita in this century, the first and third points are clearly alluded to.

> Our real nature is mukti. But we are imagining that we are bound and are making various strenuous attempts to become free, while we are all the time free. This will be understood only when we reach that stage. We will be surprised that we frantically were trying to attain something, which we have always been and are. An illustration will make this clear. A man goes to sleep in this hall. He dreams he had gone on a world tour, is roaming over hill and dale, forest and country, desert and sea, across various continents and, after many years of weary and strenuous travel, returns to this country, reaches Triuvannamalai, enters the Ashram and walks into the hall. Just at that moment he wakes up and he had not moved an inch, but was sleeping where he lay down. He had not returned after great effort to the hall but is and always has been in the hall. It is exactly like that. If it is asked why being free we imagine we are bound, I answer: "Why being in the hall did you imagine you were on a world adventure, crossing hill and dale, desert and sea?" It is all mind or maya.[17]

As for "our heart of hearts," the following comment of Ramana comes very close to Zimmer:

> The entire universe is condensed in the body and the entire body in the Heart. Thus the Heart is the nucleus of the whole

> universe. This world is not other than the mind, the mind is not other than the Heart; that is the whole truth.[18]

It is clear then that at least three meanings can be read imaginatively into the parable involving the rabbi: the one drawn by Zimmer; the one that could be unraveled through Jungian psychology; and the one that could be teased out through Advaita Vedānta à la Ramana Maharshi.

None of these represent the direction in which we wish to move the parable. Zimmer represents the application of the hermeneutical method, Jung the psychological method, and Ramana the philosophical method. The dialogical method may draw attention to the fact that the Jew came to see the light through a Christian, for the Bohemian captain is identified as such. We would, however, like to see the significance of the parable in terms of reciprocal illumination. From the point of view of reciprocal illumination the parable itself would have a different ending. From the point of view of reciprocal illumination, the story would end as follows:

> And just as the rabbi went home and found the treasure in his hearth, the captain, his curiosity piqued by the rabbi's dream, excavated the bridge and discovered a treasure for himself. The rabbi got his treasure and the captain got his; the rabbi got his through the captain, and the captain got his through the rabbi; each caused light to fall on the path of the other.

II

The fact that reciprocal illumination is part and parcel of the lived experience of our religious life requires that we draw a distinction between two forms of reciprocal illumination—between a first-order reciprocal illumination, which forms a part of religious experience itself, and a second-order reciprocal illumination, which belongs not to the world of religious life and religious experience but to the *study* of such religious life and religious experience, which is now regularly carried on in the branch of humanities under several names but most often under the rubric "religious studies" or "the study of religion."

In this book we are concerned with reciprocal illumination of the second order. These and allied points are explored in more detail in the next chapter.

> universe. This world is not other than the mind, the mind is not other than the Heart that is the whole truth."

It is clear then that at least three meanings can be read imaginatively into the parable involving the rabbi: the one drawn by Zimmer, the one that could be unraveled through Jungian psychiatry, and the one that could be raised from through Advaita Vedānta à la Ramana Maharshi.

None of these represent the direction in which we wish to move the parable. Zimmer's approach is the application of the hermeneutical method; Jung's, the psychological method; and Ramana's, the philosophical method. The dialogical method may draw attention to the fact that the Jew came to see the light through a Christian, for the Bohemian captain is identified as such. We would, however, like to see the significance of the parable in terms of reciprocal illumination. From the point of view of reciprocal illumination the parable itself would have a different ending. From the point of view of reciprocal illumination, the story would end as follows:

> And just as the rabbi went home and dug up the treasure in his hearth, the captain, his curiosity piqued by the rabbi's dream, excavated the bridge and discovered a treasure for himself. The rabbi got his treasure and the captain got one too, but the one got his through another's hand, and the dream of the one and the rabbi, each caused light to fall on the path of the other.

II

The fact that reciprocal illumination is part and parcel of the lived experience of our religious life requires that we draw a distinction between two forms of reciprocal illumination—between a first order reciprocal illumination, which forms a part of religious experience itself, and a second order reciprocal illumination, which belongs not to the world of religious life and religious experience but to the study of such religious life and religious experience, which is now regularly carried on in the branch of humanities under several names but most often under the rubric "religious studies" or "the study of religion."

In this book we are concerned with reciprocal illumination of the second order. These and allied points are explored in more detail in the next chapter.

5

Reciprocal Illumination and Comparative Religion

I would like to begin this chapter in a somewhat unusual manner, by trying to indicate what *reciprocal illumination* may not be, rather than by indicating what it is. The fact that one should endeavor, in defining a concept, to state both what it is and what it is not is not an unknown procedure and may even be a laudable one. It is the propaedeutic for any proper understanding according to the Mīmāṁsā school of Hindu thought. According to it, "[A] mere positive description is not adequate to define 'a thing,' for a thing can be truly known as that which it is only by being distinguished from that which it is not."[1]

What is unusual, then, about what I am about to do is not that I intend to describe reciprocal illumination both negatively and positively, but rather that I intend to begin by describing it negatively (by what it is not) rather than positively (by what it is). Even this is not unusual in certain fields of study. The *via negativa* constitutes a standard mystical procedure, and the Hindu penchant for it is clearly reflected in the *neti neti* (not so, not so) of some Upanishadic thinkers who would define the real as indefinable. I have set out to talk about reciprocal illumination first in terms of what it is not rather than what it is, not out of a desire to indulge any latent mystical tendencies of my own but simply out of a desire to prevent an elementary consideration from clouding the issue—namely, that the study of religion should not be confused with religion, or that the activity of studying religion should not be mistaken for a religious activity in itself. Now, it is indeed a question worth debating (and a question that has been debated) as to whether the study of religion itself qualifies as a religious activity. It may or may not, but here it is our intention to recognize the distinction without pronouncing a judgment on the point in any way.

If religion is about truth, then the study of religion is about the truth-claims of the religion or religions involved; religious studies is about the study of religion, not the religion of study; and the student of religion is different from one seeking or finding religion. Allow me to illustrate the point.

A book published in 1935 entitled *A Search in Secret India* did much to stimulate an interest in Indian spirituality in the West. It was through this book that Western readers perhaps obtained their first credible account of a Hindu sage whose body was "almost nude, except for a thin, narrow loin-cloth," whose skin was "slightly copper-coloured, yet quite fair in comparison with that of the average South Indian," who was "a tall man; his age, then somewhere in the early fifties," whose head was "covered with closely cropped, grey hair" and "well formed" and whose forehead gave "intellectual distinction to his personality."[2] The person so described was to become widely known in the years to come as Ramana Maharshi.

The author of the book, Paul Brunton, refers to two occasions when his own understanding of Christianity was vivified, first in an encounter with Ramana himself, and then in an encounter with a disciple of Ramana. After some effort Brunton succeeded in obtaining an interview with the Maharshi. We plug into the interview at a point where the Maharshi is speaking:

> "You ask me to describe this true self to you. What can be said? It is That out of which the sense of the personal 'I' arises, and into which it shall have to disappear."
>
> "Disappear?" I echo back. "How can one lose the feeling of one's personality?"
>
> "The first and foremost of all thoughts, the primeval thought in the mind of every man, is the thought 'I.' It is only after the birth of this thought that any other thoughts can arise at all. It is only after the first personal pronoun 'I' has arisen in the mind, that the second personal pronoun 'You' can make its appearance. If you could mentally follow the 'I' thread until it leads you back to its source, you would discover that, just as it is the first thought to appear, so is it the last to disappear. This is a matter which can be experienced."

> "You mean that it is perfectly possible to conduct such a mental investigation into oneself?"
>
> "Assuredly! It is possible to go inwards until the last thought 'I' gradually vanishes." "What is left?" I query. "Will a man then become quite unconscious, or will he become an idiot?"
>
> "Not so! On the contrary, he will attain that consciousness which is immortal, and he will become truly wise, when he has awakened to his true self, which is the real nature of man."
>
> "But surely the sense of 'I' must also pertain to that?" I persist.
>
> "The sense of 'I,' pertains to the person, the body and brain," replies the Maharishee calmly. "When a man knows his true self for the first time, something else arises from the depths of his being and takes possession of him. That something is behind the mind; it is infinite, divine, eternal. Some people call it the kingdom of heaven, others call it the soul, still others name it Nirvana, and we Hindus call it Liberation; you may give it what name you wish. When this happens a man has not really lost himself; rather, he has found himself."[3]

Brunton describes his reaction to the last words of the Maharshi as follows:

> As the last word falls from the interpreter's lips, there flashes across my mind those memorable words which were uttered by a wandering Teacher in Galilee, words which have puzzled so many good persons: *Whosoever shall seek to save his life shall lose it; and whosoever shall lose his life shall preserve it.*
>
> How strangely similar are the two sentences! Yet the Indian sage has arrived at the thought in his own non-Christian way, through a psychological path, which seems exceedingly difficult and appears unfamiliar.[4]

It is clear that contact with a Hindu sage had animated a piece of Christian teaching for Brunton. A similar incident occurred when Brunton received a piece of disturbing news but was calmed telepathically by a disciple of Ramana Maharshi, Ramiah by name. Ramiah had undertaken a vow of silence. Nevertheless, he took Brunton by hand and led him to a pool in the jungle. There he sat the agitated Brunton on the sandy bank, sat down himself beside him, and began to meditate. Brunton writes:

> It is not much longer before I become acutely susceptible to the silence of our lonely surroundings and to the amazing calm of my companion. Little by little, with an insidious but persistent gentleness, peace weaves itself into the texture of my soul.
>
> The mood of serene triumph over personal distresses, which I could not reach before, now comes to me more easily. In his own mysterious way the Yogi is helping me; I cannot doubt that. Barely a breath comes from his quiet form, so sunk is he in deepest contemplation. What is the secret of this beneficent radiation, which emanates from him?[5]

The outcome of the experience leads Brunton to spotlight a statement of his own tradition.

> I perceive with startling clarity that a man can look serenely upon his tribulations, if only he can find the standpoint of his deeper self; that it is foolish to cling to the transient comfort of worldly hopes when the unchanging certainty of a diviner protection awaits his acceptance; and that the reason why the wise Galilean told his disciples to take no thought for the morrow was because a higher power had taken thought for them. I perceive, too, that once a man accepts this invitation to place his confidence in the prophetic element within his being, he may pass through the vicissitudes of human life in this world without fear and without faltering. And I feel that somewhere close at hand there is the fundamental value of life, in whose calm air no cares may exist. Thus the burden, which lay so heavy on my mind, vanishes with this change of spiritual atmosphere.[6]

At this point a distinction must be drawn that will remain pivotal for the rest of this study. It is the distinction between *Homo religiosus* and *Homo academicus*,[7] between the man of religion and the student of religion ("using the term 'student' in the widest sense").[8] The student of religion studies the man of religion. This epigrammatic summation, however, stands in need of explanation; actually, both of its constitutive terms—"man of religion" and "study of religion"—need to be explained.

By men—or, more properly, human beings—of religion two categories of people are meant: (1) the believers of a tradition encompassing all from the saint to the formal believer; and (2) human beings in search of religious truth, or to press Ugo Bianchi's expression into my service, people "seeking a dialogue with the transcendent."[9] That is, human beings committed to a particular religious tradition or in general to religious truth are comprised within this term. The distinction between the two categories rests on the fact that "to test one's beliefs is different from testing oneself as a believer." J. N. Barnhart states: "[T]o ask whether one really does believe in what he professes to believe is one thing. To ask whether what one believes in deserves rational commitment is another."[10] I would like to replace the word "rational" by "existential" here to make my point. These groups of people constitute that subject of the study of religion.

But what about the term "the study of religion" itself? It can mean either the study of religion to attain religious truth in the sense of either knowledge of a tradition or insight into reality per se, or the academic study of religion, which does not aim at attaining truth but at "understanding" religion. Even if the latter leads to the former, or the former to the latter, the analytical distinction must be clearly maintained even in the face of any existential overlap or blurring. Now, inasmuch as the method of reciprocal illumination is being developed here in the context of the academic study of religion, its application will only be discussed in the following pages as confined to this field of study. In other words it is context-bound for the purposes of this book. This, of course, is not meant to deny it a wider applicability but only to clarify that no such applicability will be canvassed in these pages.

Once this clarification is made—that by reciprocal illumination is here meant such illumination in the academic study of religion—a complicating consideration emerges that must now be faced.

The recognition of an interior dimension is integral to an understanding of religion itself. Ugo Bianchi and Wilfred Cantwell Smith both have upheld this position. Initially it was from a historical point of view, but it appears to have taken on a phenomenological coloring in the case of the former and a theological hue in the case of the latter. Thus, Bianchi criticizes the sociology of religion for overlooking this dimension when he remarks that the student of religion must take into account "an inner life to which, no less than to social and historical cultural structures, however important these may be, is entrusted the essential dynamism of the religious phenomenon in history, in spite of the theories of sociologists who follow Durkheim."[11] He goes on to state how for him "religion, in the great universalist as well as in primitive religions, . . . presents itself as the total meaning of life, even in man's most intimate self, his conscience."[12]

W. C. Smith has consistently focused his and our attention on this interior dimension through his concern with the role of faith. In his *The Meaning and End of Religion* (1963) he took pains to distinguish faith from religion, on the one hand, and from cumulative tradition, on the other. In a later work, *Faith and Belief* (1979), he endeavored to clarify the understanding of faith and to distinguish it from belief. Whereas the distinguishing feature of belief is its content, faith is directed toward an object ultimately transcendent, and as such the study of religion can not only not be divorced from the dimension of faith but will turn out to be a contrived exercise if it proceeds without taking this dimension into account. Its importance becomes at once clear when it is shown how faith might directly bear on the study of religion. For while it is "always possible for the well-informed historian to see how the shape of faith" varies over time or with persons,

> If the historian is religiously insensitive, he may see no more than this. He may report the specific historical form, and fail to see or to mention the timeless substance. On the other hand, if the historian is studying a person whose faith is of the same tradition as his own, he may then see the transcendent element so vividly that he emphasizes it primarily, and underestimates, or underreports, the historical particularity. Muslims may do this of a Ghazzali, Catholic Christians of an Aquinas, Protestants of a Luther, Marxists of a Lenin. A less limited vision, however, offering a comprehensive and fairly readily demonstrable assessment, is that in each particular case faith has been the confluence of both time and what one may wish to call eternity; it is the locus of man's transcendence, a channel of particularized shape by which man has reached, been reached by, a truth that transcends those and all particulars.[13]

If this is so, then how can we exclude the grappling with truth or transcendence from the purview of the academic study of religion?

It should be clearly recognized that the interior dimension of religion falls well within the scope of the study of religion, but the acceptance of this dimension does not thereby imply the extension of reciprocal illumination as espoused here beyond the frontiers outlined earlier. This will become clear if the distinction is kept in mind between the case of a religious seeker like Brunton, whose interiority is illumined by reciprocal illumination, and the case of two religious seekers whose inner travail is reciprocally illuminating. The former is excluded from our study and the latter is included, because in the case of the latter it has implications for the religions with which they are associated.

This latter case may be illustrated with examples from the lives of Prophet Muḥammad and the mystic Rāmakṛṣṇa. It is said that after the reception of the first revelation, the Prophet was on the verge of taking his own life. lbn Isḥāq reports that after Gabriel had asked Muḥammad to recite to what is now Sūrah 96:1–5, Muḥammad described what followed thus:

> So I read it, and he departed from me. And I awoke from my sleep, and it was as though these words were written on my heart. (T. Now none of God's creatures was more hateful to me than an [ecstatic] poet or a man possessed: I could not even look at them. I thought, Woe is me poet or possessed—Never shall Quraysh say this of me! I will go to the top of the mountain and throw myself down that I may kill myself and gain rest. So I went forth to do so and then) when I was midway on the mountain, I heard a voice from heaven saying, "O Muhammad! Thou art the apostle of God and I am Gabriel." I raised my head towards heaven to see (who was speaking), and lo, Gabriel in the form of a man with feet astride the horizon, saying, "O Muhammad! Thou art the apostle of God and I am Gabriel." I stood gazing at him, (T. and that turned me from my purpose) moving neither forward nor backward; then I began to turn my face away from him, but towards whatever region of the sky I looked, I saw him as before. And I continued standing there, neither advancing nor turning back, until Khadīja sent her messengers in search of me and they gained the high ground above Mecca and returned to her while I was standing in the same place; then he parted from me and I from him, returning to my family.[14]

It should be noted here that, according to this account, suicidal despair did not precede but followed the revelation, when the Prophet felt that he might have been deluded. Then the vision of Gabriel occurred.

This experience may be compared with that of Rāmakṛṣṇa, who longed for a vision of the goddess Kālī but was constantly disappointed. Finally, one day he could take it no more:

> There was then an intolerable anguish in my heart because I could not have Her vision. Just as a man wrings a towel forcibly to squeeze out all the water from it, I felt as if somebody caught hold of my heart and mind and was doing so with them. Greatly afflicted with the thought that I might never

> have Mother's vision, I was dying of despair. Being in agony I thought that there was then no use in living this life. My eyes suddenly fell upon the sword that was there in the Mother's temple. I made up my mind to put an end to my life with it that very moment. Like one mad, I ran and caught hold of it, when suddenly I had the wonderful vision of the Mother, and fell down unconscious. I did not know what happened then in the external world—how that day and the next slipped away. But, in my heart of hearts, there was flowing a current of intense bliss, never experienced before, and I had the immediate knowledge of the Light that was Mother.[15]

Rāmakṛṣṇa also described how the Mother spoke to him.[16]

These accounts are illuminating, as one can see how; in each case, divine despair was crowned by a spiritual breakthrough.[17] It is also apparent, moreover, that both the visual and auditory modes were involved in each case, for Muḥammad saw Gabriel too and Rāmakṛṣṇa "talked" to Kālī. One may thus conclude that the psychological longing channelized spiritual energies primarily but not exclusively in the preferred mode of encounter in these cases. The reciprocal illumination consists in the realization that the auditory mode may be preceded by the visual and that the visual mode may be followed by the auditory.

It may be helpful here to point out how a slight shift in perspective would move this example into another methodological domain. Thus, if now the revelations of the Qur'ān are seen as transcripts from the Tablet in Heaven—presumably of stone,[18] and a comparison is instituted with the *stone* image of Kālī, one is led into the area of lapidary hierophanies and thus into the phenomenology of religion. Similarly, if one regards the Qur'ān as coming not from God[19] but from Muḥammad's unconscious and the vision of Kālī by Rāmakṛṣṇa as a life-saving trance,[20] then we have passed into the arena of the psychology of religion.

At the other end of the spectrum there is a second complicating factor. The proper understanding of reciprocal illumination must not only be disengaged from the religious nature of the content but also from some aspects of the academic nature of the study. The emergence of the study of religion itself serves to shed light on this point, for, as John Hick says, its very existence represents

> a way of thinking that in less clearly defined forms is widespread today and is, indeed, characteristic of our culture. The

> way of thinking is epitomized in the way in which the word "religion" (or "faith" used virtually as a synonym) has largely come to replace the word "God." In contexts in which formerly questions were raised and debated concerning God, God's existence, attributes, purpose, and deeds, the corresponding questions today typically concern religion, its nature, function, forms and pragmatic value. A shift has taken place from the term "God": as the head of a certain group of words and locutions to the term "religion," as the head of the same linguistic family.[21]

He goes on to say:

> Indeed in many universities and colleges there are departments devoted to studying the history and varieties of this phenomenon and the contribution that it has brought to our culture in general. Among the ideas treated in this connection, along with cult, priesthood, taboo, and many others, is the concept of God. For academic study, God is thus conceived as a subtopic within the larger subject of religion.[22]

The point I would like to make is that we have excluded the application of reciprocal illumination from the area of religiosity per se from our study, although it doubtless occurs in that context, on account of the fact that, at the moment, we are engaged in the subject of religion and not in the search of religious salvation. It is true that such academic study of religion essentially forms part of the study of human culture and

> The historical sources of the now prevalent and perhaps even dominant view of religion as essentially an aspect of human culture are fairly evident. This view of religion represents a logical development, within an increasingly technological society, of what has been variously called scientism, positivism, and naturalism. This development is based upon the assumption—engendered by the tremendous, dramatic, and still accelerating growth of scientific knowledge and achievement—that the truth concerning any aspect or alleged aspect of reality is to be found by the application of the methods of scientific investigations to the relevant phenomena,—God is not a phenomenon available for scientific study, but religion is. There can be a history, a phenomenology, a psychology, a sociology, and a

> comparative study of religion. Hence, religion has become an object of intensive investigation and God is perforce identified as an idea that occurs within this complex phenomenon of religion.[23]

It is precisely this association of the study of human culture that makes the delineation of the point so delicate, for human culture for the past few centuries has been dominated by the paradigm of the scientific method in the academic world, and the study of religion has not remained untouched by it. In fact the time when it came under its influence can be stated with some precision—it was during the decade of 1859 to 1869. Eric J. Sharpe sums up the development as follows in his own inimitable style:

> The decade began, of course, with the publication of Darwin's *Origin of Species*. Before its end, Herbert Spencer was well started on his elaborate *System of Synthetic Philosophy*, Thomas Huxley had confronted Bishop Wilberforce before the British Association in the name of Science, E.B. Taylor had launched his theory of "animism," Benjamin Disraeli had announced that he was on the side of the angels, J.F. M'Lennan had borrowed the term "totemism" and set it adrift in the scholarly world, and an expatriate German philologist resident in Oxford, Friedrich Max Müller, had begun to publish a definitive edition of the Sanskrit text of the *Rig Veda*, written a celebrated book on *Comparative Mythology*, and suggested to the English-speaking world that, so far from science and religion being irreconcilable opposites, there might be a "Science of Religion" which would do justice to both. In short, comparative religion (at first a synonym for the science of religion) did not exist in 1859; by 1869 it did.[24]

The synonymous use of the terms "science of religion" and "comparative religion" provides the clue for developing the argument in the direction it needs to be developed. For the "science of religion" resulted from the application of the scientific model as then conceived to the data available at the time.[25]

In the present context I would particularly like to emphasize the comparative dimension of the method, for "as in language, as in any science, the absolutely vital principle is that of comparison. . . . In short, as Max Müller so often said, 'he who knows one, knows none.' "[26] Thus, comparative religion is nothing if not comparative. A rapid survey of how comparison has been used in the context of religious plurality in the ancient, the medieval, and the modern world will pave the way for developing a special understanding of reciprocal illumination in the context of comparative religion we wish to develop. In the ancient world, comparison contributed to the identification of gods when similarities were emphasized, and thus to polytheism and to religious syncretism; and it contributed to monotheism and religious exclusivism, when differences were emphasized. This latter trend dominated the medieval period as well, though sometimes similarities were recognized. It was in modern times that comparison was first used for identification, for differentiation, and for evaluation as a basis for classifying "information" and gaining knowledge. This attitude contributed to the rise of the Science of Religion or Comparative Religion.[27] Comparative religion employs comparison as a means of knowing at various levels: (1) as when a single datum is taken and compared historically with the preceding or succeeding manifestations or both within a tradition; (2) when a single datum is compared thematically with similar data from other religious traditions; (3) when a single datum is first viewed historically and then thematically; or (4) when it is first viewed thematically and then historically.

At another level, the traditions themselves can be compared. Here again comparison can be used to focus on differences or similarities. When differences become the focus, the uniqueness of each tradition gets highlighted. When both differences and similarities are kept in view in relation to the various traditions, they are classified in different ways depending on the criteria employed. When similarities as a whole are emphasized, the category of religion becomes a key concern. It is even set beside that of ideology. This then helps differentiate between religion and surrogates for religion. Marxism, Jungian psychology, civil religion, and so on, have to be taken into account in this context. These points have an important bearing on the definition of religion.

To recapitulate: comparative religion is based on comparison, when such comparison is carried out on the basis of material that has been subjected to the most rigorous tests to establish its accuracy or authenticity. In comparative religion, such comparison is used either to derive universal laws or categories or to study the particular by comparing it with other particulars across time. In other words, the specific feature of a tradition, say the Bible within Christianity, could be critically studied in the context of its own tradition and compared in terms of its role or form over various phases of the history of the tradition. Or it could be studied as a scripture by placing it alongside other scriptures such as the Qur'ān and the Vedas and examined as a sample or species of the genus scripture. It could thus either be compared to itself through history or it could be compared with other sacred books through the category of scripture, thematically rather than historically. If this may be called the historical comparative approach, correctly perhaps if somewhat clumsily, then at least four possibilities present themselves for further investigation, as mentioned earlier.

1. A particular datum could be examined in its historical context alone;
2. a particular datum could be examined in its phenomenological or categorical context alone;
3. a particular datum could first be examined in the historical context and then placed in the phenomenological perspective; or
4. a particular datum could first be examined in the phenomenological context and then placed in a historical perspective.

All of these possibilities may now be explored further.

I. A Particular Datum Examined in the Historical Context

One of the most widely known provisions of Islamic law is the permission provided for having up to four wives simultaneously. The revelation was received after the battle of Uḥud in which the Muslims of Medina barely survived the Meccan assault. The revelation runs as follows (Qur'ān 4. 3):

> 3. And if ye fear that ye will not deal fairly by the orphans, marry of the women, who seem good to you, two or three or four; and if ye fear that ye cannot do justice (to so many) then one (only) or (the captives) that your right hands possess. Thus it is more likely that ye will not do injustice.[28]

Various explanations have been offered in justification of this provision and they possess their own merit and interest. There can be little doubt, however, that from the point of view of *Religionswissenschaft* the following statement of W. Montgomery Watt will have to be accorded pride of place. He says, documenting the reforms introduced by the Prophet:

> The most interesting reforms are in the sphere of marriage and the family. The previous situation was complex and has not been sufficiently studied by scholars with the relevant anthropological skills. A likely hypothesis, however, is that a formerly widespread matriliny was being replaced by patriliny, which fits in better with an individualistic outlook. As practiced in Arabia, matriliny did not imply matriarchy, for the head of a matrilineal household was the uterine brother of the senior woman. Under this system, since physical paternity was not important, loose forms of polyandric marriage were permitted, some little different from prostitution. The basic reform of the Qur'ān was to restrict a woman to one "husband" at a time, so that physical paternity would be certain (2:228, 2:234). The Qur'ān encouraged Muslims to have up to four wives at once (4:3), not as a restriction on a supposedly unlimited polygamy but to prevent women from relapsing into some of the former polyandric practices. Muḥammad himself is said to have had fourteen wives or concubines, of whom nine survived him, but for each of his marriages there was a social or political reason; thus he bound his two chief lieutenants, Abū Bakr and 'Umar, more closely to him by marrying their daughters, 'Ā'ishah and Ḥafṣah. By arranging for his wives to have separate apartments within his house, Muḥammad helped to make virilocal marriage the norm, as against uxorilocal marriage in matrilineal society.[29]

The appeal of the passage lies in the comparisons embedded between pre- and post-Islamic society—in the comparison between matriarchy and matriliny and in the comparison between the four wives permitted to a Muslim and many more to the Prophet. And then there is the comparison between the contemporary facts and modern apologetics. It is, as it were, through a network of comparisons located within the compass of the tradition that the historical significance of an important social arrangement is communicated.

II. A Particular Datum Examined in a Phenomenological Context

The datum concerns the expulsion of Eve and Adam from Paradise (Genesis 3):

1. Now the serpent was more subtil than any beast of the field, which the Lord God had made. And he said unto the woman. Yea hath God said. Ye shall not eat of every tree of the garden?
2. And the woman said unto the serpent. We may eat of the fruit of the trees of the garden:
3. But of the fruit of the tree, which is in the midst of the garden, God hath said. Ye shall not eat of it; neither shall ye touch it, lest ye die.
4. And the serpent said unto the woman. Ye shall not surely die:
5. For God doth know that in the day ye eat thereof, then your eyes shall be opened, and ye shall be as gods, knowing good and evil.
6. And when the woman saw that the tree was good for food, and that it was pleasant to the eyes, and a tree to be desired to make one wise, she took of the fruit thereof, and did eat, and gave also unto her husband with her; and he did eat.
7. And the eyes of them both were opened, and they knew that they were naked; and they sewed fig leaves together, and made themselves aprons.
8. And they heard the voice of the Lord God walking in the garden in the cool of the day: and Adam and his wife hid themselves from the presence of the Lord God amongst the trees of the garden.
9. And the Lord God called unto Adam, and said unto him. Where art thou?
10. And he said, I heard thy voice in the garden, and I was afraid, because I was naked; and I hid myself.
11. And he said, who told thee that thou wast naked? Hast thou eaten of the tree, whereof I commanded thee that thou shouldest not eat?
12. And the man said. The woman whom thou gavest to be with me, she gave me of the tree, and I did eat.

13. And the Lord God said unto the woman. What is this that thou hast done? And the woman said. The serpent beguiled me, and I did eat.

14. And the Lord God said unto the serpent. Because thou hast done this, thou art cursed above all cattle, and above every beast of the field; upon thy belly shall thou go, and dust shall thou eat all the days of thy life:

15. And I will put enmity between thee and the woman, and between thy seed and her seed; it shall bruise thy head, and thou shalt bruise his heel.

16. Unto the woman he said, I will greatly multiply thy sorrow and thy conception; in sorrow thou shalt bring forth children; and thy desire shall be to thy husband, and he shall rule over thee.

17. And unto Adam he said. Because thou hast hearkened unto the voice of thy wife, and hast eaten of the tree, of which I commanded thee, saying. Thou shalt not eat of it: cursed is the ground for thy sake; in sorrow shalt thou eat of it all the days of thy life;

18. Thorns also and thistles shall it bring forth to thee; and thou shalt eat the herb of the field;

19. In the sweat of thy face shalt thou eat bread, till thou return unto the ground; for out of it wast thou taken: for dust thou art, and unto dust shalt thou return.

20. And Adam called his wife's name Eve; because she was the mother of all living.

21. Unto Adam also and to his wife did the Lord God make coats of skins, and clothed them.

22. And the Lord God said. Behold, the man is become as one of us, to know good and evil; and now, lest he put forth his hand, and take also of the tree of life, and eat, and live for ever:

23. Therefore the Lord God sent him forth from the Garden of Eden, to till the ground from whence he was taken.

24. So he drove out the man and he placed at the east of the Garden of Eden Cherubims and a flaming sword, which turned every way, to keep the way of the tree of life.[30]

Ricoeur uses this event to distinguish the category of "myth" from that of symbol thus:

> The final criterion: how to distinguish myths from symbols? M. Pepin contrasts myth to allegory, but does not clearly distinguish myth from symbol. It seems sometimes that the symbol is a non-allegorical way of getting hold of a myth. Symbol and allegory would thus be two intellectual attitudes or dispositions proper to hermeneutics. Symbolic interpretation and allegorical interpretation would be two directions taken by an interpretation concerned with the same content of myths. I however take symbol in Eliade's more radical meaning of analogical significations spontaneously formed and given, as for instance the meaning of water as threatening in the deluge and purifying in baptism—and so with all the primitive hierophanies. I take myth to be a species of symbol, a symbol developed into narrative form, articulated within a time and space that cannot be coordinated with critical history and geography. The Exile, for instance, is a primary symbol of human alienation, but the story of Adam and Eve being driven from Paradise is a mythical narrative of the second level, bringing into play fabled persons, places, time and episodes. It seems to me that this added depth is essential to the myth—not to mention the attempt at explanation found in the etiological myths. Basically I am pretty much in agreement with the schema of Jaspers, who distinguishes the primitive language of number (what I call symbols), the language of myths, which mediate the primary symbols, and finally the symbols of the third level, which are more speculative, as for instance the representation of evil as "war" in Heraclitus, or "body" in Plato's *Phaedo*, or "hereditary original sin" in Saint Augustine.[31]

One might ask: where is the comparison? It is not outside—in terms of other motifs of exile from other religions, which could well be included—but it is rather within. Ricoeur establishes his point by comparing the categories of symbol, myth, and explanation within the passage as phenomenological givens.

III. A Particular Datum First Examined Historically and Then Placed in a Phenomenological Perspective

The datum is provided by the following verse of the Kaṭha Upaniṣad—one of the "verse" Upaniṣads.[32]

14. *uttiṣṭhata jāgrata prāpya varān nibodhata: kṣurasya dhārā niśitā duratyavā; durgam pathas tat kavayo vadanti.*

> 14. Arise, awake, having attained thy boons, understand (them). Sharp as the edge of a razor and hard to cross, difficult to tread is that path (so) sages declare.

This is the exhortation delivered by Yama, the god of death, to the young Naciketas. The datum that concerns us here is "sharp as the edge of a razor," an expression that provided the title of one of Somerset Maugham's novels.[33] Apart from saying that the "way of religion is never easy. It is steep and hard,"[34] does it resonate with some message beyond this apparent one?

A phenomenological perspective, such as the one provided by Mircea Eliade in what follows, suggests that it does. Eliade points out that one of "the most important functions of religious symbolism" lies in its capacity of expressing "certain structures of ultimate reality, otherwise quite inexpressible."[35] He goes on to say:

> The most frequent images are: passing between two rocks or two icebergs that bump together continuously, between two mountains in continual motion, between the jaws of a monster, or penetrating and withdrawing unhurt from a vagina dentate, or entering a mountain that has no opening. We understand what all these images point to; if there exists the possibility of a "passage," this cannot be realized except "in spirit," giving this term all the meanings that it has in archaic societies, i.e., referring to a disincarnated mode of being as well as the imaginary world and the world of ideas. One can pass through a Symplegade insofar as one is able to act "spiritually," insofar as one proves that one possesses imagination and intelligence and consequently, is capable of detaching oneself from immediate reality. *No other symbol of the "difficult passage"—not even the celebrated motif of the thin bridge like the blade of a sword or the edge of the razor to which allusion is made in the Katha Upanishad (iii, 14)—reveals better than the Symplegades that there is a mode of being inaccessible to immediate experience, and that one cannot attain to this mode of being except through renouncing the naive belief in the inexpungeability of matter.*[36]

IV. A Particular Datum First Examined Phenomenologically and Then Placed in Historical Perspective

I choose for this section the symbol of the Cosmic Tree. Let the particular datum be any one of several concerning the Indonesian or the Altaic or the Indian Cosmic Tree.

> Thus the question is posed: Is there, in either instance, some innovation, obscuration of meaning, or a loss of the original meaning? Since we know what the Cosmic Tree means in Mesopotamia, in India, or in Siberia, the question arises: Because of what religio-historical circumstances, or by what interior reason, does the same symbol in Indonesia reveal a different meaning? Diffusion as such does not solve the problem. For even if one could demonstrate that the symbol had been diffused from a single centre, one could still not give the reason why certain cultures have retained certain primary meanings, whereas others have forgotten, rejected, modified, or enriched them. One can come to understand the process of enrichment only by disengaging the structure of the symbol.[37]

Eliade goes on to say:

> It is because the Tree symbolizes the mystery of a world in perpetual regeneration that it can symbolize, at the same time or successively, the pillar of the world and the cradle of the human race, the cosmic renovation and the lunar rhythms, the Centre of the World and the path by which one can pass from Earth to Heaven, etc. Each one of these new valorizations is possible because from the beginning the symbol of the Cosmic Tree reveals itself as a "cipher" of the world grasped as a living reality, sacred and inexhaustible. The historian of religions will have to elucidate the reasons why such a culture has retained, developed or forgotten a symbolic aspect of the Cosmic Tree. In so doing, he will be led to penetrate more deeply into the soul of this culture, and will learn to differentiate it from others.[38]

The inverted Aśvattha tree appears as an image of the cosmos in the Kaṭha Upaniṣad (6.1–4) and even more conspicuously in the Bhagavadgītā (15.1–3):

1. They say there is an eternal pipal-tree
    with roots on high and branches downward.
The verses of Scripture are its leaves.
    Who understands this tree understands the Scriptures.

2. It stretches its branches
Upward and downward.
The states of all things
Nurture the young shoots.
The young shoots are
The nourishment of our senses.
And below,
The roots go far
Into the world of men;
They are the sequences of actions.

3. This understanding
Of the tree's shape—
Its end and its beginning,
And its ground is not open to
The ordinary world.
The roots of that pipal
Have spread far.
With the strong ax
Of detachment
A man should cut
That tree.[39]

This particular variant of the symbol of the Cosmic Tree demonstrates how particular circumstances modify the general symbol. The inverted Aśvattha tree of the Gītā continues to symbolize "the mystery of a world in perpetual regeneration," but as "a cipher of the world grasped as a living reality" it exemplifies a markedly Hindu appropriation. First of all, there is the inversion of the tree. This has caused some confusion, and one commentator, J. C. Thomson, "makes the mistake of believing the *aśvattha* to be the banyan tree, and writes of its branches descending to become new roots. This, though mistaken, is at least an attempt at suggesting why the *aśvattha* in particular should be said to have 'roots above and branches below'; it is noticeable that commentators neglect this point altogether."[40]

W. Douglas P. Hill tries to offer the following explanation of the inversion in terms of the Aśvattha tree:

> The *aśvattha* (probably derived from *aśva-stha*—the tree under which horses stand) is the Ficus Religiosa, or *pīpal* tree, well known to those who live in India as a tree held in great reverence among Hindus. It does not, like its cousin the banyan, drop aerial rootlets to take fresh root in the earth. Why, then is it said to have roots above and branches below? The formation of the tree is peculiar; in that its roots (which often stand in part above the ground) do not altogether, as in other trees, lose themselves in a central rounded trunk, but to a great extent retaining their separate form, climb up in a cluster, each to spread out into a separate branch. Each root is thus continuous with its own branch; and therefore, root and branch being inseparably one, it is possible to speak of the branch as descending to the earth, and of the root as rising aloft. This interpretation of the phrase not only explains the choice of the *aśvattha* as a symbol, but is an aid to the understanding of the figure.[41]

Apart from the horticultural, there is also a cultural angle involved. The Aśvattha is a *sacred* tree, and the universe, from such a point of view, exhibits a curious anomaly in relation to the ultimate reality—which is both above and beyond it, as well as its source. In the description in the Kaṭha Upaniṣad, "[T]here is no dichotomy between the Cosmic Tree and the immortal Being which is its source. It may paralyse through fear, yet it is none the less the ladder by which and through which the immortal can be found."[42] In the Gītā, however, the contrast between the noumenal and the phenomenal is emphasized; the mutability of the tree is meant to contrast with the immutability of the noumenal. In fact, Śaṅkara and other commentators as well derive "*aśvattha* from *a-śvaḥ-stha* (*na śvo'pi sthātā*), because though" *saṁsāra*, the phenomenal word "is *avyaya* as being without beginning or end, the world is in a constant state of change or flux."[43]

The exercises carried out in the previous section, whatever their intrinsic interest, may or may not represent examples of reciprocal illumination. Reciprocal illumination involves comparative religion; comparative religion may include reciprocal illumination but involves much more than reciprocal illumination. *Reciprocal illumination represents comparison of a particular kind.* It dispenses with the element of historical development, which is assumed in the historical method, and with the role of the mediating category (such as sacred space, etc.) that is utilized in the thematic study of religion. It involves a one-to-one comparison without any necessary temporal or categorical mediation. It seems only fair to alert the reader that this thread, now relinquished, will be picked up later, and spun further on the warp and woof of the historical and phenomenological approaches to the study of religion.

6

Reciprocal Illumination in Relation to the Views of W. C. Smith and Mircea Eliade

It has already been indicated how, in some ways, the semantic aura of the concept of reciprocal illumination shares some of its light with that generated by Professor W. C. Smith's approach to the study of religion. For instance, Smith recognizes that coming to understand another tradition may lead you to what "was in your own heritage all along but that previously you personally had not seen."[1] In fact, the concept of reciprocal illumination enables one to develop the idea further by pointing out that this flash of understanding can take three forms: of memory, recognition, or potentiality. A Hindu might discover, for instance, that the passages that condone violence in the Qur'ān, which so offend him, have a parallel in his or her own tradition. The parallel, however, lies buried in the distant past and has to be retrieved by an act of memory. But when Swami Śraddhānanda was killed by a Muslim youth for reconverting Muslims to Hinduism, thereby confirming the image of Islam as a violently fanatical religion in the eyes of many, Mahatma Gandhi reached deep into the recesses of history of Hinduism to declare:

> But I do regard Islam to be a religion of peace in the same sense as Christianity, Buddhism and Hinduism are. No doubt there are differences in degree, but the object of these religions is peace. I know the passages that can be quoted from the Koran to the contrary. But so is it possible to quote passages

> from the Vedas to the contrary. What is the meaning of imprecations pronounced against the Anaryas? Of course these passages bear today a different meaning but at one time they did wear a dreadful aspect.[2]

Hindu thought distinguishes between memory and recognition on the basis that while with memory the object is not immediately perceived but is only recalled, with recognition the object to which memory relates is immediately perceived. Such recognition is apparent for a Christian in the case of Jesus Christ as suffering savior and the bodhisattva of Mahāyāna Buddhism, who vows:

> I take it upon myself . . . the deeds of all beings, even those in hells, in other worlds, in the realms of punishment . . . I take their suffering upon me . . . I bear it, I do not draw back from it, I do not tremble at it . . . I have no fear of it . . . I do not lose heart . . . I must bear the burden of all beings, for I have vowed to save all things living, to bring them safe through the forest of birth, age, disease, death and rebirth. I think not of my own salvation, but strive to bestow on all beings the royalty of supreme wisdom. So I take upon myself all the sorrows of all beings. I resolve to bear every torment in every purgatory of the universe. For it is better that I alone suffer than the multitude of living beings. I give myself in exchange. I redeem the universe from the forest of purgatory, from the womb of flesh, from the realm of death. *I agree to suffer as a ransom for all beings, for the sake of all beings*. Truly I will not abandon them. For I have resolved to gain supreme wisdom for the sake of all that lives, to save the world.[3]

The correspondence of this idea of the suffering savior with Jesus Christ and the suffering servant in Isaiah is so close that it prevented Professor Basham from dismissing the "possibility that the doctrine was borrowed by Buddhism from Christianity."[4]

Again, the Hindu may recognize the missionary possibilities for the future within his own tradition, when contemplating the past success of Buddhism and the present success of Christianity and Islam, a possibility that may not have been perceived by the Hindu in his own heritage. If Christianity could liberate itself from its Judaic confines and Islam from its Arabian pale, what is there to prevent Hinduism from overflowing the boundaries of India, especially when Hinduism itself might be the product of Indo-European expansion?

It is clear, therefore, that Smith's approach is not inconsistent with reciprocal illumination. It does, however, differ from it. In the passage quoted earlier, for instance, Smith mentions how "our own heritage" may be illumined by the knowledge of another. Commendable as it is, it is still only *unilateral* illumination. Smith does not go on to say how our knowledge of our own tradition may illumine another. When he does bring the interaction of traditions into play he goes for what may be called *commonality* rather than reciprocity. He writes:

> What the [religious] communities have had in common is that their several histories, individually already complex, can be understood only in terms of each other; as strands in a more complex whole. What they have in common is that the history of each has been what it is in significant part because the history of the other has been what it has been.[5]

This point, however, can be incorporated into the approach we have characterized as the reciprocal illumination approach, if the statement is broken down into constituent propositions. These can be stated as follows:

(A) Tradition A is what it is because tradition B was what it was;

(B) Tradition B is what it is because tradition A was what it was.

Thus, it is reasonable to suggest that Hindu valorization of Vedic authority was an act of scriptural overcompensation because of the attacks on the Vedas[6] by the Indian materialists, the Buddhists, and the Jainas and that the Buddhist scriptural formula *evam me sutam* was an implied appropriation of the canonical status of *śruti* for the Buddhist scriptures.

Smith, however, goes even further in developing his global theology, and in so doing goes far beyond the circumference of the circle of light represented by reciprocal illumination. He speaks of man in the singular, he speaks of man's self-consciousness, and he speaks of God. He writes:

> I personally have done something, perhaps, to popularize the phrase, "The faith of other men"; and I continue earnestly to advocate an apprehension of the faith of all who share this planet: faith at the deepest, most personal, the truest level. I

> have come, to see, however, that to succeed in apprehending such faith, even intellectually, is to discover that a new formulation becomes required. The first step is to recognise the faith of the other men. Once that step has been truly taken, the next step is the recognition that there are no other men.[7]

In reciprocal illumination there are always other men. Elsewhere he writes:

> We are being faced with something as revolutionary intellectually as was science. The history of religion is vast; comparative religion is deep. The history of religion is the history of man (the humane history of man); comparative religion is the profound self-awareness of man in his or her unintegrated wholeness.[8]

Reciprocal illumination involves self-awareness, but it is the altered self-awareness brought about by contact with the other. It is like someone else holding up a mirror to one. Now on to God:

> Religious life begins in the fact of God: a fact that includes His initiative, His agony, His love for all of us without any exception, without discrimination, without favour, without remainder. Given that fact—and it is given; absolutely, and quite independently of whether or how we human beings recognize it; given that irremovable fact, religious life then consists in the quality of our response.[9]

The position here is too theological from the point of view of reciprocal illumination, which can no doubt take place among traditions that believe in God but can as well occur among those that don't.

Smith's approach from the point of view of reciprocal illumination is too integrative (just as that of Eliade will be found to be too aggregative).[10]

Another point of difference between the method of reciprocal illumination and the views of W. C. Smith lies in the importance attached to the views of the insiders of a tradition. There has been quite some discussion on the relative roles of the outsider and the insider in the study of religion. It is sufficient to recognize at this point that the insider's view is not only taken into account but also serves as a key referent, in both the historical method[11] as pursued by W. C. Smith and in the application of the phenomenological method.[12] It is also respected in reciprocal illumination. Given this common feature, it is important to note the differences. The difference between the phenomenological method and the historical method practiced à la Smith may be pinpointed only after both have been distinguished from another approach in which the scholars of a tradition *alone* may speak for it. This may be called the Morgan principle in the light of the following remark by Wilford Cantwell Smith:

> An illustrative development has been the publication for Western students of the Morgan series on comparative religion, in which Hindus, Buddhists, and Muslims present their own faiths: Kenneth W. Morgan (ed.), *The Religion of the Hindus* (New York, 1953); *The Path of the Buddha: Buddhism Interpreted by Buddhists* (New York, 1958); *Islam—the Straight Path: Islam Interpreted by Muslims* (New York, 1958). There are many other examples of the growing recognition in the West that to understand an alien religion one should allow its adherents to speak for themselves.[13]

Wilfred Cantwell Smith also developed the idea that any statement about a tradition made by the outsider must be acceptable to the insider, but not vice versa.[14] Thus three positions can be distinguished here: (1) the insider's own testimony; (2) the historian-phenomenologist's testimony as an outsider, which claims to provide an empathetic understanding of the insider's experience; and (3) the insider's right to react to such testimony. In this context the method of reciprocal illumination suggests a fourth position: (4A) the illumination an insider receives about his or her own tradition through comparison with another, and (4B) the illumination the empathetic outsider, the historian-phenomenologist, receives from the empathized tradition.

We now turn to the comparison of reciprocal illumination with the phenomenological method by examining the views of a representative figure associated with that method in our own times, namely, Mircea Eliade.[15] As the names of Smith and Eliade have been mentioned in quick succession, it may not be out of place to wonder aloud whether their own mode of induction into religious studies—Protestant Christianity and Islam in the case of the former and primal religions and the Indian religious tradition in the case of the latter—may not have influenced their methodological orientations. Be that as it may, and despite occasional disavowal,[16] Mircea Eliade is often associated with the practice of the phenomenological method. Although it is difficult to summarize Eliade's thought briefly "in that his interests are so wide ranging through fiction writing, Eastern religion, shamanism, alchemy, phenomenology of religion, hermeneutics, primal religions, history of religion, and the renewal of Western man's religiousness," it can nevertheless be claimed that "Eliade's comparative method is basically that of phenomenological typology. He puts side by side religious phenomena drawn from all parts of the world in order to ascertain their fundamental structure and their archetypal significance."[17] Inasmuch as Eliade puts religious phenomena side by side, room is created for reciprocal illumination, but inasmuch as the purpose of the exercise is to identify structures and types, such an academic goal goes beyond reciprocal illumination.

The insights resulting from the juxtaposition of individual items by Eliade are often remarkable. At one point, for instance, he remarks on modern man's obsession with history and compares it with the near-death experience of drowning men, whose whole life is said to flash before their eyes. This tempts Eliade to ask whether modern man is in the process of drowning. Now, this last comment reflects Eliade's interest in hermeneutics, but the comparison between the experience of the drowning man and Western preoccupation with history is extremely suggestive, at least to a Hindu. One does not have to believe in the imminent demise of the West to see that history at the level of the race may be taken to correspond to memory at the level of the individual.

If one tries to develop this clue a little further, one discovers that the comparison of near-death experiences with even classical religious texts can sometimes be surprisingly suggestive. Consider for instance, the following verses of the Bhagavadgītā (8.5–10):

5. And at the hour of death, on Me alone
    Meditating, leaving the body
Whoso dies, to My estate he
    Goes; there is no doubt of that.
6. Whatsoever state (of being) meditating upon
    He leaves the body at death,
To just that he goes, son of Kuntī,
    Always, being made to be in the condition of that.
7. Therefore at all times
    Think on Me, and fight:
With thought-organ and consciousness fixed on Me
    Thou shalt go just to Me without a doubt.
8. If disciplined in the discipline of practice
    By one's mind, straying to no other object.
To the supreme *divine* Spirit
    He goes, son of Pṛthā, meditating thereon.

9. The ancient seer, the governor,
    Finer than an atom—who meditates on Him.
  The establisher of all, of unthinkable Form.
    Sun-coloured, beyond darkness.
10. At the time of death with unswerving thought.
    Disciplined with devotion and the power of discipline,
  Making the breath to enter altogether between the eye-brows,
    He goes to that supreme divine Spirit.[18]

These verses associate the moment of death with the experience of a being of light. The Sanskrit word *divya,* which occurs twice in these verses and is translated as "divine," is formed from a root (*div*) that means to shine. The last line of verse 9 is conclusive if the etymological argument is tentative. The being is described as possessing the color of the sun (*ādityavarṇam*) and as beyond darkness.

The experience of light is perhaps capable of a mystical explanation,[19] but it is its juxtaposition with death, which seems to impart to the accounts of near-death experiences an uncanny relevance in the present context.

Eliade's willingness to compare what one would not normally regard as comparable is exciting from the point of view of reciprocal illumination, as demonstrated by the above example, which took its cue from Eliade's willingness to draw material from near-death experiences to shed light on the predicament of modern man. The same approach seems capable of being extended to sacred texts. In a similar fashion Eliade does not hesitate to draw on the experience of archaic religions for what light they may shed on the beliefs and practices of historical religions and on modern times (even though he mediates this understanding often through phenomenological structures).[20] That such comparisons between prehistoric and historical religions may be reciprocally illuminating can also be demonstrated. While discussing the prevalence of the bear cult in the Paleolithic age, Johannes Maringer remarks:

> The hunting artists of the upper Paleolithic sometimes painted or engraved pictures of the bear on cave walls. Such pictures are rare, however, and certain peculiarities are associated with them. The bear is sometimes shown with a wolf's head or a bison's tail, *as though the artists had feared to portray it as it really was.* They may also have intended to portray men disguised as bears, and in some cases the intention is unmistakable. Sometimes they drew only the head of a bear. Such works would seem to suggest a bear cult. On that hypothesis, the ice-age

> hunter artists *would have avoided any naturalistic portrayal of the bear because, like the bear-hunting peoples of our own day, they feared to call it by its own name*. . . .[21]

This aversion to pictographic portrayal may be compared with the reluctance in the early Jewish tradition to pronouncing the name of Yahweh. Even the act of transcribing the name was hedged with apotropaic ritual. This phenomenon may be called the *mana* of the name and form (or *nāma-rūpa,* if you wish, of the Hindu-Buddhist tradition). A domesticated version of it is found in Hinduism wherein, in an earlier age, wives did not utter the name of the husband. One is tempted here to go beyond reciprocal illumination to wonder if the creative or procreative functions are in some way involved: the bear as the God; Yahweh as God; and the husband as God.

But in attempting anything along these lines, one is beginning to indulge in Eliade's "penchant for structuring data into phenomenological typologies." Nevertheless, the principle underlying the Eliadian enterprise is acceptable in reciprocal illumination—though in a different sense. Eliade writes: "[N]o man of science has waited until *all* the facts were assembled before trying to understand the facts already known."[22] This is said in justification for offering generalizations on the basis of available data instead of falling into the trap of a perfectionistic but sterile encyclopedism. The same principle applies a fortiori to reciprocal illumination—*two* facts may suffice to shed light on each other. As such the approach, though less grand, is more cautious.

It also seems that Eliade's own ideas can be brought within the ambit of reciprocal illumination. One of the key categories in Eliade's thinking is the dichotomy between the sacred and the profane.[23] This opposition between the sacred and the profane is suggestive, at the sacred level, of the distinction between saṁsāra and nirvāṇa in Buddhism and at the profane level, the distinction between the classes in Marxism. The point to note here is that such distinctions tend to dissolve in the further dialectic of a system. Thus in the case of Buddhism the distinction between saṁsāra and nirvāṇa collapses; the two are identified through *śūnyatā.* In the case of Marxism, the distinction between the bourgeoisie and the proletariat is annulled in the classless society. Moreover, this dialectic, which annuls the distinctions, is propelled by one of the two elements in opposition: by the seeking of nirvāṇa in the case of Buddhism and by the proletariat in the case of Marxism. One is then left with the question: can a similar movement be expected to follow from within Eliade's scheme? And will the movement come from the sacred side (via fundamentalism) or from the profane side (via secularization and civil religion), or will Eliade's dichotomy escape the intellectual fate of the analogous concepts cited earlier. In any case, Eliade's distinction, when juxtaposed with nirvāṇa and saṁsāra, does shed some light on R. C. Zaehner's comment that the Communist takeover of China represented "the triumph of the claims of *saṁsāra* against *nirvāṇa*."[24]

In Eliadean terms it is the opposition between the sacred and the profane, which is at stake here, and the Communist takeover represents the process of desacralization and the continuing unidimensionalization of the life of modern man.

Another example of reciprocal illumination in relation to Eliade's ideas about the sacred and the profane is generated when the contrast between the two in his thought is contrasted with certain Hindu concepts. Eliade writes: "[W]hat men do of their own initiative, what they do without a mythical model belongs to the sphere of the profane: hence it is vain and illusory activity, and, in the last *analysis unreal*."[25]

The equation of the profane with the illusory is reminiscent of the concept of māyā, and the sacred then can be equated with "brahman," an equation with some etymological justification if it is borne in mind that the early meaning of the word "brahman" was sacred utterance or prayer. Brahman is taken to stand for changeless reality in Hindu thought, in contradistinction to the world of change represented by māyā. Eliade seems to reproduce the same ideological configuration when he explains his method as follows:

> I have not tried to study religious phenomena in their historical framework, but merely as hierophanies. That is why, in order to throw light on the nature of water hierophanies, I did not scruple to place Christian Baptism side by side with the myths and rites of Oceania, America or Greco-Oriental antiquity, *ignoring the differences between them—or, in other words, history* . . . there is no hierophany that is not, from the date of its first becoming manifest, "historical" . . . yet their structure remains the same in spite of this and it is precisely this permanence of structure that makes it possible to know them.[26]

It is worth remarking that the Advaita school of Hindu philosophy also dismisses differences, though for a different reason: "The idea of difference between A and B (say) presupposes a knowledge of these two entities; but that knowledge, since it points to them as two, already involves the idea of difference. There is thus mutual dependence between the notion of difference and that of the things, which differ, and neither can therefore be fully understood without the other. The advaitins accordingly regard the idea of 'difference' as self-discrepant, and dismiss it as but an appearance."[27]

But history becomes secondary, if not illusory, in both the systems. However, when Eliade's methodological illusionism is compared with Hindu metaphysical illusionism, an interesting result follows. Whereas, for Advaita Vedānta, the whole of history is in a sense illusory, can it not be said on an Eliadean application that only a segment of it is so—the segment represented by modern man who has lost a sense of the sacred?

We noticed early in this section how some aspects of Eliade's approach are hospitable to reciprocal illumination. Subsequently we saw how some of Eliade's own ideas on the nature of religion lent themselves to reciprocal illumination. Those aspects of Eliade's approach that are problematical from the point of view of reciprocal illumination may now also be identified before concluding this section. It has already been pointed out that Eliade's use of archetypes, while valid in itself, falls outside the scope of reciprocal illumination as a method. Further difficulties are presented by the following aspects of his thought.

> Eliade's approach minimizes the importance of the religious apprehensions of particular persons or specific traditions. His emphasis is placed upon phenomena and structures rather than persons or communities. This can be a helpful way of understanding religion. For example, it may help a Christian to enlarge his understanding of the cross to know that it belongs to the hierophany of the cosmic tree, and it may help a Muslim to widen his vision of the Ḥajj if he is aware that it belongs to a wider structure of pilgrimage. Moreover, Eliade's approach is inherently general in its unconcern for the insights of particular traditions, and in its assumption that religious symbols and structures transcend man's consciousness and have to do more properly with the "transconscious" part of his nature. Parochial insularity is overcome at a stroke. The problems with this approach are twofold. For most people and groups, religious or otherwise, their own self-awareness is important. They see their own religiousness in the light of their own religious experience, and understand aspects of their own tradition in the light of other aspects of that same tradition. It is a moot point, both for the scholar and the believer, whether the cross and the Ḥajj can be better understood within

> phenomenological typologies or within particular religious contexts. Perhaps the answer lies in both.[28]

It is obvious that reciprocal illumination encompasses both comparison between religious traditions and comparisons within religious traditions. Thus Hindu *tīrthayātrā* and Islamic *ḥajj* can be mutually illuminating, and Hindu pilgrimage within the framework of Hinduism itself can reciprocally illumine other aspects of it.

One of the issues that got al-Ḥallāj into trouble with Muslim authorities was his interiorization of the Ḥajj. That he was not the first to do so is clear from the following account of the conversation between Junayd and a man who had returned from the pilgrimage. Junayd asked:

> "From the hour when you first journeyed from your home have you also been journeying away from all sins?" He said, "No." "Then," said Junyad, "you have made no journey. At every stage where you halted for the night did you traverse a station on the way to God?" "No," he replied. "Then," replied Junyad, "you have not trodden the road, stage by stage. When you put on the pilgrim's garb at the proper place, did you discard the qualities of human nature as you cast off your clothes?" "No." "Then you have not put on the pilgrim's garb. When you stood at 'Arafāt,' did you stand one moment in contemplation of God?" "No." "Then you have not stood at 'Arafāt.' When you went to Muzdalifa and achieved your desire, did you renounce all sensual desires?" "No." "Then you have not gone to Muzdalifa. When you circumambulated the Ka'ba, did you behold the immortal beauty of God in the abode of purification?" "No." "Then you have not circumambulated the Ka'ba. When you ran between Safā and Marwa, did you attain to purity (*safā*) and virtue (*murawwat*)?" "No." "Then you have not run. When you came to Minā, did all your wishes (*munā*) cease?" "No." "Then you have not yet visited Minā. When you reached the slaughter-place and offered sacrifice, did you sacrifice the objects of worldly desire?" "No." "Then you have not sacrificed. When you threw the pebbles, did you throw away whatever sensual thoughts were accompanying you?" "No." "Then you have not yet thrown the pebbles, and you have not yet performed the pilgrimage."[29]

Nor was al-Ḥallāj the last. Abū Sa'id ibn Abi 'l-Khayr (died AD 1049) "referred to the *Kaba* as 'a stone house.' "[30] However, Junayd did not run down the practice of pilgrimage but only showed its spiritual emptiness when not accompanied by virtuous states of mind. And Abū Sa'id flourished in a more liberal age. Such interiorization is also a regular feature of Hindu reform movements.

The insights this comparison offers are that the more historical the character of a religion, the less liberal it tends to be; that mysticism tends to rise above the temporal and historical plane, and this may have led Ḥallāj and Hinduism in the direction they went; and that reform within Islam consists in restoring its literal character, for the persecutors of Ḥallāj presumably looked upon themselves as reforming Islam from the corruption Ḥallāj represented, while reform within Hinduism seemed to imply the assertion of its semiotic character. Reform in Islam involved the literalization of the ritual; by contrast, reform within Hinduism consisted of its deliteralization. This contrast is confirmed by the developments within the two traditions in the nineteenth century; Wahhābī movement in Saudi Arabia and neo-Hindu movements in India.

7

Reciprocal Illumination and the Historical Method

The historical method is a key component of the study of religion. It may therefore be useful to place the suggestion of reciprocal illumination alongside it and examine the points of convergence and divergence between them.

It is obvious that, when we say two or more traditions can shed light on each other, what we really imply is that it is the *knowledge* of these traditions that accomplishes this task. And more often than not, such knowledge is *historical* knowledge in the broadest sense of the term. That is to say, all factual knowledge in its broadest sense is historical knowledge.[1] When we write the history of a myth, or when we describe the myths about history or historiography in a culture, the distinction between history as what actually happened and myth as what is fancifully supposed to have happened helps fill in the total picture rather than having history and myth exist in mutually destructive opposition. In this sense, the data on which reciprocal illumination is based is inevitably historical.

When history is distinguished from myth and sets out to establish what actually happened as distinguished from what is believed to have happened, the historical method continues to provide the building blocks with which comparisons may be instituted at all three levels: (1) at the level of what actually happened in two or more traditions, (2) at the level of what was supposed to have happened in two or more traditions, and (3) at the level of the relationship between what happened and what was supposed to have happened in the context of two or more traditions. These points may now be suitably illustrated.

The historical method was influenced by an implicit teleology for quite some time, perhaps as a result of the powerful and pervasive influence exercised by the concepts of Darwinism and unilinear evolution in the intellectual ethos of the post-Darwinian era. Under the influence of such concepts, scholars sought to detect some underlying pattern beneath the surface of historical developments. G. W. F. Hegel provides a good example here. In his *Lectures on the Philosophy of History*, Hegel proposed that the history of the world could be seen as a progress toward the consciousness of freedom. This freedom, restricted to the head of the empire in Persia, became more widely diffused in the city-states of Greece. The Roman Empire contributed less to this freedom by itself than through the reaction it provoked—toward nature in Roman philosophy or through God in Christianity. It is no accident; therefore, that it is in Augustinian thought that one finds the first clear articulation of the person. The torch was carried forward by the Reformation, when the Roman Catholic Church became restrictive of freedom, a freedom that, according to Hegel, found its full expression in the culture of the country he represented.[2]

Other accounts, less predictably nationalistic in outcome, like Spengler's *Decline of the West*, adhere to the same idea of a telos underlying *historia*. The idea is persistent and attractive and surfaces again in Marx, but possesses little interest in the context of reciprocal illumination by itself, for the simple reason that under its influence the comparisons that are instituted are not meant to shed light on the items compared but to capture a movement beyond what the items represent. Or, in other words—although it may be too much to say that the scholar has a hidden agenda underlying the comparison instituted— the comparisons are only grist for the mill of generalization. From the point of view of reciprocal illumination they are merely exploited, or bent to serve a favored teleology.

A comparison of such historical teleologies themselves, however, can be illuminating. Let us consider, for instance, some grand summations of history involving religion. Frazer saw all humanity progressing from magic through religion to science;[3] Comte saw the same journey undertaken also through three stages, but this time through the theological, the metaphysical, and the positivistic phases.[4] Hegel saw religion *itself* undergoing three phases: of undifferentiated universality, of particularistic opposition to religions other than Christianity, and of reflective synthesis in Christianity.[5] One immediately sees a pattern underlying these patterns—that the scholar's own pet attraction comes out on top of the heap (although it could be casuistically argued that it is the pet because it comes out on top). The enhancement of understanding attained through this exercise is not through reciprocal understanding but through a more *general* procedure; call it phenomenological or hermeneutical. It is even capable of extension. Thus, Islam considers itself the culmination of the Judeo-Christian prophetic tradition;[6] Christianity considers itself the fulfillment or crown of other religious traditions;[7] and some forms of Hinduism have adopted a similar attitude.[8]

What might constitute reciprocal illumination would be an enlightening contrast between some forms of Judaism, with their commitment to an original revelation, and Islam's commitment to a *final* revelation; the former may explain the pertinacity of Judaism as one of the oldest major religions of the world, and the latter the missionary zeal of Islam as the youngest major religion of the world. This brings us to a second point of difference between the historical method and reciprocal illumination. Although reciprocal illumination may involve a time dimension and may shed light on the circumstances in which religions originated, it is not concerned with the question of origins per se.[9]

Although the reading of grand designs in history, which unfold through stages, is not without interest and may even shed light on various aspects of a tradition, this light has its source in lamps other than what we have called reciprocal illumination. But once the various stages have been divested of an immanent telos and are merely considered as extended chronological periods, one such period may be reciprocally illuminating in comparison with another. The idea that a wife's complete submission to the husband may help her achieve liberation is anathema not only to modern feminists but also to all modern women. But how such an idea in a classical Hindu worldview *could* have made sense in terms of the tradition itself can be understood by considering a modern explanation of comparable phenomenon—that abject submission to the will of the guru secures enlightenment for the discipline. The following explanation of the efficacy of this method has been offered in modern times by Ramana Maharshi:

> This is the meaning conveyed by the story of Ashtavakra and Janaka. The anecdotes differ in different books. We are not concerned with the names and the embellishments. The tatva, i.e., the moral, must not be lost sight of. The disciple surrenders himself to the master. That means there is no vestige of individuality retained by the discipline. If the surrender is

> complete all sense of individuality is lost and there is thus no cause for misery. The eternal being is only happiness. That is revealed.
>
> Without understanding it aright, people write that the Guru teaches the disciple something like "TATVAMSI" and that the disciple realizes "I am Brahman." In their ignorance they conceive of Brahman as something more huge and powerful than anything else. With a limited "I" the man is so stuck up and wild. What will be the case if the same "I" grows up enormous? He will be enormously ignorant and foolish! This false "I" must perish. Its annihilation is the fruit of Guru *seva*.[10]

The logic of this case illuminates the case of surrendering of one's will to the husband.[11] Of course, it can similarly be argued that the surrender of will on the part of the husband to the wife as a *devī* could be spiritually as efficacious.[12]

An illustration used by W. C. Smith shows the difference between the historical method and reciprocal illumination. He cites a parable that is said to have changed the course of Tolstoy's life.

> In this tale, the human condition is portrayed as like that of a man who, fleeing from a furious beast, falls into a well and is held from dropping into the jaws of a devouring dragon below only by clinging to a bush that will, he sees, presently inevitably give way, since it is being nibbled at by two mice, one white and one black, that go round and round and slowly but relentlessly gnaw at its roots. The two mice are day and night; the bush, which tastes sweet at first but soon loses its savour, is one's worldly position; man knows that he or she must in due course die.[13]

From this point onward, Smith's argument can be moved in a forward and backward direction. The forward movement consists of acknowledging the profound influence Tolstoy exerted on Mahatma Gandhi. Gandhi himself identifies Tolstoy, along with Ruskin and Rajchandra, as three figures who influenced the course of his life above all others.[14] A biographer of Gandhi, Robert Payne, suggests that Gandhi may have given more credit to Tolstoy than he deserves by declaring him to be the *fons et origo* of his own doctrine of nonviolence. Payne points out that Gandhi was a man of action by contrast with the pure moralism of Tolstoy. He, nevertheless, acknowledges that Tolstoy's "influence was so deep, so pervasive, that Gandhi could scarely tell where his own ideas began and Tolstoy's ended."[15] Gandhi's response to reading *The Kingdom of God Is Within You*, by Gandhi's own account, reads like a conversion experience.[16] This, then, is the central point to bear in mind—that Gandhi's reading of Tolstoy's book constituted a "turning-point"[17] in Gandhi's life, just as reading the parable of "The Man in the Well" constituted a turning point in the life of Tolstoy.

Now Smith's argument can be moved backward to ancient India. He shows how the parable that so changed Tolstoy's life (who so changed Gandhi's life) originated in India, though it reached Tolstoy in its Christian incarnation. In India, the story is found not only in the Mahābhārata[18] but also in a seventh-century text,[19] and even a Buddhist source has been suggested for it.[20]

The conclusion Smith draws from this narrative of parabolic persistence through several incarnations is the sense of a completed circle—an Indian parable journeys to the West and influences Tolstoy, who influences Gandhi, who comes from India.[21]

This is a result yielded by the historical method. The application of the method of reciprocal illumination will involve a different procedure and may or may not yield a different result. One might now wish to compare the conversion experience of Gandhi through reading Tolstoy and the conversion experience of Tolstoy through reading the parable for any reciprocal illumination that might result from such a comparison. The process may now be set in motion.

It strikes one right away that while Tolstoy was influenced by a parable—a "myth"—Gandhi was influenced by a historical figure. (The man in the well is not a historical figure.) But Gandhi never met Tolstoy and actually "there had been little communication between them: four letters from Gandhi, and only two from Tolstoy until his long last letter was written. When Gandhi received it in Johannesburg, Tolstoy had only a few more days to live."[22] In other words, Gandhi's encounter with Tolstoy was more *historic* than *historical*, and borders on the mythical, in the sense that the historicity of Tolstoy was perhaps of little value per se to Gandhi, just as the historicity of the Kṛṣṇa of the Gītā was a nonissue with him. And it turns out that the parable of "The Man in the Well" was something more than a fable for Tolstoy, too. For he wrote of it: "This is no fable. It is a real unanswerable truth."[23] In other words, the conversion experiences of Gandhi and Tolstoy yield potentially fascinating perspectives on the mythicizing of history and the historicizing of a myth, and give a new turn to the paradoxical vision of treating history as myth and myth as history. This discussion holds the promise of becoming even more fascinating, when placed against the larger backdrop of Christianity being regarded as a historical religion and Hinduism as one prone to believing in myths.

It should be noted that the comparison of the two conversion experiences was not mediated through the category, far less the typology, of conversion experience. That would belong to the realm of the phenomenological method, from which reciprocal illumination must be as constantly and consciously distinguished as from the historical method. This is, of course, not to deny that moments of reciprocal illumination might light up the chamber of these methods as well.

8

Reciprocal Illumination and the Phenomenological Method

The phenomenological method has become as significant a factor in the study of religion as the historical,[1] and is sometimes described as its thematic counterpart.[2] It is a method difficult to define and has sometimes been called an approach rather than a method.[3] Thus, it might be helpful to distinguish between the phenomenological approach and the phenomenological method in the study of religion. It may then be said that, while as an approach it wishes "to combine complete accuracy of scholarship with complete sympathy of treatment to ensure complete understanding of the religious beliefs and practices of other human beings,"[4] as a method its aspiration is somewhat more precise. Here the key word is structure,[5] not to be confused with its esoteric Straussian usage. In the phenomenology of religion it denotes the manner in which the phenomenologist comes to understand a given religious phenomenon by identifying the structure of his or her experience of it. The phenomenon is immediately experienced: "[S]tructure is certainly experienced but not immediately; it is indeed constructed, but not logically, causally and abstractly. Structure is reality significantly organized."[6] G. van der Leeuw packs the suitcase perhaps a little too tightly, but packs it well when he goes on to say:

> The appearance, to continue, subsists as an image. It possesses backgrounds and associated planes; it is "related" to other entities that appear, either by similarity, by contrast, or by a

> hundred *nuances* that can arise here: conditions, peripheral or central position, competition, distance, *etc.* These relationships, however, are always *perceptible* relationships, "*structural connections*": they are never factual relationships nor causal connections. They do not, of course, exclude the latter, but neither do they enunciate anything about them, they are valid only within the structural relations. Such a relation, finally, whether it concerns a person, a historical situation or a religion, is called a *type*, or an *ideal type*.[7]

As this condensed (and some might uncharitably say, dense) passage suggests, phenomenology may not be everyone's cup of tea. Yet, though the debate on the definition of the phenomenological method shows every sign of continuing in scholarly circles, three features of the method can be confidently identified; and each is enshrined in a term: *epoche, eidos,* and *type. Epoche* consists in suspending any value judgments about the phenomenon under observation; *eidos* consists of seeking the essence of the phenomenon in its manifestation; and *type* consists in understanding this essence through a typology. To illustrate: one looks at a savior figure such as Dionysus; one sees the essence in his manifestation both as representing the saving act in nature and history—in the young god's form as *kouros,* life renews itself, but "visionary feelings" also attached themselves to the "old *kouros* form of Dionysus," so that "from the periodic epiphany of the saviour there developed the historic event of the god of ecstasy's entry, overcoming the resistance of a prosaic and suspicious people."[8] And this figure of Dionysus belongs to the "type" of savior myth constituted of (a) *Birth, Epiphany,* (b) *Deed of Salvation,* and (c) *Resurrection: Parousia.* Its analysis discloses the following structural element: that the "saviour, whose being is not of this world—for just as he 'returns,' so also he has existed from the beginning (pre-existence)—is born when the time is 'fulfilled.' It is this fatefulness of the time of salvation that links the periodic form of the savior with the historic."[9]

The method of reciprocal illumination does not mediate its understanding of comparable religious phenomena through a "type" but compares them and their structures directly; it is open on the issue of whether the essence of the phenomenon is disclosed through the manifestation or underlies it, and while it does suspend value judgments, it does not suspend the comparison of such judgments or acts embodying them if such comparison is illuminating. Thus type, *eidos,* and *epoche* (to list them in reverse) play their role in reciprocal illumination, but in a manner that may differ from their role in the phenomenology of religion. To illustrate the difference with reference to *epoche*, it will acknowledge the illuminatory force of the contrast that the same "general principle of respect for parents may produce a stringent ban on parricide in a technically advanced society but may lead to a custom of abandoning infirm or very elderly parents in hunter-gatherer cultures where there is no provision for sustaining the disabled and where dependency is regarded by all as shameful."[10]

The difference between the phenomenological method and reciprocal illumination can also be illustrated with reference to *eidos* or eidetic vision, for the simple reason that although the "phenomenon is what 'appears,' *to phainomenon*, but it is not sure at all what appears to us really constitutes the essentials behind or within the phenomenon. Very often we must try to search behind the phenomenon in order to find the essentials."[11] Let us consider two instances of obeisance to political authority with religious connotations: that by the Buddhist monks in North China during the Northern Wei Empire (386–534) and that by the Muslim soldiers of the Vijayanagar Empire during the reign of Devarāya II (1426–46). The Buddhist monks offered salutations to the emperor who was identified with the Buddha, an equation that also received sculptural expression. "The most noteworthy objects at Yun-kang are the five gigantic figures of the Buddha, with the tallest standing about seventy feet in height. These five Buddhas were regarded by the Northern Wei people as the representatives of the first five emperors of the dynasty, in accordance with an idea formulated by the Buddhists that the rulers were the present-day manifestations of the Tathagatas."[12] Now, a phenomenological approach might suggest that this merely constitutes a recognition of the optional destiny of the Buddha—that he will either be a universal emperor (*cakravartī*)[13] or set the Wheel of Dharma in motion. Indeed, accounts of Buddha's life are shot through with royal symbolism,[14] and his nativity itself is not free from this glorious uncertainty about his destiny.

> The written explanation of the doubt is that, though the horoscope forecasted the greatness of the newborn baby, it did not specify what form it was to take. Our Middle Ages would have stated it as possible becoming one or the other of "the two halves of God, the Pope or the Emperor," and the Indian idiom was "Universal Monarch or Saviour." Because the Brahmans were unable to decide between the two conjectures, the gods were called upon. But even they were hesitant, and it was left to an old rishi to come down from his mountain

> hermitage and settle the question. This version became so popular that it was the subject of numerous pictorial representations, which still remain. For Hsuan Tsang, our Chinese traveler, there is no doubt that it was Asita, the rishi, who alone was clairvoyant enough to forecast clearly the Bodhisattva's destiny.[15]

But such an explanation would be misleading, because the manifestation here does not represent the essence of the situation. As Buddhism spread through China during the post-Han period, the Saṅgha was able to assert its authority vis-à-vis the state in the south but not in the north. In the south, Hui-yüan (334–416/417) "staunchly defended the autonomy of the Saṅgha against the estate, insisting that the monk is not obliged to kowtow to the ruler,"[16] but in the north, "unlike Hui-yuan in the south, the monk appointed did not fight for the independence of the Saṅgha from the state but kowtowed to the emperor and justified this seeming contravention of the monastic rule by identifying the emperor with the Tathāgata!"[17] The essence of the situation is political, the manifestation is religious.

Similarly, the case of the Muslim soldiers saluting the Hindu king has to be approached with caution. At a phenomenological level, this could be seen as reflecting a Caesar-God accommodation even within Islam, in which the prophetic and temporal roles of Muḥammad are combined.[18] At a historical level, it could serve as an example of an accommodation on the part of Islam as it grappled with Hindu religious pluralism[19] and a plural Hindu polity, for we find Hindus in the service of Muslim rulers and Muslim troops engaged by Hindu emperors of Vijayanagar. Both these explanations, however, are misleading. Manifestation once again does not reflect either the phenomenological or historical essence of the situation, for the reality was military.

> The Vijayanagar armies were so consistently defeated in their contests with Bahmani forces that Devaraya held a council of his nobility to explore the causes of Muslim successes and devise means of counteracting them. As a result, Mussalmans were thenceforth eligible for service in his army and allowed the free exercise of their religion; a Koran was placed before his throne that they "might perform the ceremony of obeisance in his presence, without sinning against their laws." Further, the Hindu soldiers received better training, particularly in archery. After this reorganization, the army became a more efficient striking force.[20]

However, although the application of the phenomenological *eidos* is problematic here, the two examples from North China and South India are mutually illuminating in an unsuspected way—and in a way that enables the further point to be made that whereas reciprocal illumination is not routed through a "type" that is a phenomenological modality, yet two types, when set side by side, may spark reciprocal illumination. For if (following Max Weber and extending his typology) one identified the world-wandering mendicant monk as an ideal type from Buddhism and the world-conquering warrior as that from Islam, then it is clear that the state was recruiting the "ideal type" of each tradition into not merely formal but ideological service, perhaps consciously in the case of China and unconsciously in the case of India. It is only fair to add, however, that Weber himself does not regard his description as ideal types in this context but identifies the monk and the warrior as "primary carriers" of the tradition. In both the cases, the State, by appropriating the primary carriers of the traditions, was trying to further its own end in terms of this idiom. It is, however, important to note that the method of reciprocal illumination, although it may compare types as items, does not compare items through a "type." It institutes such comparisons directly, and in this shares W. C. Smith's concern regarding phenomenological typologies, "namely, that a deep knowledge and understanding of two particular traditions may lead to the recognition that authentic comparison need not necessarily follow typological lines—for example, the sacred text of one, the Qur'an, may be equivalent to the sacred founder of another, Christ."[21]

9

Parallelisms between Hinduism and Christianity as Further Examples of Reciprocal Illumination

As I have maintained all along, sometimes while we are engaged in the study of another tradition we encounter something in that other tradition that has the effect of enhancing our understanding of our own tradition. I trust this experience, if not common among students of comparative religion, is certainly not unknown to some, or indeed, to many of them. For some years now I have been endeavoring to define this experience and to refine its cognitive mechanism to a degree of precision that, I hope, will someday approach the status of a method in the study of religion. That remains a distant goal and may well turn out to be the academic equivalent for the search of the holy grail—but just as that search, even when it did not succeed, sometimes led to many unexpected, worthwhile discoveries, I am now ready to share some of my adventures or misadventures with you once again.

I alluded earlier to the fact of our knowledge of another religious tradition enhancing, or deepening, our understanding of our own. I have referred to this phenomenon in this book as that of reciprocal illumination. And I will like to share with you in this chapter some more examples of this phenomenon—cases in which, I think, my understanding of Hinduism was, if not enriched, enhanced, or enlarged, at least affected and influenced by what I learned of Christianity. Some of the examples I have chosen most of us would be inclined to regard as cases of religious pathology rather than religiosity, as they involve (1) the practice of suttee; (2) the caste system; (3) the practice of untouchability; and (4) trial by ordeal. However, just as the study of illness advances that of health, perhaps the examination of even these "dark spots" of Hinduism with a comparative lens might throw some light on reciprocal illumination.

Suttee

I would like to begin the discussion here with a verbal clarification. The question might be raised as to why I am choosing the form "suttee" over "sati" in referring to this rite. My reasons for doing so are historical and lexicographical. The anglicized form "suttee" has become firmly associated with the rite as it was performed when it was abolished in the dominions of India under the British in 1829. I find the historical vintage of the word worth retaining in the context in which the argument is being made. The lexical argument pertains to the fact that use of the word "sati" for the rite contains the potential risk of confusing the person with the performance, apart from overloading the word with a Western layer of meaning by some kind of a semantic ricochet effect.[1] I will reserve the Hindu term *satī* for the wife who performs suttee.

The practice of suttee, in which the widow burns herself alive on the funeral pyre of the husband, provokes great outrage and, among the more restrained, revulsion. This has unfortunately made it difficult to discuss the issue the way I propose to. In order for me to make my point, it is vital to emphasize that the practice of suttee was *always* (in theory and, usually, in practice), voluntary. It was the widow's decision, and if she made such a decision it was also the duty of all around her—ranging from the members of the family to the priests—to dissuade her from such an undertaking. A seventh-century Sanskrit text contains a moving account of how a royal widow refused to be dissuaded. If what I am going to say is going to make any sense, this fact must be borne in mind: that the act was meant to be performed voluntarily. By performing the act, which epitomized conjugal virtue, a woman ensured the following:

1. Reunion with her husband in heaven, irrespective of the moral standing of her husband. In other words, she was generating such virtue by this act as not only wiped out her own sins, such as they might be, but also those of her husband.
2. Her act was supposed to similarly redeem the community of which she was a member, and the locality in which it

was being performed, from sin and evil, and she came to be worshipped as a goddess.

3. According to some texts, the forces of virtue her act released operated not merely spatially but temporally—purifying seven generations backwards and forwards.[2]

It had always baffled me as to why a woman would commit suttee till it occurred to me that she might, like Jesus Christ, be viewed as dying for the sins of others. Once I looked upon the *satī*, or widow performing suttee, as a *mini female Christ*, my appreciation of the whole phenomenon underwent considerable modification. Christianity had made me understand an aspect of my own tradition, which had remained, until then, essentially incomprehensible. It should also be borne in mind that both the *satī* and Jesus did their duty as they saw it—the *satī* exemplified *strī-dharma*, or duties of a devoted wife in its best (though to us, extreme) form, and Jesus exemplified the *dharma* of a prophet, especially an eschatological prophet, by dying for others just as the *satī* dies for the husband. It could, of course, be argued of the *satī* that she suffers from messianic delusions, even megalomaniacal delusions, in terms of her personal psychology; but then only a cultural bias would prevent us from then attributing the same to Jesus. It could also be argued that the *satī* probably succumbs to societal pressures and the "satianic" (and for Christians satanic) expectations of Hinduism: but that is like arguing that Jesus simply internalized the messianic and apocalyptic expectations of Judaism. To look upon a *satī* merely as a widow burnt to death with her husband is tantamount to looking upon Jesus as a common criminal crucified for stirring up trouble, which has led some cynics to dub him the best-known convicted felon in history.

Caste System

The caste system has had a terrible press in the West and in India as well. And perhaps not without good reason. But here again, discounting its pathology for the moment, one may ask oneself the question: what is really going on here? A possible answer came to me from a rather unexpected source: Ephesians 4:15–16. I quote from the Good News Bible:

> [W]e must grow in every way to Christ, who is the head. Under his control all the different parts of the body fit together,

> and the whole body is held together by every joint with which it is provided. So when each separate part works as it should, the whole body grows and builds itself up through love.[3]

I was immediately reminded of the fact that the earliest textual reference to the caste system in the entire corpus of sacred literature in Hinduism employs the same metaphor. This reference occurs in the Puruṣa Sūkta or Hymn to the Primeval Man that is found in the ṚgVeda (10.90). The following remarks help clarify the context:

> There is no clearly defined creator-god in the main body of the ṚgVeda. By the end of the ṚgVedic period, however, such a god had developed, whether wholly from the speculations of the brahmans or from non-Aryan influences. This god was *Prajāpati*, "the Lord of Beings," later called *Brahmā*, the masculine form of the neuter *brahman*. Prajāpati was thought of as a primeval man (*puruṣa*), who existed before the foundation of the universe. The man was sacrificed, presumably to himself, by the gods, who apparently were his children. From the body of the divine victim the universe was produced. The great "Hymn of the Primeval Man" in which the first cosmic sacrifice is described explains how the four "castes" arose from his sacrifice. In the verses which follow "Man" stands for the cosmic being and it is tempting to compare it with the appellation "son of Man" applied to Jesus, who was also sacrificed. The relevant verses (ṚgVeda X.90.11–12), which were cited earlier in another context, are now quoted again (in translation)
>
> "When they divided the Man,
> into how many parts did they divide him?
> What was his mouth, what were his arms,
> What were his thighs and his feet called?
>
> "The brāhmaṇ was his mouth,
> of his arms was made the warrior,
> his thighs became the vaiśya,
> of his feet the śūdra was born."[4]

The enumeration is hierarchical; the Brāhmaṇa associated with the mouth stands at the top like Jesus (who is, I find, referred to as first-born in the Bible, just as the Brahmins are first-born).

Thus parallel suggests the possibility that the original conception of castes was one of constituent elements of a functioning social organism on the analogy of the body.

Untouchability

Most students of Indian culture and of Hinduism are aware of the existence of a class of people within Hindu society whose touch was considered polluting, and who were therefore segregated and known as untouchables. Many are also aware of the efforts of Mahatma Gandhi directed toward the removal of untouchability—an opposition he first expressed to his parents at the age of fourteen.[5] The question I had to ask myself was: How did it come into existence? It should be borne in mind that pollution is a key element in the situation here—contact with untouchables was considered polluting.

Here again a passage from the Bible gave one reason to pause and reflect. It is the passage in which the bleeding woman touches Jesus. I present the account according to Luke (8:42–46):

> As Jesus went along, the people were crowding him from every side. Among them was a woman who had suffered from severe bleeding for twelve years; she had spent all she had on doctors, but no one had been able to cure her. She came up in the crowd behind Jesus and touched the edge of his cloak, and her bleeding stopped at once, Jesus asked, "Who touched me?"
>
> Everyone denied it, and Peter said, "Master, the people are all around you and crowding in on you."
>
> But Jesus said, "Someone touched me, for I knew it when *power went out of me*." The woman saw that she had been found out, so she came trembling and threw herself at Jesus' feet. There in front of everybody, she told him why she had touched him and how she had been healed at once, Jesus said to her, "My daughter, your faith has made you well. Go in peace."[6]

If one were to connect pollution with loss of power, and power with ritual purity, one can see how the concept of untouchability might develop, especially when we realize that "Often in the *Ṛg Veda* we read of a mysterious entity called *brahman*; in some contexts *brahman* is the magical power in the sacred utterance (*mantra*), but often it has a wider connotation, and implies a sort of supernatural electricity, known to students of primitive religion as *mana*. The possessor of *brahman*, by a common process of secondary word formation in Sanskrit, became known as *brāhmaṇa,* the tribal priest and magician."[7] However, untouchability itself is not mentioned in the ṚgVeda at all.[8] What I am suggesting is that the biblical passage turned my thoughts in that direction. That passage has a kind ending, but at some point in its history was Hinduism convulsed by an equivalent of the AIDS scare of today?

Trial by Ordeal

The following passage occurs in the Chāndogya Upaniṣad (6.16.1–3)

1. Also, my dear, they lead up a man seized by the hand, saying, "he has stolen, he has committed a theft, heat the axe for him." If he is the doer thereof (i.e. if he has committed the theft) then he makes himself untrue (a liar). Being given to untruth, covering himself by untruth he takes hold of the heated axe and is burnt. Then he is killed.
2. But if he is not the doer thereof, thereupon he makes himself true. Being given to truth, covering himself by truth, he takes hold of the heated axe he is not burnt. Then he is released.
3. And as in this case he would not be burnt, thus has all this that for its self. That is the true. That is the self. That art thou, Śvetaketu. Then he understood it from him, yea, he understood.[9]

This is clearly a reference to trial by ordeal, and the temptation to cite John 8:32 is irresistible: "You will know the truth and the truth will set you free." It is, however, not truth but *faith* that possesses miraculous powers in Christianity, while in the passage above one has the miraculous power of remaining unharmed if one possesses the *truth.*

I will now endeavor to show that the Christian belief in faith, when understood as the Hindu counterpart to belief in truth, enables one to appreciate the instances of veridical therapeutics sometimes found in Hinduism. Let me explain. There is a Hindu practice known as an Act of Truth, whereby miraculous cures and even miracles are performed. This Act of Truth is not a *moral* force like Mahatma Gandhi's *satyāgraha;* it is physical and metaphysical. An appropriate illustration must wait until I have recounted the story of the healing of the ten men by Jesus (Luke 17:11–19):

> As Jesus made his way to Jerusalem, he went along the border between Samaria and Galilee. He was going into a village when he was met by ten men suffering from a dreaded skin disease. They stood at a distance and shouted, "Jesus! Master! Have pity on us!"
>
> Jesus saw them and said to them, "Go and let the priests examine you."
>
> On the way they were made clean. When one of them saw that he was healed, he came back, praising God in a loud voice. He threw himself to the ground at Jesus' feet and thanked him. The man was a Samaritan. Jesus spoke up, "There were ten men who were healed, where are the other nine? Why is this foreigner the only one who came back to give thanks to God?" And Jesus said to him, "Get up and go; your faith has made you well."[10]

In the healing story from the Hindu side (which is really Buddhist), the healing is effected by truth rather than faith. Heinrich Zimmer narrates it as follows, prefacing it with a remark on the Hindu concept of *dharma*:

> Though dharma, the fulfillment of one's inherited role in life, is the traditional basis of this Hindu feat of virtue, nevertheless, a heartfelt truth of any order has its force. Even a shameful truth is better than a decent falsehood—as we shall learn from the following witty Buddhist tale.
>
> The youth Yaññadatta had been bitten by a poisonous snake. His parents carried him to the feet of an ascetic, laid him down, and said, "Reverend sir, monks know simples and charms; heal our son."
>
> "I know no simples; I am not a physician."
>
> "But you are a monk; therefore out of charity for this youth perform an Act of Truth"
>
> The ascetic replied, "Very well, I will perform an Act of Truth." He laid his hand on Yaññadatta's head and recited the following stanza:
>
> For but a week I lived the holy life
> With tranquil heart in quest of merit.
>
> The life I've lived for fifty years
> Since then, I've lived against my will.
>
> By this truth, health!
> Poison is struck down! Let Yaññadatta live!

> Immediately the poison came out of Yaññadatta's breast and sank into the ground.[11]

I pass over the rest of the account—the point has been made. The monk uttered a shameful truth—but the truth—and that truth acted as an antidote to the poison. In this respect the Hindu position is not very different from the Buddhist—as will become clear from another example. But this must wait till I have cited the story of Jesus healing the official's son (John 4:46–53):

> Then Jesus went back to Cana in Galilee, where he had turned the water into wine. A government official was there whose son was sick in Capernaum. When he heard that Jesus had come from Judea to Galilee, he went to him and asked him to go to Capernaum and heal his son, who was about to die. Jesus said to him, "None of you will ever believe unless you see miracles and wonders."
>
> "Sir," replied the official, "come with me before my child dies."
>
> Jesus said to him, "Go; your son will live!"
>
> *The man believed Jesus' words and went.* On his way home his servants met him with the news, "Your boy is going to live!"
>
> He asked them what time it was when his son got better, and they answered, "It was one o'clock yesterday afternoon when the fever left him." Then the father remembered that it was at that very hour when Jesus had told him, "Your son will live." So he and all his family believed.[12]

The Hindu parallel is provided by the case of

> The story of Parikshit. He was a stillborn child. The ladies cried and appealed to Sri Krishna to save the child. The sages round about wondered how Krishna was going to save the child from the effects of the arrows (*apandavastra*) of Asvatthama. Krishna said, "If the child be touched by one eternally celibate (*nityabrahmachari*) the child would be brought to life." Even Suka dared not touch the child. Finding no one among the reputed saints bold enough to touch the child, Krishna went and touched it, saying, "If I am eternally celibate (*nityabrahmachari*) may the child be brought to life." The child began to breathe and later grew up to be Parikshit.[13]

Thus the child was restored to life by an Act of Truth. In the light of the Act of Truth and its recognition in Hinduism, it is indeed a striking fact that "one surprising omission in the lists of virtues mentioned in the Bible and other Christian works is the virtue of truthfulness. By truth the N.T. generally means the truth of the doctrine or the truth of Christ's teaching. This we read in 2 Jn. 1.2: 'I rejoiced greatly and I found thy children walking in the truth.' And again: 'Then said Jesus to those Jews who believed on him, if ye continue in my word, then are ye my disciples indeed; And ye shall know the truth, and the truth shall make you free.' (Jn. VIII. 31–32)."[14]

Once *truth* in Hinduism and *faith* in Christianity have been placed side by side, an interesting insight ensues—that as the pivotal concepts in their two traditions, both the concepts are liable to what one might call ideological excess. In Christianity this could lead to the view that if one has faith in Jesus Christ and in his having died for our sins, one now has a carte blanche for sinning! It is true that Paul opposes such antinomianism, but the tendency for slippage here is obvious. In fact, it was encountered by Gandhi when he met Mr. Coates in England. Earlier, to help Gandhi get rid of his "superstition," Mr. Coates had tried to break the necklace of Tulsi-beads Gandhi's mother had given to Gandhi but Gandhi would not let him. Now he wanted to convince Gandhi that salvation was impossible for Gandhi unless Gandhi "accepted Christianity which represented *the* truth, and that Gandhi's sins would not be washed away except by the intercession of Jesus, and that all *goods works were useless*."[15] He also heard the following statement from another Christian:

> You cannot understand the beauty of our religion. From what you say it appears that you must be brooding over your transgressions every moment of your life, always mending them and atoning for them. How can this ceaseless cycle of action bring you redemption? You can never have peace. You admit that we are all sinners. Now look at the perfection of our belief. Our attempts at improvement and atonement are futile. And yet redemption we must have. How can we bear the burden of sin? We can but throw it on Jesus. He is the only sinless Son of God. It is His word that those who believe in Him shall have everlasting life. Therein lies God's infinite mercy. And as we believe in the atonement of Jesus, our own sins do not bind us. Sin we must. It is impossible to live in this world sinless. And therefore Jesus suffered and atoned for all

> the sins of mankind. Only he who accepts His great redemption can have eternal peace. Think what a life of restlessness is yours, and what a promise of peace we have.[16]

Gandhi was not convinced.

> The argument utterly failed to convince me. I humbly replied:
>
> "If this be the Christianity acknowledged by all Christians, I cannot accept it. I don't seek redemption from the consequences of my sin. I seek to be redeemed from sin itself, or rather from the very thought of sin. Until I have attained that end, I shall be content to be restless."
>
> To which the Plymouth Brother rejoined: "I assure you, your attempt is fruitless. Think again over what I have said."
>
> And the Brother proved as good as his word. He knowingly committed transgressions, and showed me that he was undisturbed by the thought of them.[17]

N. K. Devaraja also cites this encounter in his book *Hinduism and Christianity* and remarks:

> The episode seems to constitute a *reductio ad absurdum* of insistent emphasis on the doctrines of faith and grace. It proves how the doctrine of redemption through Christ may lead to the weakening of the will to improve morally and spiritually. Dr. Radhakrishnan reports that some followers of the Tengalai School of *Bhakti* adopted "the dangerous doctrine of *dosha-bhogya*, namely, that God enjoys sin, since it gives a larger scope for the display of his grace." Fortunately, in India, the doctrine of Karma has been far too prevalent to permit any such doctrine to gain currency among the people.[18]

We thus see the contorted face of extreme and reckless faith, and I venture to suggest that this grotesqueness is a pathological expression of its centrality, just as trial by ordeal is a bizarre manifestation of confidence in the power of truth. The illustration cited earlier from the Chāndogya Upaniṣad appears at the end of a series of examples through which Śvetaketu has been repeatedly instructed in eternal verities. I cite the final passage again in a different translation, which highlights the *truth* factor more clearly than the previous one.

1. "Again, my dear boy, people bring a man handcuffed [to face the ordeal], crying out, 'He has committed a robbery, he has stolen, heat the axe for him!' if he is guilty, he makes himself out to be what he is not (*anṛtam ātmānam kurute*), speaks untruly (*anṛta*), clothes [him]self (*ātmānam*) in untruth. He takes hold of the red-hot axe and is burnt. Then he is killed.

2. "If, however, he is innocent, he shows himself to be what he is (*satya*), speaks the truth (*satya*), clothes [him]self in truth. He takes hold of the red-hot axe and is not burnt. Then he is released (*muc-*).

3. "So, just as such a man is not burnt [because he embodies Truth], so does this whole universe have this [Truth], as its Self. That is the Real (*satya*, Truth): That is the Self: that you are, Śvetaketu!" This did he understand from him,—this did he understand.[19]

In its own way this represents the reductio ad absurdum of the truth principle.

Resurrection and Rebirth

The concepts of resurrection in Christianity and rebirth in Hinduism have often been compared and contrasted;[20] and sometimes an effort has even been made to integrate them.[21] In what I am going to say, however, the reciprocal illumination is gained not by a static apposition of the two, but by focusing on a turning point in the development of the doctrines in their early stages. It is as if the arcs of light from two swinging lamps have suddenly intersected to produce an extra flash of light.

It is well known that the early church understood the resurrection quite literally. Indeed, "the resurrection appearances convinced the disciples that Jesus had been raised from the dead so that he might soon return on the clouds of heaven as the promised Son of Man, who should judge the nations at the great assize of the Last Day."[22] However, this does *not* seem to have been the case with Paul.

> The earliest extant account of the appearances of Jesus after the resurrection is that of Saint Paul. About the year 54 A.D. he wrote to the church that he had founded in Corinth:

> "Now I want to remind you, brothers . . . [that] I passed on to you, as of first importance, the account I had received, that Christ died for our sins, as the Scriptures foretold, that he was buried, on the third day he was raised from the dead, as the Scriptures foretold, and that he was seen by Cephas [Peter], and then by the Twelve. After that he was seen by more than five hundred brothers at one time, most of whom are still alive, although some of them have fallen asleep. Then he was seen by James, then by all the apostles, and finally he was seen by me also, as though I were born at the wrong time."[23]

Now,

> the interesting thing about what Paul says next is that he goes on the assumption that Jesus rose in a spiritual body, not in a physical one. "It is so with the resurrection of the dead. The body is sown in decay, it is raised free from decay . . . It is a physical body that is sown, it is a spiritual body that is raised . . . I can tell you this, brothers: flesh and blood cannot share in the Kingdom of God, and decay will not share in what is imperishable."—This is not what the Church later declared about the resurrection of Jesus, namely, that it was a resurrection of his physical body; nor is it the view of Luke and John; but it is worth noting that one who was converted two years after Jesus' death should hold it.[24]

The point of interest here is that despite the general and overwhelmingly literal acceptance of physical resurrection, even at a very early stage the possibility of a spiritual interpretation had been mooted.

An interesting parallel to this phenomenon, but in reverse, can be identified on the Hindu side. Despite the general and overwhelmingly spiritual understanding of rebirth in Hinduism, in the very text in which the doctrine is propounded unambiguously for the first time[25] we also encounter the view that the departing father is, in a sense, reborn in his own son! The doctrine of metempsychosis is discussed in Bṛhadāraṇyaka 3.2.13; earlier in Bṛhadāraṇyaka 1.5.17 we read:

> 17. Now therefore the transmission. When a man thinks that he is about to depart, he says to his son, "you are Brahman, you are the sacrifice and you are the world." The son answers, "I am Brahman, I am the sacrifice, I am the world." Verily, whatever has been learnt, all that taken as

one is knowledge (Brahman). Verily, whatever sacrifices have been made, all those taken as one are the world. All this is indeed, this much. Being thus the all, let him (the son) preserve me from (the ties of) this world, thus (the father thinks). Therefore they call a son who is instructed "world-procuring" and therefore they instruct him. *When one who knows this departs from this world he enters into his son together with his breaths.* Whatever wrong has been done by him, his son frees him from it all, therefore he is called a son. By his son a father stands firm in this world. Then into him enter those divine immortal breaths.[26]

The Savior and Saving Knowledge

The role of Jesus Christ as the Redeemer is central to Christianity and the doctrine of virgin birth is closely associated with the nativity of Jesus. Although the Gospel of Mark "shows no interest in Jesus' birth and youth,"[27] the Gospels of Matthew and Luke "both relate to stories of the Virgin Birth."[28] The Apostle's Creed referred to Jesus Christ as "born of the Holy Spirit and the Virgin Mary,"[29] and the doctrinal formulation at Chalcedon in 451 also referred to Jesus Christ as "begotten in these last days of Mary the Virgin."[30]

On this point Gandhi offers a striking comment. He writes:

> If you read the Quran, you must read it with the eye of the Muslim; if you read the Bible, you must read it with the eye of a Christian; if you read the Gita, you must read it with the eye of a Hindu. Where is the use of scanning details and then holding up a religion to ridicule? *Take the very first chapter of Genesis or of Matthew. We read a long pedigree and then at the end we are told Jesus was born of a virgin. You come up against a blind wall.* But I must read it with the eye of a Christian.[31]

The point obviously is that if Jesus' birth was a case of parthenogenesis, then what is one to make of all the Davidic genealogy, except perhaps as the fulfillment of the prophetic pro forma requirement that the Messiah be born in the house of David? Logically it does not make much sense, howsoever significant it may be traditionally.

A curious parallel to this can be identified on the Hindu side—at least in that part of it represented by Advaita Vedānta. In Advaita Vedānta there is no savior as such, but there is saving knowledge, and it is contained in the Vedas, which are designated *apauruṣeya*—that is to say, they are not the work of any author, human or divine. And saving knowledge, according to the standard Advaitin position, must be mediated through them. Two points must be clarified here. The first is that although the creator-god Brahmā promulgates the Vedas at the beginning of each aeon, he is not their composer; nor is it composed by the sages, who merely intuit the sacred word. So although the process of the transmission of the Vedas is associated with gods and human beings, its composition is not. The text exists by itself from beginningless time. The second point is that knowledge of the Vedas by itself does not secure salvation—only the realization of the ultimate reality called Brahman, which is expounded therein, can bring it about. But according to a standard Advaitic view, Brahman can *only* be known through the Vedas. It must also be added that the Śūdras were excluded from studying the Vedas in classical Hinduism.

This sets up the background for the comparison. In Christianity we have the elaborate delineation of the genealogy of Jesus, *only to be told that he was born of a virgin*! In Advaitic Hinduism we have numerous statements by its main exponent, Śaṅkara, that Brahman can only be known through *śruti* or the Vedas. At the same time, however, he is quite willing to say that such saving knowledge can also be acquired from other sources! This is dramatized in an incident found in his hagiographies, which may now be narrated:

> In Kāśī on an occasion while Śaṅkara, accompanied by his disciples, was going towards the Gaṅgā for a holy bath and prayers, he saw a pariah with ferocious dogs coming across his path and shouted to him: Move away! Move away! But the pariah replied:
>
> When hundreds of Upaniṣadic texts speak about the unique, pure, relationless, indivisible One Reality of the nature of truth, awareness and happiness (*satyabodhasukharupamakhaṇḍam*), your imagining Difference is surprising. Some wear dress of recluses and act like them; without any real knowledge they deceive householders. When you shouted, "Move away," were you addressing the body or the self? All bodies are made of food, they are all material, and do not differ from one another. As for the inner witness Self, how is the consideration of its difference in a pariah and a brahmana appropriate? As there is no difference in the sun's reflections in the divine Gaṅgā and toddy, so there is none among the One Self's reflections in various bodies. Neglecting the one perfect, eternal and

bodiless Person in all the bodies, why this false apprehension, "I am a pure *brahma,* O Dog-eater, get away"?

Surprised and deeply shaken, Śaṅkara immediately recognised the truth of this and replied: "O You best among the embodied, you have but asserted what is Truth, so because of the words of you who are the knower of the Self, I am at once abandoning the notion 'this is an outcaste.' "[32]

Śaṅkara then uttered five verses with the refrain: "[H]e who has such steadfast knowledge is my guru whether he be an outcaste or a brāhmaṇa." According to the story, "while Śaṅkara was thus rhapsodizing about Oneness, he was blessed with a vision of Śiva in the untouchable, and his four dogs appeared to him as the four Vedas. Śaṅkara's encounter with the *caṇḍāla* must have been as 'creative' as the Maritzburg experience was for Mahatma Gandhi."[33]

So much for the historical element in the argument. What is curious is the fact that

> In his bhāṣya on the *Brahmasūtras,* which exclude Śūdras from access to the supreme liberating knowledge in the Veda, Śaṅkara cites the cases of Vidura and the righteous butcher of *Mahābhārata* and explains: "As in them there was generation of sublime knowledge due to the impressions of their past actions (*pūrvakṛtasaṁskāra*), their attaining the fruit of it cannot be prohibited or prevented. Knowledge must culminate in its fruit. Further, according to the smritis, the four castes have a right of access to Itihāsa-Purāṇas; so through them they can attain the highest knowledge, but not through the Veda." Such was Śaṅkara's conclusion, which, in fact, makes the prohibition of Vedic study for śūdras ridiculous, for they may get the very same knowledge from other sources![34]

The genealogy of Jesus and the monopoly of the Vedas is both established and then undermined by its very instigators!

The Kali Yuga and the Apocalypse

It appears that the centuries succeeding the Christian era were such difficult periods for Hinduism and Christianity that they generated the sense of an imminent end in both. In the case of Christianity, the Gospel records

> represent Jesus as both predicting his imminent return (Matthew xvi, 28; Mark xiii, 26) and refraining from giving any precise indication of when it would take place (Mark viii, 38; Luke xii, 40; xvii, 24). A possible solution of this problem may be that Jesus did indeed foretell his return, while disclaiming knowledge of its date, and that those passages which intimate the contrary are due to a reading back of a belief which first arose in the apostolic age. If this were correct, we must then seek an explanation of how such a belief could have come into being if Jesus himself had not given it countenance. There are four main factors, which have operated to transform a prophecy of return into a prophecy of an *immediate* return. These are (1) the certainty, characteristic of apocalyptic literature, that what is predicted is close at hand: "the time will come and will not tarry" (*Apocalypse of Baruch*, xx, 6); "my salvation has truly drawn nigh, and it is no longer distant as formerly" (*ibid.* xxiii, 7; of *Revelation* i, I); (ii) the influence of Old Testament prophecy with its eager expectancy; (iii) the rapid progress of the Gospel, which would suggest a speedy preparation of mankind for the Second Coming; (iv) the outbreak of persecution, which would lead to a quickened faith in the divine vindication, and in the revelation of Christ in glory to judge and punish the persecutors.[35]

If we now turn to India we find that around the beginning of the Christian era, much of northwestern India had been overrun by foreign invaders, such as the Śakas and the Kuṣāṇas, to mention only a few. With this historical fact in the background, the Hindu version of the Apocalypse, the Kali Yuga, the Dark Age, can be seen in a new light.

> The end of the Kali-yuga, according to many epic passages, is marked by confusion of all religious rites, and the rule of cruel and alien kings. This view is propounded strongly in texts, which date from about the beginning of the Christian era, when alien kings did in fact rule much of India, and established practices were shaken by heresies such as Buddhism and Jainism. An earlier tradition would place the Mahābhārata War c. 900 B.C., according to which the 1,200 years of Kali-yuga, if read as human years and not as "years of the gods" would at this time be nearing their end. Evidently some pious Hindus thought that the dissolution of the cosmos was imminent.[36]

But the parallel does not end there. It has been argued that when the Second Coming did not eventuate, one of the challenges the early church had to face was to accommodate itself to this fact.[37] For the Hindus the crisis also passed and the adjustment, which had to be made in terms of *theology* in Christianity, was made in terms of *chronology* in Hinduism. According to Hindu tradition, the Kali Yuga commenced around the time of the Mahābhārata war and its end would mark the cataclysmic end of the whole period comprising of four *yugas*, of which it is the fourth. If that war were placed circa 900 BC then 1,200 human years would bring it close to the Christian era. This would be the case if one spoke of the ages in *human* years; but texts now speak of them in terms of *divine* years, which prolongs the duration of the age involved considerably, even prodigiously (to 432,000 years!). This has led A. L. Basham to make the plausible suggestion that once the fear of imminent collapse of the socioeconomic order generated by foreign invasions had passed, "perhaps it is to the departure of this fear in later times that we must attribute the devising of the 'years of the gods,' which made the dissolution of the world comfortably distant. Most medieval texts state that the cosmic dissolution occurs only after the last cycle of the kalpa, and that the transition from one aeon to the next takes place rapidly and calmly; the expectation of the Kalkin, who will not destroy but regenerate the world, could not otherwise be harmonized with the scheme of the yugas."[38]

Baptism: Christian and Hindu

The role of baptism as a Christian sacrament is well known. For our purposes it is important to bear in mind that it originally involved (and still does, in the case of many denominations) complete immersion. Michel Meslin identifies its symbolic significance as follows:

> It was Paul who first defined the theological and symbolic significance of Christian baptism, joining the neophyte's ritual descent into water to Christ's death and rebirth to a new and spiritual life through his resurrection (Rom. 6:3–4). Sin is not carried away by the flowing water but by the Lord's death and resurrection; through baptismal immersion, the Christian is able to participate in this new existence (Col. 2:12). In Titus 3:5, Paul describes baptism as the gift of "a bath of regeneration and renewal"; the baptismal water is at once the water of death in which the old, sinful man is immersed and the water

> of life from which he emerges renewed. In fact, Paul rediscovers the meaning of a very ancient symbolism of death and resurrection found in archaic initiation rituals, a symbolism that has been admirably analysed by Mircea Eliade. . . .[39]

Basically, then, baptism brings about spiritual regeneration by washing away sin. This does not seem far-removed from one Hindu point of view according to which water can only remove physical impurity (although the water of holy places and rivers is said to be charged with spiritual potency). However, in the context of baptism, the following Hindu anecdote contained in a dialogue between Bankim and Rāmakṛṣṇa seems to have the effect of deepening its significance.

> Bankim (to the Master): "Sir, how can one develop divine love?"
>
> Master: "Through restlessness—the restlessness a child feels for his mother. The child feels bewildered when he is separated from his mother, and weeps longingly for her. If a man can weep like that for God he can even see Him.
>
> "At the approach of dawn the eastern horizon becomes red. Then one knows it will soon be sunrise. Likewise, if you see a person restless for God, you can be pretty certain that he hasn't long to wait for His vision.
>
> "A disciple asked his teacher, 'Sir, please tell me how I can see God.' 'Come with me,' said the guru, 'and I shall show you.' He took the disciple to a lake, and both of them got into the water. Suddenly the teacher pressed the disciple's head under the water. After a few moments he released him and the disciple raised his head and stood up. The guru asked him, 'How did you feel?' The disciple said, 'Oh! I thought I should die, I was panting for breath.' The teacher said, 'When you feel like that for God, then you will know you haven't long to wait for His vision.'
>
> (To Bankim) "Let me tell you something. What will you gain by floating on the surface? Dive a little under the water. The gems lie deep under the water, so what is the good of throwing your arms and legs about on the surface? A real gem is heavy. It doesn't float; it sinks to the bottom. To get the real gem you must dive deep."
>
> Bankim: "Sir, what can we do? We are tied to a cork. It prevents us from diving." (*All laugh.*)
>
> Master: "All sins vanish if one only remembers God, His name breaks the fetters of death. You must dive; otherwise you can't get the gem. Listen to a song."

The Master sang in his sweet voice:

> Dive deep, O mind,
> Dive deep in the Ocean of God's Beauty;
> If you descend to the uttermost depths,
> There you will find the gem of Love.[40]

The parallel is also capable of being moved around a bit with a slight adjustment in the lens. For one thing, one may focus more on diving into the water; for another, one may take into account the observation that has become virtually a commonplace in comparative studies of Christianity and Hinduism: that the role played by *sin* in the Christian scheme of things is often, in Hinduism, played by ignorance, which is considered as "the root-basis of human plight or human bondage."[41]

In the context of philosophic Hinduism, diving into the water almost takes on a baptismal aspect. "Controlling speech and breath, and diving deep within oneself as a man dives into water to recover therefrom something that has fallen there, one must find out the source whence the ego rises, by means of keen insight."[42] Another interesting point to consider is the fact that while Christ was baptized, Christ himself is not known to have baptized. Similarly, some Hindu sages, who had the reputation of being Realized, never conferred Realization on others, as it is not something that can be conferred.

Part II

10

Reciprocal Illumination within a Tradition

Within a Tradition: Hinduism

The neo-Hindu attitude toward religious tolerance and the classical school of Hindu thought known as Advaita Vedānta offer a case of reciprocal illumination between two segments within a tradition. The main point to be considered is the treatment accorded to diversity, or multiplicity, or plurality. The problematic in Advaita Vedānta, which regards the ultimate reality as nondual (*advaita*), is to reconcile the apparent diversity of the world around us with the nonduality of the ultimate principle. In the case of the neo-Hindu attitude to religious tolerance, the problematic is to reconcile the diversity represented by the exclusive claims of sects within Hinduism or religions outside it.

Advaita Vedānta tries to solve the problem by simultaneously asserting the "non-duality of *Brahman*," or the ultimate, and "the non-reality of the world."[1] What E. J. Thomas says elsewhere of Yogācāra idealism applies here: "Such idealism, like other Indian idealistic systems, does not look to find reality in the fullest and most harmonious statement of the facts of experience, but in emphasizing one fact (itself an abstraction), and in brushing away the rest as illusion."[2] It is apparent, then, that Advaita Vedānta deals with the problem of plurality in the face of nonduality by denying the reality of such plurality.

By contrast, the neo-Hindu attitude to religious plurality does not allege the falsity of such plurality as a monotheistically dogmatic tradition might, but accepts it as consistent with the realization of the unity of the Godhead. S. Radhakrishnan remarks:

> Differences in name become immaterial for the Hindu, since every name, at its best, connotes the same metaphysical and

> moral perfections. The identity of content signified by the different names is conveyed to the people at large by an identification of the names. Brahmā, Viṣṇu, Śiva, Kṛṣṇa, Kālī, Buddha and other historical names are used indiscriminately for the Absolute Reality. "May Hari, the ruler of the three worlds worshipped by the Śaivites as Śiva, by the Naiyāyikas as the chief agent, by the Jainas as the liberated, by the ritualists as the principle of law, may he, grant our prayers." Śaṁkara, the great philosopher, refers to the one Reality, who, owing to the diversity of intellects (*matibheda*) is conventionally spoken of (*parikalpya*) in various ways as Brahmā, Viṣṇu and Maheśvara.[3]

Radhakrishnan then goes on to cite the following South Indian folksong:

> Into the bosom of the one great sea
> Flow streams that come from hills on every side,
> Their names are various as their springs.
> And thus in every land do men bow down
> To one great God, though known by many names.[4]

Several significant points arise at this stage. First of all, Radhikrishan quotes Śaṅkara in support of a religious tolerance that accepts devotional plurality, but it is the same Śaṅkara who, as the proponent of Advaita Vedānta, negates metaphysical plurality. Is Śaṅkara then religiously tolerant or not? Not according to K. Satchindananda Murty, who implies that according to Śaṅkara "the Vedic faith is exclusive,"[5] "as exclusive as the Semitic faiths and brooks no rivals." Further investigation suggests that three aspects of Śaṅkara's thought are involved here: (1) ontological absolution; (2) penultimate theism and; (3) scriptural dogmatism. From the point of ontological absolutism, represented by the doctrine of *nirguṇa brahma*, plurality is negated. From the point of view of theism, represented by the doctrine of *saguṇa brahma*, plurality of the names of one God is accepted. From the point of view of scriptural dogmatism, Vedic authority is upheld, just as Christians might uphold biblical authority and Muslims Qur'ānic authority. However, although the Vedas are upheld exclusively, the Vedas are to be transcended,[6] hence Murty's conclusion, even if conceded (although open to question),[7] does not follow as the night the day but comes to rest in a twilight zone. It does help to show, however, how aspects of the thoughts of the same thinker within a tradition may be related in different ways to the same topic.

The next point worth considering is the question of theism and religious tolerance. It is tempting to contrast Semitic monotheism with "Hindu polytheism"[8] here, the former often being associated with intolerance.[9] By way of contrast with exclusive monotheism, Hindu polytheism is said to be organized in a monistic way. That is to say, it is not a rigid monotheism enjoining on its adherents the most complete intolerance for those holding a different view.[10] The reciprocal illumination that such an interfaith comparison can provide may be saved for a later occasion. The point to bear in mind in the intrafaith context is that Hindu theism turns out to be more hospitable in some ways to religious tolerance than Hindu absolutism.

A further point now calls for consideration. Some interpreters of nondualism have maintained that the negation of plurality in relation to the absolute is to be followed by a still profounder realization—the affirmation of that plurality as not apart from the nondual reality. Thus, the same Śaṅkara cited earlier "says that after filling our sight with wisdom, let us see the world as *Brahman*. Such a vision is fruitful, not a vision which looks solely at the tip of the nose."[11]

11

Reciprocal Illumination between Traditions

Buddhism and Confucianism

I

The question has been raised regarding both Buddhism and Confucianism whether they may be regarded as religions.[1] This in a large measure because both tend to assume an agnostic attitude toward issues that in other religions are regarded as central—such as the existence of God or of a soul.

II

In early Buddhism this attitude is represented by the Buddha's refusal to answer a certain class of questions.

> The questions were: Is the world eternal (sassata)? Is the world not eternal? Is the world finite (antavā)? Is the world infinite? Is the soul (jīva) the same as the body? Is the soul distinct from the body? Does he who has won through to the truth (Tathāgata) continue to live after this life's death (param maraṇā)? Does he not live after death? Does he neither live nor not live again after death?[2]

These ten questions are later extended to fourteen, as in the *Abhidharmakośa* of Vasubandhu.

(1–4): Is the world constant?
Or not?
Or both?
Or none of both?

(5–8): Is the world limited in time
Or not?
Or both?
Or none of both?
(9–12): Does the Tathāgata exist after death?
Or not?
Or both?
Or none of both?
(13–14): Are life and body identical?
Or not?[3]

Buddha's silence in this respect has been interpreted variously.[4] There can be little doubt, however, that one of the chief reasons—if not the only one—for the Buddha's refusal to answer these questions was because "this profits not, nor has to do with the fundamentals of religion, nor tends to aversion, absence of passion, cessation, quiescence, the supernatural faculties, supreme wisdom and Nirvāṇa."[5]

It is not entirely certain whether Buddha did not answer the questions because he did not know the answers, or because be thought it best not to reveal the answers. Māluṅkyāputta clearly tells him,

> If the Blessed One knows that the saint both exists and does not exist after death, let the Blessed One elucidate to me that the saint both exists and does not exist after death: if the Blessed One knows that saint neither exists nor does not exist after death, let the Blessed One elucidate to me that the saint neither exists nor does not exist after death. If the Blessed One does not know either that the saint both exists and does not exist after death, or that the saint neither exists nor does not exist after death, the only upright thing for one who does not know, or who has not that insight, is to say, "I do not know; I have not that insight."[6]

At this point the Buddha skirts the issue with a parable:

> "It is if, Māluṅkyāputta, a man had been wounded by an arrow thickly smeared with poison, and his friends and companions, his relatives and kinsfolk, were to procure for him a physician or surgeon; and the sick man were to say, 'I will not have this arrow taken out until I have learnt whether the man who wounded me belonged to the warrior caste, or to the Brahman caste, or to the agricultural caste, or to the menial caste.'

"Or again he were to say, 'I will not have this arrow taken out until I have learnt the name of the man who wounded me, and to what clan he belongs.'

"Or again he were to say, 'I will not have this arrow taken out until I have learnt whether the man who wounded me was tall, or short, or of the middle height.'

"Or again he were to say, 'I will not have this arrow taken out until I have learnt whether the man who wounded me was black, or dusky, or of a yellow skin.'

"Or again he were to say, 'I will not have this arrow taken out until I have learnt whether the man who wounded me was from this or that village, or town, or city.'

"Or again he were to say, 'I will not have this arrow take out until I have learnt whether the man who wounded me was a cāpa, or a kodaṇḍa.'

"Or again he were to say, 'I will not have this arrow taken out until I have learnt whether the bow-string which wounded me was made from swallow-wort, or bamboo, or sinew, or maruva, or from milk-weed.'

"Or again he were to say, 'I will not have this arrow taken out until I have learnt whether the shaft which wounded me was a kaccha or ropima.'

"Or again he were to say, 'I will not have this arrow taken out until I have learnt whether the shaft which wounded me was feathered from the wings of a vulture, or of a heron, or of a falcon, or of a peacock, or of a sithilahanu.'

"Or again he were to say, 'I will not have this arrow taken out until I have learnt whether the shaft which wounded me was wound round with the sinews of an ox, or of a buffalo, or of a ruru deer, or of a monkey.'

"Or again he were to say, 'I will not have this arrow taken out until I have learnt whether the arrow which wounded me was an ordinary arrow, or a claw-headed arrow, or a vekaṇḍa, or an iron arrow, or a calf-tooth arrow, or a karavīrapatta.' That man would die, Māluṅkyāputta, without ever having learnt this.

"In exactly the same way, Māluṅkyāputta, any one who should say, 'I will not lead the religious life under The Blessed One until The Blessed One shall elucidate to me either that the world is eternal, or that the world is not eternal . . . or that the saint neither exists nor does not exist after death;'—that person would die, Māluṅkyāputta, before The Tathāgata had ever elucidated this to him."[7]

It may also be recalled here that "Not all Buddhists seem to have believed that strict omniscience on the part of the Buddha would be necessary to invest his religion with reputed authority. If he knew everything that was essential for salvation, that would be sufficient to make him into a trustworthy guide. In some passages of the Pali Scriptures, as a matter of fact, the Buddha expressly disclaims any other kind of omniscience."[8]

In any case, it is clear that the Buddha's agnosticism was a part of his pragmatism.

III

Confucius seems to have entertained a somewhat similar attitude toward metaphysical speculation. In fact, he lived in an age when "Men still cowed before the eclipse and the age when human sacrifices were carried out on the death of a ruler were less than a century past. In such an atmosphere, Confucius chose to direct attention away from the supernatural and toward the vital problems of human society and the ordering of the state."[9] The following selections from the Lun Yü give us an idea of his approach to the supernatural and the metaphysical:

> Tzu Lu asked about the worship of ghosts and spirits. Confucius said: "We don't know yet how to serve men, how can we know about serving the spirits?" "What about death," was the next question. Confucius said: "We don't know yet about life, how can we know about death?" [11.2]
>
> Fan Ch'ih asked about wisdom. Confucius said: "Devote yourself to the proper demands of the people, respect the ghosts and spirits but keep them at a distance—this may be called wisdom." [6.20]
>
> The Master did not talk about weird things, physical exploits, disorders, and spirits. [7.20][10]

It is well known that when Confucius was asked: "Do the dead have knowledge or are they without knowledge?" he refused to give a definite reply.[11] It is easy to see how the Buddha would have done the same. We also have a perhaps even more candid admission of the lack of omniscience on the part of Confucius than on that of the Buddha, if the Book of Lieh Tzu is to be believed. The incident refers to a point of astronomical detail, which Confucius failed to answer to the amusement of the gathered: "Is the sun nearer to the earth at dawn, when it is larger, or at noon, when it is hotter?"[12] One wonders how the Buddha would have responded.[13]

It is clear, however, that the Buddha and Confucius shared a certain agnosticism regarding the supernatural and the metaphysical, and that they did so on account of a certain pragmatism.

This is not to imply that both of them lacked what might be called a sense of regulative order if they did not believe in God the way most religions do; the Buddha believed in karma,[14] and Confucius in heaven or *t'ien*.[15] They also seemed to have favored the "Middle Way" in their own way.[16] But in one crucial way they part company, though sharing an agnosticism rooted in pragmatism.

IV

Although Buddha and Confucius were pragmatically agnostic,[17] their pragmatism was oriented toward different ends. If Confucius' orientation was toward this world, the Buddha's was very much "out of this world." If Confucius was "this-worldly," the Buddha was "otherworldly." These terms, however, have become debased through overuse. What one might say is that while Confucius's goals were secular, those of the Buddha were transcendental. Both, in a sense, were not only agnostic and pragmatists, but also humanists. Confucius said: "It is man that makes truth great and not truth that makes man great."[18] And the Buddha said: "Within this very body, small as it is and only six feet in length, I do declare to you are the world and the origin of the world, and the ceasing of the world, and likewise the Path that leads to the cessation thereof"[19]—the truth. And yet if we had asked them "what is truth?" without jesting like Pilate, we might have obtained different answers. Reciprocal illumination emerges from the consideration that while the agnosticism of the Buddha is tied to soteriological pragmatism, that of Confucius is tied to sociopolitical pragmaticism. Thus, a similar agnosticism is connected with different orientations of pragmatism—more soteriological in the case of the Buddha, and more sociopolitical in the case of Confucius.

Hinduism and Judeo-Christianity

I

The purpose of this exercise is to identify an etiological homology between the account of the Puruṣasūkta[20] and the account of Eve's emergence from a rib of Adam,[21] and to see if such an exercise provides any measure of reciprocal illumination.

II

In order to detect the underlying connection, one needs to commence with the realization that any given society is usually marked by two forms of internal differentiation[22]—one based on class and another based on sex. Thus, society consists of, say, the nobles, the peasants, and so forth,[23] on the one hand, and of men and women, on the other.[24]

Religions have to explain the fact of this fundamental differentiation. Vedism explains the emergence of one form of differentiation, the sociological, in terms similar to those used in Judeo-Christianity to explain another form of differentiation, the biological.

III

According to the Puruṣasūkta, the universe has emerged, and along with it society as well—indeed, all creatures—from a primeval man or *puruṣa*. This *puruṣa* was sacrificed. Then a question is asked and an answer is given.

> When they divided Puruṣa, how may portions did they make?
>
> What do they call his mouth, his arms? What do they call his thighs and feet?
>
> The Brāhmaṇa was his mouth, of both his arms was the Rājanya made.
>
> His thighs became the Vaiśya; from his feet the Śūdra was produced.[25]

Thus the emergence of the four *varṇas* is depicted here as resulting from the sacrifice of the primeval man.[26] More specifically, they are depicted as emerging from parts of the primeval man.

IV

According to the biblical account, Adam is the primeval man. Eve, the primeval woman, was "manufactured" or rather "Godfactured" from his rib.

> And the *Lord God* caused a deep sleep to fall upon Adam, and he slept: and he took one of his ribs, and closed up the flesh instead thereof:
>
> And the rib, which the *Lord God* had taken from man, made he a woman, and brought her unto the man.
>
> And Adam said, This *is* now bone of my bones, and flesh of my flesh; she shall be called woman, because she was taken out of Man.[27]

Thus the emergence of the two sexes is depicted as proceeding from a part of the body of the primeval man.[28]

V

There are, indeed, differences in the two accounts. The Puruṣasūkta is a comprehensive and general account of creation; the biblical account is a particular and specific to the emergence of Eve; and so on. But all the same, a certain etiological homology in the explanation of fundamental differences in society is discernible. Reciprocal illumination consists in the recognition of how Adam's rib provides a mythological complementariness to the Puruṣasūkta; and how the Puruṣasūkta illustrates the possibility of a social as opposed to a biological dismemberment of the primeval Man,[29] thereby opening up the scope for the possibility of a social interpretation of Genesis 2:21–23, which indeed has been offered:

> Eve, or, in Hebrew, Havvah: the first woman in the Creation narratives of the Hebrew Bible, according to which she was formed from one of the ribs of Adam, the first man (Gn.2:21–23). In this account the creator god wished for Adam to have a mate and so brought all the beasts of the field and birds of the sky before him to see what he would call each one (Gn.2:19). However, among these creatures the man found no one to be his companion (Gn.2:20). Accordingly, this episode is not solely an etiology of the primal naming of all creatures by the male ancestor of the human race but an account of how this man (ish) found no helpmeet until a woman was formed from one of his ribs, whom he named "woman" (ishish; Gn.2:23). This account is juxtaposed with a comment that serves etiologically to establish a social institution of marriage wherein a male leaves his father and mother and cleaves to his wife so that

> they become "one flesh" together (Gn.2:24). The matrimonial union is thus a re-union of a primordial situation when the woman was, literally and figuratively, flesh of man's flesh.[30]

Buddhism and Hinduism

I

The doctrine of *trikāya* or the three bodies of the Buddha[31] is an important component of Mahāyāna Buddhism.[32] It is, however, not as commonly realized that there also exists an Advaita Vedantic doctrine of the three bodies as well. It is a doctrine of the three bodies—not of the Buddha, to be sure, but of the *jīva,* the embodied soul.[33]

The purpose of this investigation is to demonstrate the logical connection that seems to exist between the doctrine of the three bodies of the Buddha in Mahāyāna Buddhism and the doctrine of the three bodies of the *jīva* in Advaita Vedānta.

II

As preparation for a comparison of these two doctrines, brief statements of the essentials thereof may be noted.

The doctrine of the three bodies of the Buddha may be summarized as follows. The core of this doctrine consists of the belief that the Buddha

> has three bodies; a Body of Essence (*Dharmakāya*), a Body of Bliss (*Sambhogakāya*) and a Created Body (*Nirmāṇakāya*), and of these only the last was seen on earth. The Body of Essence eternally penetrates and permeates the universe: it is the ultimate Buddha, of which the other two bodies are emanations, more or less unreal. The Body of Bliss exists in the heavens, and will continue until the final resolution of all things in the Body of Essence. The Created Body was a mere emanation of the Body of Bliss.[34]

Alongside this may now be placed a brief statement of the doctrine of the three bodies of the *jīva* as it obtains in Advaita Vedānta.

> The self having avidyā as the adjunct is the jīva. It is endowed with a psychophysical organism for the sake of enjoyment. It is said to possess three bodies, causal, subtle and gross. The

> causal body (kāraṇaśarīra) is so called because, as a particular aspect of prakṛti, which is the parent of the subtle and gross bodies etc., it is the cause (kāraṇa). . . .
>
> The subtle body (sūkṣma-śarīra) consists of the five organs of sense, the five of action, the five vital airs, mind and intellect. . . . The gross body (sthūla-śarīra) of the jīva is its particular physical frame. . . . Thus the three forms of the jīva are conditioned by the three vestures it wears.[35]

III

These statements of the doctrine of the three bodies in Mahāyāna Buddhism and Advaita Vedānta can now be placed side by side. In doing so, however, it is helpful to bear in mind certain fundamental differences between these two philosophical systems. First, while the description of the three bodies in Advaita Vedānta is centred on the *jīvātman*, Buddhism does not recognize any such entity. Rather, Buddhism, including Mahāyāna Buddhism, is known for its doctrine of *nairātmya* or ātman-lessness,[36] on the one hand, and *puḍgala-śūnyatā*, on the other. Second, while Buddhism does not believe in the *ātman* or the reality of the individual soul, it does believe in an Ultimate Reality, and in explicating it the Mahāyāna Buddhism seems at times to come close to something like the Hindu Brahman, so much so that in Mahāyāna Buddhism the "Body of Bliss was identified with Nirvāṇa. It was in fact the World Soul, the Brahman of the Upanishads, in a new form."[37] Whether one regards the Dharmakāya as the Brahman in disguise or not—"a blessing in disguise" in a theological rather than colloquial way—there can be little doubt that Mahāyāna Buddhism does concede the existence of an Ultimate Reality of some sort—identified with or identical to the Dharmakāya.

If, now, in keeping with this predisposition of Buddhism to exclude *jīvātman*, we replace the *jīvātman* with the Buddha in the scheme of the three bodies in Advaita Vedānta, then the correspondence between this new configuration with the traditional Buddhist doctrine of the three bodies becomes remarkable.

1. The Dharmakāya now begins to correspond to the *kāraṇaśarīra*. The Dharmakāya is the first Cause of the Universe, just as the *kāraṇaśarīra* is the cause of the *jīva*. Similarly, just as the other *kāyas* emanate from the Dharmakāya, the other two bodies originate in the *kāraṇaśarīra*.

2. The Sambhogakāya now corresponds to the *sūkṣmaśarīra*. It is the Sambhogakāya of the Buddha, that rules over the heavens; it is the *sūkṣma-śarīra* that, upon death, enjoys a sojourn in heaven so far as the *jīva* is concerned.
3. The Nirmāṇakaya corresponds to the *sthūlaśarīra*. The Nirmāṇakāya was the Buddha in flesh and blood so it is the *jīvātman* with the *sthūlaśarīra*.

There are, of course, divergences. For instance, the salvation of the *jīvātman* consists in getting rid of three bodies, but salvation in Mahāyāna Buddhism is identified with the Dharmakāya. But on reflection, most of these differences will seem to flow from the fact that in the Mahāyāna Buddhism the *jīvātman* has been replaced by the Buddha. What needs to be realized is that the essential model of the three bodies is common in structure in both the systems; the difference is in content, arising out of the philosophical presuppositions of the two systems. The real parallel, in this sense, to the doctrine of the three bodies of the Buddha is not the Trinity of Christianity,[38] or the Trimūrti of Hinduism, but the doctrine of the three *śarīras* of the Upaniṣads.

IV

To conclude:

1. There is a morphological and not merely numerical similarity between the doctrine of *trikāya* in Mahāyāna Buddhism and the doctrine of *triśarīra* in Advaita Vedānta.
2. This similarity becomes clear if the *jīvātman* in the doctrine of *triśarīra* is replaced by the Buddha. This induces a shift from the microcosmic to the macrocosmic.

Hinduism and Taoism

One of the questions Ramana Maharshi was often asked had to do with the social usefulness of the *jñānī* or the Realized being. To all appearances such a person seemed socially useless, of no real use to the world. Ramana Maharshi's conversation with the well-known scholar Evans-Wentz is relevant here (E.W. obviously stands for Evans-Wentz, B. stands for *Bhagavān* Ramana Maharshi, as he was reverentially called):

E.W.: They say that there are many saints in Tibet who remain in solitude and are still very helpful to the world. How can that be?

B.: It can be so. Realization of the Self is the greatest help that can be rendered to humanity. Therefore saints are said to be helpful even though they remain in the forests. But it should not be forgotten that solitude is not to be found in the forests only. It can be had even in town in the thick of worldly occupation.

E.W.: Isn't it necessary that saints should mix with people and be helpful of them?

B: The Self alone is the Reality; the world and the rest of it are not. *The Realized Being does not see the world as different from himself.*

E.W.: Then does that mean that a man's Realization leads to the uplift of mankind without their being aware of it?

B: Yes; the help is imperceptible but is still there. A Realized Man helps the whole of mankind although without their knowledge.

E.W.: Wouldn't it be better if he mixed with others?

B.: There are no others to mix with. The Self is the one and only Reality.

E.W.: If there were a hundred Self-realized men, wouldn't it be to the greater benefit of the world?

B.: When you say "Self" you refer to the unlimited, but when you say add "men" to it, you limit the meaning. There is only one Infinite Self. . . .

E.W.: In Europe people do not understand that a man can be helpful in solitude. They imagine that only men who work in the world can be useful. When will this confusion cease? Will the European mind continue wading in the morass or will it realize the Truth?

B.: Never mind about Europe or America. Where are they but in the mind? Realize your Self and then all is realized. If you see a number of men in a dream and then wake up and recall your dream, do you try to find out whether the persons of your dream-creation are also awake?

A self-realized being cannot help benefiting the world. His very existence is the highest good.[39]

The Self-Realized Man is a natural, perhaps supernatural resource—elemental like water. Or perhaps such a person influences the world the way the moon influences the tides. Notwithstanding such claims, the suspicion lingers that such a person is of little use to the world

The Taoist classic, Tao Te Ching, seems to hold a similar position, though at times it seems to advocate timely withdrawal rather than total inaction on the part of the sage.[40] Chapter 24 also notes that "he that possesses the Tao does not linger."[41] These sentiments would probably find a friendly echo in Ramana, as also the suggestion in chapter 34 that the sage acts though in a self-effacing way,[42] and in chapter 17 that although the sage is instrumental in accomplishing his task either people think that it happened of its own accord,[43] or that they did it themselves.[44] These passages, however, do not quite hit the bull's-eye. From the point of view of finding a proper point of comparison for Ramana's position, chapter 27 is the more helpful. Arthur Waley notes in this connection that "the commonest charge brought against Taoists was that of being merely interested in self-perfection without regard to the welfare of the community as a whole."[45] Ramana could perhaps relate to such a charge. Chapter 27 "is devoted to rebutting that charge" and is cited below. It seems especially relevant, as the term "Light" in the passage "has been defined as self-knowledge. 'This' means the way the Sage saves the world, though apparently shunning it."[46]

> Perfect activity leaves no track behind it;
> Perfect speech is like a jade-worker whose tool leaves no mark.
> The perfect reckoner needs no counting-slips;
> The perfect door has neither rope nor twine,
> Yet cannot be untied.
> Therefore the Sage
> Is all the time in the most perfect way helping men,
> He certainly does not turn his back on creatures.
> This is called resorting to the Light.
> Truly, "the perfect man is the teacher of the imperfect;
> But the imperfect is the stock-in-trade of the perfect man."
> He who does not respect his teacher,
> He who does not take care of his stock-in-trade,
> Much learning though he may possess, is far astray.
> This is the essential secret.[47]

Ramana is regarded as an Advaitin, and Advaitins regard Brahman as the ultimate reality (the term connoting the "highest," even when not applied to the ultimate).[48] The following statement about the Tao in chapter 25 of the Tao Te Ching is strikingly reminiscent of statements about Brahman in Advaita.[49]

> There was something formless yet complete,
> That existed before heaven and earth;
> Without sound, without substance,
> Dependent on nothing, unchanging,
> All pervading, unfailing.
> One may think of it as the mother of all things under heaven.
> Its true name we do not know;
> "Way" is the by-name that we give it.
> Were I forced to say to what class of things it belongs I should call it Great (*ta*),
> Now *ta* also means passing on,
> And passing on means going Far Away,
> And going far away means returning,
> Thus just as Tao has "this greatness" and as earth has it and as heaven has it, so may the ruler also have "greatness," and one belongs to the king. The ways of men are conditioned by those of earth. The ways of earth, by those of heaven. The ways of heaven by those of Tao, and the ways of Tao by the Self-so.[50]

Thus ancient China provides a context, which improves our understanding of mysticism in modern India. There are differences, to be sure. Ramana's position is based on a clearly articulated philosophical school. In his statement, "If you see a number of men in a dream and then wake up and recall your dream, do you try to find out whether the persons of your dream-creation are also awake," Ramana can even be accused of being solipsistic, though he is more cautious elsewhere. Taoism does not seem to go that far philosophically. Similarly, the Taoist sage, though less inclined to actively intervene politically than the Confucian scholar, is more inclined to do so than Ramana. In other words, the movement from the primal philosophical point was more political in the case of Taoism and philosophical in the case of Hinduism; but once this is acknowledged, it is possible to identify the implicit metaphysical idealism of Taoism and the implicit political activism of the Advaita of Ramana. We possess an account of an interview of Ramana with two Indian freedom fighters on August 14, 1938. The conversation ends as follows:

> D. Is there not any Power on earth, which can bestow Grace on its devotees so that they may grow strong to work for the

> country and gain *swaraj*? (Sri Maharshi remained silent. This he later said signified that such was the case.)
>
> D.: Is not the *tapasya* of the ancient *mahatmas* of the land available for the benefit of its present-day inheritors?
>
> M.: It is, but the fact must not be overlooked that no one can claim to be the sole beneficiary. The benefits are shared by all alike. (After a pause) Is it without such saving Grace that the present awakening has come into being? (Here Sri Bhagavan said that before His arrival in Tiruvannamalai in 1896, there was not any clear political thought in India, only Dababhai Nauroji had become an M.P.)[51]

The implication of the parenthetical remark is astonishing and seems to imply that Ramana, like a Taoist sage, notwithstanding his apparent inactivity, had set the political leaven at work.

Buddhism and Islam

How contrastive comparisons can be illuminating is demonstrated by a consideration of the concept of revelation in Buddhism and Islam. Here, too, one must first go beyond homonymous correspondence to arrive at synonymous correspondence, before the illuminating power of contrastive comparisons can be revealed. The Qur'ān is held to be the revealed word of God, and, as such, infallible. A similar infallibility has also been claimed on behalf of the words of the Buddha in some forms of Mahāyāna Buddhism. A little consideration shows, however, that such common claim to infallibility based on the omniscience of Allah and Buddha is, at best, superficial. At least in Theravāda Buddhism, Buddha's omniscience is claimed only with respect to diagnosing the cause of *dukkha* and prescribing the way of removing it, the further wrinkle being that the Buddha, unlike other arhats, knew this remedy in each individual case, whereas the arhants by and large relied on the Four Noble Truths, which in any case had been propounded by the Buddha. In Mahāyāna Buddhism, Buddha's omniscience rested on the metaphysical identity of the subject with the object known. Thus the exact content of omniscience in the case of Theravāda Buddhism and its nature in the case of Mahāyāna Buddhism are very different from the Islamic kind of omniscience.

The proper comparison here may lie between the silence of the Buddha and revelation from God (such as is represented by the transmission of the Qur'ān by Muḥammad, for instance). The following considerations point in such a direction.

(1.) According to the Qur'ān, a prophet has been vouchsafed to all the peoples of the earth by God, who spoke to them in their own language. This may be compared with the following statement of the Tathāgata Guhya Sūtra:

> During the night, O Śāntamati, in which the perfected one became perfectly enlightened with the unsurpassed, perfect enlightenment, during the night in which he passed totally into nirvana, not one syllable was uttered or used by the perfected-one, neither did he address anyone, nor will he. Yet all creatures, according to their propensities, perceive the voice of the perfected one as it issues forth in the various dialects of their homelands; for them it takes special forms . . . a perfected one is freed . . . from everything with name.[52]

(2.) The very *fact* of revelation, according to the Qur'ān, authenticates, irrespective of the content. This statement may initially sound exaggerated, but a little reflection might establish its reasonableness. The Qur'ān claims that revelations prior to it, such as the Torah and the Gospels, have been corrupted, but this does not apparently compromise their standing as revelation, because this allegation is made against the Jews and Christians (that they have corrupted the texts) and yet they are accorded the status of "people with a book." Similarly, even if the content of all revelation is claimed to be monotheistic, then although prophets have been sent to all the peoples, yet apparently monotheism was not a universal phenomenon according to the Qur'ān. Even when Satan contaminated such revelation, as in the case of the Qur'ān itself, such verses were abrogated but not discarded. In other words, revelation is revelation, irrespective of error in this sense.

The same point is made in Buddhism regarding Buddha's preaching of Absolute Truth, when recourse is taken to words rather than silence in the Viśeṣa-Cintā-Brahma-Paripṛcchā:

> "Manjusri," said the God Brahma, "Is what you have been telling me the Absolute Truth?" "All words are true," said Manjusri. "Are lies then also true?" asked Brahma. "They are," said Manjusri. "And why?" "Good sir, all words are empty and vain and belong to no point in space. To be empty and vain and belong to no point in space is the characteristic of the Absolute Truth. So in that sense all words are true."[53]

(3.) One may compare the statement in the same text "all possible words are the words of the Tathāgata" with the Islamic view that while the Qur'ān is the speech of God, God is always speaking, even if his words are not, as in the case of the Qur'ān, becoming human words. Similarly, Seng Chao's statement that the "Holy man always speaks and never speaks"[54] may be compared with the Ḥadīths to the effect that the Ṣūfī "talks little" and "talks much."

(4.) One may also compare the fact of *one* nondual God being the source of *several* revelations with this statement: "The Tathāgata adjusts the language that he uses to the particular prejudices that have to be overcome in living being. His mind is non-dual, while his teachings are multifarious."[55]

(5.) As is well known, the word for nonbeliever in Islam is *kāfir*. Scholars have pointed out that the word really means ungrateful, the implication being that God in his grace has offered his revelation to human beings, some of whom are so perverse as to reject it. An analogous Christian sentiment would emphasize that Jesus gave his *life* for all sinful men and yet the pagans willfully disregard the enormity of his self-sacrifice made on their behalf. In both cases, God's compassion is contrasted with man's niggardliness. John Stone has commented that, in the case of Buddha, "Language, finally, is an instrument of compassion. The Buddha need not speak: having passed beyond discursive or conceptual talk, he is free to enjoy perfect, undifferentiated silence. In order to save common people, he used common words such as cause and effect, existence and non-existence, right and wrong, affirmation and denial, and empty and non-empty, to explain his teaching."[56]

He goes on to institute a comparison with Christianity as well.

> Such an attitude (mundane language, though empty has a sacred function) contrasts strongly with the Judeo-Christian tradition. As Elohim pronounces the world into being, the creative power and unmitigated reference of certain words becomes canonical. If the Buddha's descent into the void of language is an act of compassion, the Christian logos identifies the supramundane and ultimate reality with a Word into which humanity must, by the grace of God, ascend.[57]

This comparative study also sheds more light on certain developments within Buddhism. It is well known that Mahāyāna Buddhism in India basically used one language—Sanskrit—and was remarkably free from the sectarian divisions that characterized pre-Mahāyāna Buddhism, at least in India, where it bifurcated into the two main doctrinal schools of Madhyamaka and Yogācāra.

This proliferation of schools in pre-Mahāyāna Buddhism has been connected with the Buddha's discouragement of the use of Sanskrit; his own use of the popular language, and his willingness to allow his followers to preserve the teaching in their own language or dialect. One would have tended to view this as a purely social or local phenomenon, but as John Stone points out: "The obvious risk of affirmation of *prajñapti*"—namely, the use of conventional language to convey ultimate verities—"is license: the splintering of Buddhism may in part be attributed to the necessary use of conventional language for religious purposes."[58]

The role of linguistic homogeneity in preserving religious homogeneity is an interesting one. Mahāyāna Buddhism in China and Japan developed subschools, but not to the same extent as pre-Mahāyāna Buddhism in India—and India was also linguistically far more heterogeneous.

Here Buddhism and Christianity provide an interesting comparison. Both the religions, unlike Judaism, Hinduism, and Islam, dispensed with the linguistic anchor of a sacred language, but enjoyed periods of maximum doctrinal cohesion during the period they adopted a language. But these considerations perhaps take us beyond the pale of reciprocal illumination.

12

Reciprocal Illumination among Traditions

Among Three Traditions: Islam, Hinduism, and Christianity

Miracles have been associated with mystics, though they are not their hallmark. In fact, they are discouraged, even in Christianity. Nevertheless, an interesting parallel emerges when the point is raised: how are miracles performed? The key element in the question to be considered here is the following: Is the performer aware of performing them? Reynold A. Nicholson explains the position with respect to Sufism thus:

> The Moslem saint does not say that he has wrought a miracle: he says, "A miracle was granted or manifested to me." According to one view, he may be fully conscious at the time, but many Sufis hold that such "manifestation" cannot take place except in ecstasy, when the saint is entirely under divine control. His own personality is then in abeyance, and those who interfere with him oppose the Almighty Power, which speaks with his lips and smites with his hand.[1]

The Hindu mystic Ramana Maharshi made a remarkably similar statement in terms of Patañjali's yoga, which is theistic:

> This concentration is called *samyamana* in the Yoga *Sastras*. One's desires can be fulfilled by this process and it is said to be *siddhi*. It is how the so-called new discoveries are made. Even worlds can be created in this manner. *Samyamana* leads to all *siddhis*. But they do not manifest so long as the ego lasts. Concentration according to yoga ends in the destruction of the experiencer (ego), experience and the world, and then the

> quondam desires get fulfilled in due course. This concentration bestows on individuals even the powers of creating new worlds. It is illustrated in the *Aindava Upakhyana* in the *Yoga Vasistha* and in the *Ganda Saila Loka* in the *Tripura Rahasya*.[2]

When, however, one seeks the nature of this miracle-working power, paradoxically it is Islam that offers an Advaitic explanation and Hinduism that offers a theistic one.

The example from Islam refers to the case of Bayazīd of Bisṭām and is narrated by Rūmī. Bayazīd, in his ecstatic moments, had declared himself to be God. "After coming to himself on one of these occasions and learning what blasphemous language he had uttered, Bayazīd ordered his disciples to stab him with their knives if he should offend again."[3]

An account of what followed, abridged from Rūmī's *Masnavī*, runs as follows. When he uttered blasphemous language again,

> His disciples all became mad with horror,
> And struck with their knives at his holy body.
> Each one who aimed at the body of the Sheykh—
> His stroke was reversed and wounded the striker.
> No stroke took effect on that man of spiritual gifts,
> But the disciples were wounded and drowned in blood.

Here is the poet's conclusion:

> Ah! you who smite with your sword him beside himself,
> You smite yourself therewith. Beware!
> For he that is beside himself is annihilated and safe;
> Yea, he dwells in security for ever.
> His form is vanished, he is a mere mirror;
> Nothing is seen in him but the reflexion of another.
> If you spit at it, you spit at your own face,
> And if you hit that mirror, you hit yourself.
> If you see an ugly face in it, 'tis your own,
> And if you see a Jesus there, you are its mother Mary.
> He is neither this nor that—he is void of form;
> 'Tis your own form which is reflected back to you.[4]

This explanation is worthy of a nondualistic Upaniṣad, such as the Bṛhadāraṇyaka and the Chāndogya.

We turn now to the miracles of Jesus Christ. The following remarks of Ramana Maharshi are significant in this respect (D. stands for *D*evotee):

> D.: Jesus Christ cured people of their diseases.
> Is that only an occult power (*siddhi*)?
> M.: Was Jesus aware at the time that he was curing men of their diseases? He could not have been conscious of his powers. . . .
> D.: Was not Jesus a Perfected Being possessing occult powers (*siddhi*)?
> M.: He could not have been aware of his powers (*siddhis*).[5]

It is important to consider the fact in this context that Jesus held himself to be "in a unique filial relationship to God"[6] as in Luke 11.20:

> If I by the finger of God cast out devils, then is the Kingdom of God come upon you.

Thus, we have the explanation of miraculous behavior of a Muslim mystic explained in Advaitic terms by another Ṣūfī; and the explanation of the miracles of Jesus explained in yogic terms by a Hindu Advaitin. The crucial point, however, relates to the absence of the ego in all the cases, but allows for a greater recognition of the role of Jesus vis-à-vis non-Christian examples, on account of Jesus's special relation of sonship with God. Thus, one notes about miracles in the New Testament that, for the most part, the question of the relation of human to divine agency does not distinctly emerge. Jesus's miracles are the equivalents of his words in terms of deeds; a parable is a verbal miracle, and a miracle a parable. Consequently, there is close association of miracle with Jesus's agency. The problem of agency comes out more explicitly in the so-called Beealzebub Controversy (see Luke 11:14–23, Matthew 12:22–30, Mark 3:22–32), but even there the issue is not that of human vs. divine agency but of demonic (?) vs. divine authority in miracles. The disciples' surprise at their ability to perform miracles is implied in Luke 10:17–20, and the pious attribution of miracles to God and not to the human agency is instanced in Acts 19:11–20, when once again the issue of authority is primary. Jesus's agency is, however, strongly emphasized (see especially Mark 8:2–3): his agency is not distinct from God's in the context of the coming of God's Kingdom.[7]

Among Four Traditions: Buddhism, Confucianism, Christianity, and Hinduism

Comparisons assembled around the figure of Māra in Buddhism are illuminating in such a context. According to the Mārasuttas of the Pali canon, Māra sends his three daughters in the form of Taṇhā, Arati, and Rāga to seduce the Buddha, when the Buddha is on the verge of enlightenment, but they fail in the goal of foiling his meditation. However, Indra, the king of the gods in classical Hinduism, often sends his divine nymphs to seduce the sages when the accumulated penance becomes so strong as to threaten his throne, and they usually succeed.

Does this comparison reveal a tension between the sacred and the secular realms in Hinduism? The Buddha has forsaken temporal power for good, despite the fact that it was an optional destiny, and all the endeavors of Māra are directed toward preventing Buddha's march to enlightenment. When Buddha is offered a kingdom, it is *not* by Māra but by a king, Bimbisāra, who "offered him entire sovereignty, but Gotama refused, saying that he left the world with the desire for the highest enlightenment."[8] Does the fact that in Christianity temporal sovereignty is offered by Satan to Jesus (Matt. 4:8–10; Luke 4:4–8) indicate that the tension between the sacred and secular realms has not been as completely resolved in early Christianity as in early Buddhism?

But back to the contrast with Hinduism. Clearly the secular connections are stronger here. Thus, the performance of sacred penance threatens the rule of Indra—the king of the gods, no doubt, but still a king. Here sacred power has clearly "secular" consequences. Sometimes the austerities are deliberately undertaken to overthrow Indra. In Buddhist texts, however, Indra, as Śakra (fully equipped with a folk etymology) appears as an admirer rather than a rival of the Buddha—further evidence that early Buddhism had shed any pretence to political power in either the mundane or divine realm. Could it be the case that the Indo-European identity of sacred-secular (*brahma-kṣatra*) still did not totally shed its original overlap in classical Hinduism, the way it did in early Buddhism?

The use of dancing girls, first to frustrate the pure spiritual seeker (Buddha) and then to frustrate the search for power through spiritual practices of would-be-Indra *ṛṣis*, runs its full course in the early history of Confucianism, as one moves along the sacred (Buddhist), sacred-secular (Hindu), and secular-sacred (Confucian) continuum. In fact, the end of the early Confucian experiment in utopian governance is also ascribed to such a maneuver. We are told (perhaps not without some reflected glory in view of his subsequent eminence) that as Confucius rose to various appointments under the Duke of Lu,

> A transforming government went abroad. Dishonesty and dissoluteness were ashamed, and hid their heads. Loyalty and good faith became the characteristics of the men, and chastity and docility those of women. Strangers came in crowds from other States. Confucius became the idol of the people, and flew in songs through their mouths.[9]

The rest of the account is less edifying:

> But this sky of bright promise was soon overcast. As the fame of the reformations in Loo went abroad, the neighbouring princes began to be afraid. The duke of Ts'e said, "With Confucius at the head of its government, Loo will become supreme among the States, and Ts'e which is nearest to it will be the first swallowed up. Let us propitiate it by a surrender of territory." One of his ministers proposed they should first try to separate the sage and his sovereign, and to effect this, they hit upon the following scheme. *Eighty beautiful girls, with musical and dancing accomplishments, were selected, and a hundred and twenty of the finest horses that could be found, and sent as a present to Duke Ting. They were put up at first outside the city, and Ke Hwan having gone in disguise to see them, forgot the lessons of Confucius, and took the duke to look at the bait. They were both captivated. The women were received, and the sage was neglected.* For three days the duke gave no audience to his ministers.

At this turn of events

> "Master," said Tsze-loo to Confucius, "it is time for you to be going." But Confucius was very unwilling to leave. The time was drawing near when the great sacrifice to Heaven would be offered, and he determined to wait and see whether the solemnity of that would bring the duke back to his right mind. No such result followed. The ceremony was hurried through, and portions of the offerings were not sent round to the various ministers, according to the established custom. Confucius regretfully took his departure, going away slowly and by easy stages. He would have welcomed a messenger of recall. The

> duke continued in his abandonment, and the sage went forth to thirteen weary years of homeless wandering.[10]

Māra has been dubbed the Buddhist Satan. It is remarkable, however, that although in Christianity Satan is associated with spirit possession and thus with invading the body, there is only one instance in the Pali canon when Māra actually causes physical discomfort: when he enters Moggallāna's stomach.[11] On the face of it, one may connect it with the emphasis on the physical body in Christianity as the locus of resurrection and thus salvation, and the negative attitude to the physical body in Buddhism, with the emphasis is placed on *citta* as the vehicle of *nirvāṇa.* Hence Satan's defilement of the body in Christianity and hence Māra directing his attacks on the mind and not the body in Buddhism (though he does disturb Buddha's sleep in the Māra-Suttanta). Moreover, as *nirvāṇa* is supramental, it is the body that sustains one through the experience. In the ultimate trance all life signs disappear except body heat.[12] In this sense one did touch *nirvāṇa* with the body—the whole universe was said to be contained in the body.[13]

If the point of positing Satan is to recognize evil as an independent force in itself, then Māra's invasion of Moggallāna's body would seem to run counter to karma. But this is so also only on the surface, for according to early Buddhism not *all* suffering is due to karma, and natural causes are admitted. But whether supernatural causes are also admitted is the question. They are in Yoga. However, even that may not compromise karma for two reasons. Māra's action itself may have been brought about by karma and only Buddha knows what is caused karmically and what is caused naturally (or supernaturally).

It is not often realized how important a role Satan played in the religious awareness of Luther. Once Luther identified the presence of Satan with the crackling of coals of the fire in his room, he was confirmed in his faith, for where else would Satan be except testing those who were about to escape his grasp? A similar situation obtains in relation to Māra in Buddhism in connection with the Buddha. According to the Lalitavistara, for example,

> Māra the wicked one, O monks, followed close behind the Bodhisattva, as he was practicing austerities for six years, seeking and pursuing an entrance, and at no time succeeding in finding any. And finding none he departed gloomy and sorrowful.[14]

When the Buddha-to-be sat down, having resolved to obtain liberation, he was questioned by Māra. It was then that he made his famous gesture of touching the earth with his hand to bear witness to the fact that he was ready for Buddhahood, as in the following account of the Pali commentator.

> Now Māra on hearing these words (Lusts are thy first army, etc.) said, "Seeing such a yakkha as me dost thou not fear, O monk?" "Verily, I fear not, Māra." "Why does thou not fear?" "Through having performed the perfections of the merits of almsgiving and others." "Who knows that thou hast given alms?" "Is there need of a witness here, evil one? When in one birth I became Vessantara and gave alms, through the power thereof this great earth quaked seven times in six ways, and gave witness." Thereupon the great earth as far as the ocean quaked, uttering a terrible sound. And Māra terrified at hearing it like a dropped stone lowered his flag, and fled with his host.[15]

There is some difference, however, in the symbolism of the two accounts. The *earth* in the case of the Buddha is the witness of Buddha's integrity, but the *coals*, which presumably formed part of the earth, represented the fiery presence of Satan for Luther.

The use of the simile of the rock in the following passage is therefore interesting in the Pali account:

> (Māra speaks): "For seven years have I followed the Lord step by step. I can find no entrance to the All-enlightened, the watchful one.
>
> As a crow went after a stone that looked like a lump of fat, thinking, surely here I shall find a tender morsel, here perchance is something sweet,
>
> And finding no sweetness there, the crow departed thence; so like a crow attacking a rock, in disgust I leave Gotama."
>
> The lure of Māra who was overcome with grief slipped from beneath his arm. Then in dejection the Yakkha disappeared from thence.[16]

Māra and Satan as scapegoats are also comparable. Ānanda did not request the Buddha to live on for an aeon when the Buddha suggested that he could.[17] Sometimes Māra is held responsible for Ānanda's failure.[18]

One should distinguish, however, between the (1) evil wrought by the devil; (2) preordained evil as part of a divine scenario; and (3) human wickedness. When, at the Last Supper, Jesus foretold his denial by Peter and betrayal by Judas, it was not so much their own wickedness that was involved as the working of God's will.

The real comparison—the synonymous correspondence—is between Māra in early Buddhism and Indra in classical Hinduism. This was pointed out earlier, and the point may now be developed further. Indra interferes with the yogis as Māra did with the Buddha. Again, just as Māra is associated with the *khandhas* in Buddhism (*khandhamāra*), Indra is etymologically connected with the *indriyas*. Māra disguises himself as a young man in his attempt to seduce the nun (Māra-Suttana, I, 128), while Indra disguises himself as Gautama to seduce Ahalyā. Moreover, in a Jātaka story (Jātakamālā 4.4–6) Māra generates the illusion of a hell to prevent the Buddha-to-be from giving a gift to a *pratyekabuddha*; Indra does the same before Yudhiṣṭhira is allowed into heaven in the Mahābhārata.

A correspondence was established earlier between the offer of temporal authority to Jesus by Satan and to the Buddha by Bimbisāra. It is clear that there are several accounts of this encounter in both the traditions. The comparison of the results of the application of the techniques of close reading to these accounts is also a fruitful field of investigation. (I owe the following analysis of the close reading approach to the temptation of Jesus to Jean-Pierre Lavalee).

One may begin with a comparison of the portrayal of the temptation of Jesus as found in Matthew and Luke;[19]

Matthew 4:8–10	Luke 4:5–8
Again, the devil took him to a very high mountain, and showed him all the kingdoms of the world and the glory of them; and he said to him, "All these I will give you if you will fall down and worship me." Then Jesus said to him, "Begone, Satan! for it is written, 'You shall worship the Lord your God, and him only shall you serve.' "	And the devil took him up, and showed him all the kingdoms of the world in a moment of time, and said to him, "To you I will give all this authority and their glory; for it has been delivered to me, and I give it to whom I will. If you, then, will worship me, it shall all be yours." And Jesus answered him, "It is written, 'You shall worship the Lord your God, and him only shall you serve.' "

One of the most striking differences between the two sections concerns the location. In Matthew, the devil takes Jesus to the top of a mountain in order to view the world. They remain earthbound, while looking on the kingdoms from an elevated perspective. It is easy to relate to this description in Matthew. One can easily recall a dramatic panoramic view vouchsafed by such a place from one's individual experience. However, in Luke, Jesus and the devil are "up." They are detached from the earth, and it seems as if they are suspended in midair. Luke presents a much more spiritual scene, inasmuch as Jesus and the devil are not bound by earthly laws of gravity. Luke's description of showing all the kingdoms "in a moment of time" further supports the idea that Christ and Satan are beyond secular rules. It is *a* moment, a decidedly singular expression. The scene is apprehended by both in an instant.

In expressing the words of Satan, the Gospel of Luke is somewhat convoluted. In order to tempt Jesus, the devil explains: "To you I will give all this authority and this glory; for it has been delivered to me, and I give it whom I will." The construction seems very awkward. For example, in placing "To you" first, the rest of the sentence becomes a modifying clause. It states: To Z, X will give Y. It is grammatically more efficient to treat "to you" as an indirect object. For example: "I will give all this . . . to you," or X will give Y to Z. Constructions such as the one given by Luke make the reader work harder to apprehend what is being explained.

In Luke's rendering of the devil's words there is a further ambiguity. The lines: "for it has been delivered to me" bring to mind the questions: "Who did the delivering?" and "Why was it delivered?" The ambiguity brings distracting issues to mind and takes the reader's attention away from the meaning of the devil's speech. There exist schools of criticism, namely form and redactivist criticism, which might say that Luke carefully crafted the sentence in order to raise these questions. They might say that the issues are raised to guide the reader to a greater understanding. While this is possible, a new critical reading simply reveals it to be poor writing.

One other element of the temptation scene that allows for different interpretations is found in the response of Jesus to the devil's enticement. In Luke it is recounted as follows: "And Jesus answered him, 'It is written "You shall worship the Lord".' " Again, the text says: "Jesus said to him 'Begone' Satan: for it is written . . ." The appeal to "it is written" shows borrowed authority. The command present in Matthew adds an entirely new dimension to the scene. Jesus can be perceived as having far more power over Satan if he issues a direct order to leave, rather than "answering," which places the onus on Jesus to respond. In Matthew, Jesus seems immediately superior to Satan, while in Luke he is slower to condemn Satan. "Answering," incorporates a superior-to-inferior relationship, for the one party must answer to another. In portraying Jesus as answering to Satan, Luke diminishes his strength.

Edward J. Thomas offers material for a similar exercise in the case of the temptation of the Buddha. Accounts of this temptation are found in the (1) Jātakas, (2) Pabajjā-Sutta (Pali), (3) Mahāvastu, and (4) Lalitavistara. Let us first consider the Jātaka account.

> The Jātaka tells us that Gotama, after staying seven days at Anupiya, went on foot straight to Rājagaha, the Magadha capital, in one day, a distance of some two hundred miles, and began to beg. The royal officers reported his arrival to the king (Bimbisāra), who in astonishment seeing him from the palace ordered them to follow and observe. If he was a non-human being he would vanish, if a divinity he would go through the air, if a nāga into the ground, but if a man he would eat his alms. He was seen to go to the Pāṇḍava hill, and overcoming his disgust at the unusual food to eat it. The king then came, and pleased at his deportment offered him entire sovereignty, but Gotama refused, saying that he had left the world with the desire for the highest enlightenment. Yet though he rejected the repeated requests of the king, he promised to visit his kingdom first on becoming a Buddha, and then journeyed by stages to the teachers Āḷāra and Uddaka . . . .

We turn next to the Pabajjā Sutta:

> The Jātaka adds that the full account is to be found in the sutta of the Going-forth (*Pabajjā-sutta*) with its commentary. Yet this sutta, found both in the Pāli and in the *Mahāvastu*, differs curiously from the Jātaka. The king sees him first, and noticing his beauty and downcast eyes sends messengers to find where he lives, then visits him, offers him wealth, and asks of what family he is. Gotama tells him, but does not mention that he is a king's son, and says that he has no desire for pleasures, and looking on renunciation as peace, he is going to strive. Here the sutta ends, but the *Mahāvastu* adds two verses in a different metre containing Bimbisāra's request and

> Gotama's promise that he will return and preach the doctrine in his kingdom. This incident is also added by the Pāli commentator on the sutta.

The account in the Mahāvastu may now be summarized:

> But the *Mahāvastu* places this event after the visit to Āḷāra, and says that Gotama after leaving Kanthaka paid a visit to the hermitage of Vasishṭha, and then stayed with Āḷāra. It was after leaving the latter that he went to Rājagaha and saw Bimbisāra, and at the same place applied himself to the teaching of Udraka (Uddaka). But the *Mahāvastu* also gives another account, according to which, after leaving the world, he went straight to Vaiśālī without any previous visits, joined Āḷāra, and after rejecting his teaching went to Rājagaha and practised the teaching of Udraka. Here we have an earlier account, which like the earliest Pāli knows nothing of the Bimbisāra story.

We turn to the Lalitavistara for the final version:

> The *Lalita-vistara* is much more elaborate. After receiving his ascetic's robes Gotama is entertained at the hermitage of the brahmin woman Śāki, then at that of the brahmin woman Padmā, and then by the brahmin sage Raivata and by Rājaka, son of Trimaṇḍika, until he reaches Vaiśālī and joins Āḷāra. The story of meeting Bimbisāra at Rājagaha is told by the insertion of a poem in mixed Sanskrit, which concludes by saying that Gotama left the city and went to the banks of the Nerañjarā, thus ignoring the visit to Uddaka (Rudraka). The prose of the next chapter however continues with the story of his study under Uddaka in much the same language as the Pāli.[20]

One may now turn to a point of a very different kind, one in which instead of analyzing the various deceptions and manifestations of Satan, sacred or secular, in Christianity or in Buddhism, its very existence is itself called into question from one perspective within Hinduism. A correspondent once wrote to Mahatma Gandhi:

> . . . I am tempted to put you a question concerning His adversary (according to Semitic beliefs), whose name you are so often using in your writings and speeches;—not of course

> without effect, as witness the article "Snares of Satan" in your issue of 6-8-'25. If it was only rhetorical effect that was intended thereby because you were writing or speaking the language of a people who have been taught to believe in Satan's existence through the Semitic creed of Christianity, then I would have nothing to say. But the article cited, among other things, does seem to point to a belief on your part in Satan's existence,—a belief, in my humble opinion, quite un-Hindu. Asked by Arjuna what was the cause of man's continual fall, Shri Krishna said: "*Kama esha krodha esha,*" etc. (It is lust, it is anger). According to Hindu belief, it would seem, the Tempter is no person outside of us,—nor indeed is it *one*; for there are "the six enemies" of man enumerated in the Shastras: *Kama* or lust, *krodha* or anger, *lobha* or greed, *moha* or infatuation, *mada* or pride and *matsara,* i.e. envy or jealousy. So it is clear, Hinduism has no place for Satan, the Fallen Angel, the Tempter, or as he has been called by a French writer (Anatole France), "God's man-of-affairs!" How is it then that you who are a Hindu speak and write as if you believed in the real existence of the old one?[21]

Gandhi's response contains various strands. First of all, there is the suggestion that even if Hinduism does not possess such a concept or "person," it may be worth including one within its ample bosom. Then there is the suggestion that Hinduism possesses a parallel concept in the figure of Rāvaṇa in the singular, and the hundred Kauravas in the plural. Then there is the further suggestion that the personification of evil will persist despite our quibbling about it.

> In my opinion the beauty of Hinduism lies in its all-embracing inclusiveness. What the divine author of the Mahabharata said of his great creation is equally true of Hinduism. What of substance is contained in any other religion is always to be found in Hinduism. And what is not contained in it is insubstantial or unnecessary. *I do believe that there is room for Satan in Hinduism.* The Biblical conception is neither new nor original. Satan is not a personality even in the Bible. Or he is as much a personality in the Bible as Ravana or the whole brood of the *asuras* is in Hinduism. *I no more believe in a historical Ravana with ten heads and twenty arms than in a historical Satan. And even as Satan and his companions are fallen angels, so are gods, if you will.* If it be a crime to clothe evil passions and

ennobling thoughts in personalities, it is responsible. For are not the six passions referred to by my correspondent, and nameless others, embodied in Hinduism? Who or what is Dhritarashtra and his hundred sons? To the end of time imagination, that is, poetry, will play a useful and necessary part in the human evolution. *We shall continue to talk to passions as if they were persons. Do they not torment us as much as evil persons*? Therefore, as in innumerable other things in the matter under notice the letter killeth, the spirit giveth life.[22]

13

Reciprocal Illumination among Types of Traditions

I

Religions can be categorized in various ways, depending on the set of criteria used for this purpose. R. C. Zaehner uses a combination of criteria—geographical, historical, and ideological—to distinguish what he calls the Prophetic tradition from the Wisdom tradition. He writes:

> What are these two main streams and what are the subsidiary streams that run parallel to them? A glance at the map of the world religions will show that there is a fairly clear dividing line between the limits of extension of the two main religious traditions. "Western" religion, by which we in fact mean the religions originating in the Near East, owes its origin, directly or indirectly, to the Jews: "Eastern" religion either owes its origin to India or is profoundly influenced by Indian religious thought. In each case there is the parent stock from which the more widely diffused religions spring. In the West this parent stock is Israel, the Jews; in the East it is India. And just as Israel gives birth to Christianity and—less directly—to Islam, so does the national religion of India, Hinduism, give birth to Jainism and the two great forms of Buddhism, which now share between them almost the whole of South East Asia, China and Japan. In each case a religious genius appears among the "chosen" people: in the case of the Jews, Jesus Christ, in the case of the Indians, Gotama the Buddha. In each case there then springs up a new religion distinct both from the parent stock and from its great offshoot: in the one case, Islam, in the other Mahāyāna Buddhism which is so radical a transformation of early Buddhism as to constitute, almost, a religion in

> its own right. In each case again there are religions originating in lands adjacent to one of the two great religious streams: in the one case Zoroastrianism, in the other Taoism. Here, however, the parallelism ends. The resemblances are of structure, not of content. It is in the matter of content that the two streams are so radically divided.[1]

The parallel between the emergence of Islam and Mahāyāna Buddhism may seem a bit forced, but the historical structuralism of the passage is suggestive. The difference in geographical origins is then reinforced by a consideration of ideological differences between the two main streams. Judaism, Christianity, and Islam, despite their individual claims to finality, share certain presuppositions. They are summarized by Zaehner as follows:

> All three start with the premiss that God is an external, objective reality, the supreme and absolute ruler of the universe, who created it out of nothing. Further they agree that the human person was created one and indivisible, that bodily death, therefore, does not mean a final separation of body from soul, but that, in order that man's salvation shall be complete, his body must be re-united to his soul at the end of time. Thus the "prophetic" tradition, as I shall call it, is agreed on the nature of God as supreme ruler of the universe, its creator, sustainer and preserver; it is agreed that man was created for a purpose which will only be fully revealed at the end of time; and it is agreed that death, the result of sin, is not man's final condition but only a temporary separation. Man is composed of soul and body, and final beatitude must therefore include the reunion of man's severed parts: an immortal soul is only half a man; it is not the whole man. Moreover, the immortality of the soul, though it undoubtedly plays an important part in all three religions, is not quite central to any of them. Life on earth is regarded by all as being supremely important. This life is a time for testing, a preparation for life everlasting. Further, this life is unique: it is our only chance and can never be repeated. On it depends our eternal destiny of weal and woe. Earthly life, then, though only a preparation, is a preparation of immense importance; it is a deadly serious affair in which all is at stake, for—and here all three religions agree—we will be held to account by God, our sovereign Lord,

> for what we have done and left undone. In all this the three religions, which go to make up the prophetic tradition, agree.[2]

This is to be contrasted with the religions belonging to the other stream—the Wisdom religions. According to Zaehner,

> this whole tradition is fundamentally indifferent to God as external law-giver who must be obeyed: in its extreme form it denies the existence of God altogether and puts its exclusive emphasis on the deliverance of the immortal soul from the body. Its attitude is throughout conditioned by an unquestioned and unquestioning belief in re-incarnation, which it regards not as a desirable process but as the supreme evil. Human life is not God's greatest gift to man, it is a curse which inheres in the very nature of things. It is matter, the body as such, which is the persistent drag on the soul and from which the soul longs to be separated. Moreover, Indian religion in practically all its forms would go on to say that this deathless condition which is the soul's natural habitat is not something we can take on trust from an external agency; it is something that, given the right dispositions and training, can be experienced here and now. Granted, then, that the *experience* of immortality is the *sole* object of religion, the very need for a divine revelation is done away with. This extreme emphasis on the experience of immortality, that state in which all differentiation falls away from the experiencing subject, led the more extreme supporters of the Indian Vedānta to identify the human soul with the godhead, and claimed that once this condition is empirically realized the whole phenomenal world is seen to be an illusion.[3]

The contrast is useful, but unfortunately is not helped by Zaehner's lapses into inaccuracies and even prejudice. For Zaehner seems to implicitly regard the monotheistic stream as normative. The slip shows at several points. (1) While commenting on the Upaniṣads, Zaehner remarks:

> These are "mystical" treatises the object of which is to discover what the common substratum of the universe is: they are *primitive* philosophical speculations and not by any means a direct confrontation of God and man. Man, rather, is groping

> towards God, and his groping leads him to experience the immortality of his own soul. At no stage does Indian religion have any clear conception of God as Lord and maker of all things out of nothing, as an essentially moral being who demands that man shall be righteous.[4]

First of all, it is not at all clear whether the word "primitive" is used in a derogatory or technical sense—or even whether this onomastic ambiguity is being exploited to have a dig at Hinduism. Second, it could easily be said that the prophetic traditions have no clear concept of the soul. Such a statement is not made. And is not man groping toward God in the prophetic tradition as well? It can even be said that God is groping toward man. (2) Zaehner is prepared to say that "To the Western religious mind and particularly to the orthodox Protestant such an identification can only appear as blasphemy. Indeed, it has been described by the great Neo-Calvinist theologian, Hendrik Kraemer, as a repetition of the Fall; so fundamentally different are the values of Israel and India."[5] He is not prepared to say that to the Indians the idea of a God who makes things out of nothing seems patently absurd, however pivotal it may be for the prophetic traditions. (3) The fact that he regards monotheistic ideas as normative is clear from his remark that "the Indian tradition, despite its frequent theism, is ever again hankering after a more adequate concept of the deity."[6] (4) Zaehner remarks that the "great monotheistic systems of the Near East, which the West has in part inherited, never tire of emphasizing the absolute distinction of God from the created order: God and Nature are not interchangeable terms as Spinoza maintained. In the oriental systems, however, the two are in fact never clearly distinguished: God is Nature and Nature is God."[7] Zaehner here fails to distinguish clearly between pantheism and panentheism, the latter offering a more accurate statement of the Hindu position in this respect, at least according to some scholars.[8]

It is interesting that while he contrasts the two streams on so many points, he does not contrast the two traditions in terms of tolerance and intolerance. He, however, does have this to say *before* embarking on the comparison:

> At any rate since the rise of Christianity in the West, European civilization has been dominated by beliefs passionately held: toleration and "reasonableness" have been very late comers to the European scene, and even now, as the history of this century shows, their hold on our minds is the most precarious.

> For better or worse the European mind is possessed by the concept of Truth, the concept that the ultimate realities can be known at least in part, and that the possession of this truth is vital to man's well being. Such is not, and rarely has been, the Indian or Chinese way of seeing things. Indian religion has always tended to regard different religious manifestations as being all in their own way aspects of one indivisible truth which cannot be seized in its essence because it is ineffable: each religion is the same truth seen from a different angle. If this is really so, then the endless trail of persecution which has defaced the history of the West, must seem not only wicked but also incomprehensible. So the immense seriousness and awe with which the Jew or the Calvinist, for example, regards his God, must seem a trifle exaggerated to the Eastern mentality. So it is that persecution has been rare in the East since Eastern man does not see "error" as something particularly pernicious: when all is said and done, it is simply another way of looking at things.[9]

It is significant that he fails to see the connection between this aspect of the situation and the difference in the nature of theism in the two traditions. He is prepared to see the Indian tradition seeking a more adequate concept of the deity, but he fails to see that "Indian monotheism in its living forms, from the Vedic age till now, has believed *rather in the unity of the gods in God, than the denial of gods for God*. Hence Indian monotheism has a peculiarity which distinguishes it from the Christian or the Mahomedan."[10]

The nonmention of Judaism here indicates how the way the traditions are grouped changes with the criteria used. If the criteria were tolerance versus intolerance of other religions, Judaism will have to be placed in the same box as the Indian traditions. Zaehner, for instance, says that if we take "Judaism and Buddhism as the 'types' of the two great traditions the radical difference between them will become immediately apparent."[11] This is *not* how Erich Fromm sees it. Fromm distinguishes "between *authoritarian* and *humanistic* religions"[12] and goes on to say: "One of the best examples of humanistic religions is early Buddhism."[13] Then, within a few pages, he cites "a story from the Talmud 'which' expresses the unauthoritarian humanistic side of Judaism as we find it in the first centuries of the Christian era."[14] In contrast to the radical difference between Buddhism and Judaism posited by R. C. Zaehner, Erich Fromm sees a happy convergence between the early form of Buddhism and the rabbinic form of Judaism.[15]

Even a close reading of Zaehner's own chapter suggests that the two streams will be difficult to keep apart, if the obiter dicta scattered in that chapter itself are developed into criteria for distinguishing among traditions. (1) Traditions could be distinguished on the basis of theism and atheism.[16] This would move a large chunk of the Hindu tradition (Bhakti) and also Sikhism over to the Western side. (2) Traditions could be distinguished on the basis of divine revelation. The Nyāya tradition within Hinduism would have to be moved over, as also Sikhism. (3) Whether a tradition is anthropocentric (starts from man) or theocentric (starts from God) will alter the balance. This would also cause Sikhism and Bhakti in Hinduism to move to the Western side. (4) The relationship between God and Nature could form another basis for realigning the traditions. (5) Historical-mindedness of traditions could also be a criterion. This would move Confucianism probably to the Western side. Moreover, although Zaehner says that "Indian religions"[17] are "anything but historically minded,"[18] Basham regards Buddhism as historically minded in comparison with Hinduism.[19] Once again the traditions may have to be realigned.

Zaehner therefore freezes the frames prematurely, and preempts the exercise of reciprocal illumination at the level of types or clusters of traditions with his fixed typology. The next section is suggestive of the gains in insight that might flow from a more flexible approach in this respect.

II

The issue of the relationship between church and state has not dominated the discussion in religious studies as it might have done at times in the past but continues to be one of considerable interest, as evidenced by an entire journal devoted to its study.[20] When the issue is viewed in the light of the different traditions, then reciprocal illumination seems to result if these traditions are grouped in two clusters according to whether they have been marked by conflict between civil and religious authority or not, especially in their classical formulation. It would be useful to begin by examining a few specific cases.

Hinduism is not only a complex tradition, but also possesses a long history, which renders generalization even more hazardous. Let us, however, focus on an early text, the Śatapatha Brāhmaṇa which

> describes in great detail the status of the priestly class and its relation to secular authority (*rājanya*), and to the commonalty

> (*viś*). Whilst acknowledging the rights of the ruler *brāhmaṇas* claimed exemption from particular statutes of Civil Law. This claim was based on the assertion that the *brāhmaṇas* were the earthly counterpart of the gods, and when descended from a *ṛṣi* they claimed to represent all the deities (XII.4.4,6). Their prerogatives are enumerated (XI.5.7,1 *et seq.*), particularly those referring to the honour (*arcā*) and gifts (*dakṣiṇā*) due to them. They should not be subject to oppression (*ajyeyatā*) or the death penalty (*avadhyatā*), even when guilty of a capital crime.[21]

This last provision may be compared with "the quarrel of Henry II and Thomas à Becket over the non-liability of monks to punishment under Civil Law for the many murders committed by them during the king's reign."[22] There is also a long history of conflict between the Brāhmaṇas, representing religious authority, and the Kṣatriyas, representing civil authority, in the early mythology of Hinduism.[23] Buddhism also presents evidence of such potential and actual conflict. Thus

> while a householder or an ascetic should not kill, it was the duty the soldier to kill. The Buddha had to take cognizance of this condition, as illustrated in the following story. It appears that some soldiers under Bimbisara, king of Magadha, were talking to each other about the evil karma they were accumulating by their acts of war, and they decided to join the *sangha* to lead the holy life. By so doing they felt that they could avoid evil deeds. Having thus decided, they went to the monks and were ordained. When this incident was reported to King Bimbisara, he went to the Buddha and said that there were unbelieving kings who had to be kept at a distance by soldiers. Now if soldiers were to join the *sangha*, his army would be depleted and there would be no defenders left. Such a situation would be disastrous not only to the kingdom but also to the *sangha*. He therefore begged the Buddha not to receive soldiers into the *sangha*. The Buddha assented, and laid down the rule that no one in the royal service should be ordained. By this friendly compromise with the king, the Buddha acknowledged the necessity of the existence of armies whose duty it was to kill. However, the Buddha also enunciated a number of rules to guarantee that the monks' relation to the army was cut to a minimum.[24]

The case of Buddhism in China presents an even more striking example. Thus, the Chinese scholar Hsun Chi charged

> Buddhist religion with sedition, and adduced the following counts to substantiate his indictments: (1) the Buddhists were building monasteries and temples to imitate the imperial palaces; (2) they were translating seditious works; (3) they were usurping the imperial prerogative of imposing fines and punishment by saying they could save people from hell; (4) they were setting up another calendar in opposition to that of the dynasty by their days of fasting and festivals; (5) by describing the peace and happiness of the Buddhist heavens, they were indirectly criticizing the dynasty for not maintaining peace and prosperity on earth; and (6) they were imitating the imperial insignias with their banners and pennants.[25]

Similarly, Fan Chen argued against the acceptability of Buddhism on philosophical grounds[26] and Ku Huan and Ho Ch'eng-tien on cultural grounds[27] around the fourth/fifth century AD. But from the point of view of the matter under discussion, it is the question of whether the monks should pay obeisance to the emperor that deserves greater attention.

> At first this constituted no great problem, since only the most eminent monks were ever likely to meet the emperor, and these were usually foreigners who were not expected to follow full Chinese etiquette. When native Chinese came to constitute the majority of Buddhist clerics, however, the problem became more serious. The question was brought under discussion at court during the Eastern Chin period but no settlement was reached until A.D. 403. At that time the high minister Huan Hsüan (369–404), who had temporarily usurped the throne, referred the problem to one of the outstanding monks of the day, Hui-yüan (334–417), for a decision. Hui-yüan replied with a letter stating that, though Buddhist laymen, like any other laymen, were obliged to acknowledge their loyalty and respect for their sovereign by the customary etiquette, the Buddhist clergy, who by the nature of their life and aims were far removed from ordinary men, could not be expected to go through the outward signs of obeisance. Huan Hsüan accepted Hui-yüan's argument and decreed that monks need not bow before the emperor.[28]

While in South China the sangha had thus asserted its authority vis-à-vis the emperor, in North China the sangha had virtually become an appendage of the state. By contrast with the situation in the South, the monk Fa-kuo

> exercised administrative control over the monastic community in north China, with his subordinates scattered throughout the realm to carry out the orders of the central authorities. He was thus a member of the governmental bureaucracy, whose duty it was, as with any other functionary, to reverence the ruler in the accepted fashion. But the Buddhist scriptures were emphatic on the point that monks should not bow before their parents or rulers. To solve this dilemma Fa-kuo took refuge in a bold doctrine—that the ruling emperor T'ai-tsu was the Tathagata in person, so that when he offered his respects to T'sai-tsu, he was not reverencing the earthly ruler but the Tathagata himself.[29]

In the history of Christianity, the relationship between church and state has been equally problematical. Three clear phases are discernible: before it became the state religion, while it was one, and after it ceased to be one. The point to note is that even when it was the state religion the relationship was not free from internal tension. Harvey Cox writes:

> The conversion of Constantine presented the early Christians a new test. Some theologians tried to rewrite Christianity into an imperial ideology—and almost succeeded for a time. But their attempt to resacralize politics never eliminated the tension between God and the regime, which the biblical faith had planted in the consciousness of man. From now on, no political system could ever safely claim a direct and undisputed sacral legitimation, and no sovereign could infringe on that aspect of his subjects' lives, which pointed them to an authority beyond him. Indeed, the tension between Christian faith and political authority was so pointed that it has continued to bother Western political thinkers in every generation.[30]

One may now turn to Judaism and Islam. In Judaism, till modern times, there was either a fusion of civic and religious domains or their complete separation in the Diaspora. This is connected to the idea of Jewish Law as embracing the whole of life. Thus "so long as Israel existed as a more or less sovereign nation under its own king, this whole complex of political-social-religious life functioned, at least ideally as an organic unity."[31] This unity was destroyed in 586 BC, after which "In principle, the idea of divine sovereignty and absolute rule was maintained; in practice it was recognized that Caesar's will ruled the world and that the traditional law of God could only operate as the private norm of a minority which increasingly conceived itself as a religious community within the larger, ungodly, political state."[32] The same situation continued during the Middle Ages.[33] The point to note is that while the severance between the public and private realms was forced on Judaism as a political reality, the two are fused in its religious ideology.

Islamic Law or Sharī'ah is well known for its comprehensiveness and was formulated by the Ulamā on the basis of *ijmā'*. This is vital to the understanding of Islamic Law, and even more so when it is maintained that *ijmā'* ultimately became the *ijmā'* of the *'ulamā'*. At first, the Ulamā—the learned or the doctors—corresponded to the "scribes"in Judaism.

> As their authority became more firmly held and more generally conceded by the public opinion of the community, the class of Ulamā claimed (and were generally recognized) to represent the community in all matter relating to faith and law, more particularly against the authority of the State. At an early date—probably sometime in the second century—the principle was secured that the "consensus of the community" (which in practice meant that of the Ulamā) had binding force. *Ijmā'* was thus brought into the armoury of the theologians and jurists to fill up all the remaining gaps in their system. As the tradition was the integration of the Koran, so the consensus of scholars became the integration of the Tradition.[34]

H. A. R. Gibb goes on to say,

> *Ijmā'* thus intervenes more or less decisively in every branch of Islamic doctrine, law, and state-craft; it may even set aside or supersede the strict logical conclusions regarding the authenticity, meaning and application of a given text; it may give support to a tradition which strict criticism rejects as of doubtful genuineness; and though it cannot in theory abrogate a direct text of Koran or Tradition, it may (in the view of the jurists) indicate that "the law so prescribed has fallen into disuse."[35]

The comparisons made hitherto have been confined to premodern times by deliberate intention. For if one now places Hinduism, Buddhism, and Christianity in one bag, as traditions with a tradition of more marked conflict between civil and religious authorities, when compared with the traditions in the other bag, namely, Judaism and Islam, then it could be proposed that, between the two, the former cluster of traditions (comprising Hinduism, Buddhism, and Christianity) seems to possess a greater natural potential for turning secular than the latter cluster (comprising Judaism and Islam). The contemporary dimension of this discussion, however, is forbiddingly complex, as is illustrated by the case of Israel and Pakistan. (1) Both of them in some sense are regarded as religious states, but in what sense are they religious states? They were founded on religious grounds, but the grounds had more to do with communities than ideologies. They were founded on religious grounds in the sense that religious groups wanted a defined region for themselves. (2) The founders of both Israel and Pakistan were secular in their outlook. Although Theodor Herzl laid the foundation of the modern Zionist movement and Muhammad Ali Zinnah provided the leadership to Indian Muslims, both were secular in personal life. (3) The most orthodox sections of both the Jewish and the Islamic communities (in India) opposed the formation of the state. The Jewish orthodox sections opposed it on the grounds that the foundation of the State of Israel could only follow upon the fulfillment of the messianic expectation. The Muslims opposed Pakistan on the grounds that Islam is pan-nationalistic. (4) Although both these countries were created as homelands for their respective peoples, there are more Indian Muslims outside Pakistan than in Pakistan and more Jews outside of Israel than in Israel.

14

Reciprocal Illumination between Religion and the Secular Tradition

Buddhism and Science

I

One of the important themes in the encounter between Buddhism and the Western world—as represented by Christianity and science[1]—has been that Buddhism is in accord with science[2] but not with Christianity, which itself has been at loggerheads with science.[3] Thus, it has been claimed, for instance, that the "early Buddhist description of the cosmos as far as the observable universe goes . . . is remarkably close to the modern conception of the universe,"[4] and this view, it seems, has gained considerable acceptance.[5]

The purpose of this section is to indicate that apart from correspondences between modern science and Buddhist statements in matters of detail—for example, the description of the universe—a certain similarity, if not identity, can be detected between the "spirit" of Buddhism and the spirit of science. This section sets out to identify that similarity,[6] and such reciprocal illumination as might proceed from this circumstance.

II

What is the "spirit" of science?

There can perhaps be several answers to this question, but the following seems to be the distillate of as prolonged and mature a precipitation as any.

> Pre-eminently the spirit of science is the spirit of adventure and all that goes with adventure: the readiness to accept trial

> and risk error, to take new bearings. In scientific study this means not only a continued search for data; it also means a readiness to revise and even abandon theory in the light of new data. But no *method* will, of itself, ensure this spirit. On the contrary, it is possible to become so wedded to a particular hypothesis accepted as promising, that one may fail to observe that the promise is not being fulfilled.[7]

This spirit clearly underlines model-analysis—the basic method of scientific research. An integral part of this method is the readiness to abandon models with lesser explanatory power in favor of those with more. In this sense, science is the constant pursuit of truth rather than a particular truth, as there is always the possibility of an existing model being superseded by an even better model. Indeed, this aspect of modern science is too well known to require further comment.

III

The spirit of Buddhism, however, now needs to be outlined. This can be done by referring to Majjhima Nikāya 1.256, which deals with a "pernicious heresy" conceived by "a certain monk named Sāti, the son of a fisherman."[8] In the course of what follows, the Buddha addresses the assembled monks and asks somewhat rhetorically

> ". . . Right Recognition is the knowledge of the true facts as they really are?"
> "Yes, sir."
> "Now if you cling to this pure and unvitiated view, if you cherish it, treasure it, and make it your own, will you be able to develop a state of consciousness with which you can cross the stream of transmigration as on a raft, which you use but do not keep?"
> "No, sir."
> "*But only if you maintain this pure view but do not cling to it or cherish it* . . . only if you use it but are ready to give it up?"
> "Yes, sir."[9]

The significance of these remarks by the Buddha is thus elaborated by A. L. Basham:

> Buddhism is a practical system, with one aim only, to free living beings from suffering. This passage apparently implies

> that even the most fundamental doctrines of Buddhism are only means to an end, and must not be maintained dogmatically for their own sake. It suggests that there may be higher truths, which can only be realised as Nirvāṇa is approached.[10]

Such then is the "spirit" of Buddhism.

IV

This convergence in the spirit of science and Buddhism becomes dramatically apparent if a hypothetical situation is envisioned in which the growth of modern science occurs, not in a Christian but in a Buddhist country—not, say, in Great Britain but in Śrī Laṅkā. There would have been no doctrine of creation to be disapproved, and no revelation, faith in which is shaken by the advancement of science. As no appeal to miracles is involved, so no threat would have been felt either on account of disbelief in miracles generated by a scientific spirit or through the substitution of natural or scientific explanations for alleged miracles. The effect of scientific advance would thus hardly lead to atheism (though it could be argued that this is so because Buddhism is atheistic);[11] nor would it lead to an antireligious attitude (though it could be argued that this is so because Buddhism is not a religion).[12] This is not to say that there would be no problems created by the impingement of scientific advance on Buddhism. For one thing, inasmuch as science deals primarily with sensory data and the external world and Buddhism with the supresensory realm and the "internal" world, their realms of discourse are different and so is the nature of their concerns. Similarly, the question of rebirth could also pose a problem. However, accommodation might be easily achieved by dividing up the realms of discourse in the first case and by "mythic thumbing"[13] in the second. The similarity in the spirit of science and Buddhism seems to imply (1) fewer areas of confrontation, (2) easier accommodation when confrontation does occur, and (3) a convergence of method in spite of divergence of realms, which make a coordinated endeavor potentially easier on several fronts. However, there is one sense in which the outcome of the impingement does seem unpredictable. Buddhism represents a somewhat settled body of conclusions, whereas the conclusions of science are being continually unsettled by further applications of its methods. Thus, in the comparison of Buddhism and science we are really comparing an almost fixed point, or at least only a gradually moving one,[14] with a rapidly moving point, and a priori there seems to be no way of knowing whether the rapidly moving point will diverge, converge, or oscillate in relation to the more gradually moving point. Could it be that it might even settle down into an orbit of some kind around it?

Hinduism and Human Rights

I

I would first like to focus on the concept of rights from a comparative perspective.

It has been claimed that the concept of rights is a secular and Western concept. If this is indeed so, then our undertaking may turn out to be more complex than might be apparent at first sight. In order to pursue this point, allow me to raise two questions: (1) what is exactly meant by rights in current discourse? and (2) do other religions and cultures possess such a concept (or an analogous one), or are they devoid of it?

What are rights? Modern discourse seems to offer four main ways of looking at rights: (1) rights as liberties, (2) rights as claims, (3) rights as entitlements, and (4) rights as trumps. If we use the term "reproductive rights," for instance, to refer to the cluster of rights to family planning, contraception, and abortion, then it might also be of interest to determine the nature of such rights from these four points of view.

Rights as Liberties

Rights as liberties are associated with civil and political rights, such as the right against unlawful detention or interference with privacy. In sum: "Liberty rights, with which civil and political rights are associated, are negative rights in that they offer certain protections but do not necessarily generate duties, other that the duties to refrain from coercion or interference."[15]

The right to marry and to raise a family, as part of the umbrella term "reproductive rights," seems to belong here.

Rights as Claims

By comparison with rights as liberties, "Rights as claims involve a subject of the right (the person who is making the claim), what the subject has a right to, and who has responsibility for fulfilling the duty implied in the claim."[16]

The right to due process is a good example of such a concept of rights. The right to practice contraception and abortion seems to belong here.

Rights as Entitlements

"Rights as entitlements view the nature of rights not as against someone, but as for something."[17] A good example of this is provided by rights of children, where the "specific bearer of duty for the right may not be clear, but the obligation to provide protection is nevertheless valid."[18] The right to have access to *facilities* for exercising the right to contraception and abortion seems to fall under this rubric.

Rights as Trumps

Rights as trumps constitute a way of dealing with conflict among rights. "All rights talk signifies the moral weightiness of the liberty, negative or positive claim, entitlement, duty or obligation. But when there is a conflict in serious moral claims, trumps signify that some rights, while not absolute, are nevertheless based on more compelling moral grounds."[19] Such a view of rights might be helpful in "negotiating the tension between biotic rights and human reproductive rights. Human reproductive rights could trump biotic rights for the first child, or even the second. But beyond replacement, biotic rights could then trump."[20] Biotic rights may involve restorative measures to preserve a species from extinction, for instance,[21] or the protection of the biosphere.

The question of abrogation of reproductive rights under certain circumstances, or conversely, their ability to trump other rights in certain cases, may belong here.

If one examines these four concepts of rights closely, one finds that they contain some elements in common. These are an entitlement and an entitlement to remedy, when that entitlement is disregarded. The fact that we have a category called "rights as entitlement" should not obscure the fact that *all* rights involve entitlements. Unless one is entitled to liberties, or claims, one cannot claim them as rights. Similarly, rights as trumps means that some rights possess a more compelling claim or entitlement than others. Perhaps another clarifying insight here consists of the realization that rights are like legal claims, whose violation involves punishment or compensation. The corresponding question to ask in relation to non-Western societies and cultures, then, is: through which category do people make claims in these cultures, such that their violation involves punishment or compensation?

The answer: duty. In most of the traditional cultures the entitlement of others, or their claims on us, are articulated as our duties toward them, and failure to perform one's duty involves atonement (in terms of conscience), or shame (in terms of society), or in some cases, even compensation. In duties, then, we seem to possess an analogue to rights.

In fact, an even stronger statement might be possible. Duty-discourse and rights-discourse are not only comparable, but to a certain extent they may even be convertible. The fact that, in the discussion of all the views of rights, the word "duties" crops up lends credence to this view.[22] This does not mean that rights and duties are coextensive, because duties can extend beyond rights. For instance, "some duties could precede the attribution of rights,"[23] just as "there could be duties not grounded in rights."[24] Nevertheless, though not coextensive, rights and duties are correlative in that (someone's) rights are related to (someone's) duty.

Three claims can be made, at this stage, on the nature of the relationship between rights and duties, each stronger than the other. One could begin by claiming that rights and duties are *comparable* entities. One could then go on to make the stronger claim that the two are *convertible*. Finally, one could claim that the two are *coextensive*, that one invariably and reciprocally involves the other. Although for the purposes of this chapter the claim that the two are convertible will suffice, let us also examine the claim that they are coextensive, for it sheds light on the claim that they are convertible. Consider the case of infants. Infants, in relation to parents, have rights without duties. And parents, in relation to infants, have duties without rights. Parents, however, can also be said to possess rights, in the sense that they have a right not to have the infant taken away from them. This right, however, is *not* in the form of direct reciprocation for duties performed for the infant, but rather in relation to the state. It could now be argued that when the infant grows up and becomes an adult, parents do have a right to be looked after by the children, and this right is indeed located in one who is now an "infant" and *not* the state (although the state has the obligation to *enforce* the right). In this sense, the two *are* mutually implicative. The case of animals might provide another possible example. Animals may have rights against human beings (as in animal rights), without corresponding duties, at least in some cases and in the case of some animals. Even here it might be argued that some kinds of animals, such as draught animals, do have a "duty" toward the owner, although the application of the concept to animals is obviously problematical. I forbear to carry on with the exercise, because its purpose is served; even if rights and duties are not coextensive or cannot be correlated all the way, their mutual implication is difficult to deny. This is confirmed by the historical fact that the first Indian to use the English language in a major way in moral and religious discourse had no difficulty in making the switch. I refer to Raja Rammohun Roy, who, in the early part of the nineteenth century, was already talking about encroachment on the *rights* of Indian women.

II

Is it possible to develop this point further? In our search for a non-Western analogue to the concept of rights, we have come up with the concept of duties. Is that all? Does our investigation cease here, or is it capable of being carried further?

Let us select another culture for a closer comparison with the Western: the Hindu culture. We can now place two major systems of moral discourse side by side, and survey them in depth. Once this is done, one finds that each of these forms its own pattern in which rights and duties respectively find a place. We also find that the patterns differ, and, further, that such differences shed light on each other.

The results of the comparison can only be summarized here.[25] While both the modern Western and the traditional Hindu worlds seem equally eager to do the right thing, the attempt to do so seems to have led them in different directions—in the direction of rights in the West, and in the direction of righteousness in India. With the recognition of the individual in the west as "the autonomous possessor of his own person and capacities," his rights were "now conceived essentially as the instrument for the protection of the individual and her property from the rest of society in the form of entitlements, while individual interests (were) identified prior to and independently of any moral or social bonds."[26] Such socioeconomic individualism was morally recast by Kant. With him, "a rationally based conception of self-respect . . . breaks free of a notion of rights that in effect equate(d) them with privileges of membership in a civic or religious organisation. It is in such a world that the idea of human rights, rights by virtue of the moral nature of human beings alone, comes to the fore."[27] This results in a separation of "two senses of right, namely righteousness and entitlement" in Western thought, or, more accurately, the locus of the two ceases to be identical. Hindu thought, however, developed along different lines. Within it *dharma* constitutes the key category. Dharma "is the order of the entire reality . . . which both keeps the world together and maintains each thing according to its nature."[28] This carries two major implications:

> (1) the two senses of right, namely righteousness and entitlement are brought together in the Indian conception in contrast to their separation in western thought, and (2) with this convergence, the primary category is not that of moral principle but of a primordial order that is neither exclusively moral or exclusively cosmological but both together at once.[29]

This concept of order is also holistic by its very nature, encompassing the "three worlds" of the individual, society, and cosmos, as it were.

> This further subdivision of righteousness into moral and cosmic aspects helps us now to distinguish three different aspects of "right": (a) cosmic righteousness, (b) social righteousness or Sittlichkeit, to use Hegel's term, and (c) rights in the sense of entitlements. The first is defined primarily through the category of order, the second through that of norms, and the third through that of rules. And we may say that in the Indian scheme, the priority runs from order to norms to rules, whereas in the western scheme the priority is exactly reversed.
>
> The price that the Indian scheme (pays) for its priority of order is that the individual qua individual gets largely swallowed up, so that such notions as privacy, non-interference, liberty of choice, social mobility, individual rights and in general "outer freedom" are marginal to the culture. The price that the western model pays for its priority of rights is that questions about order, the common good, social cohesion and the "inner freedom" . . . are pushed into the background.[30]

III

Nowhere are these difficulties more apparent than in the current discourse on human rights. On account of the individualistic starting point of modern human rights discourse, such discourse runs into difficulties as soon as attempts are made to extend it beyond the individual to embrace social, cultural, and environmental concerns. This is not to say that such an attempt has not been made. The scheme of the three generations of human rights represents such an attempt, even though the three generations are not always uniformly stated.[31] According to one version, civil and political rights constitute the "first generation," social, cultural, and economic rights the second, and environmental and developmental rights the third. This attempt to enlarge the circumference of human rights from its individualistic center leads precisely to the kinds of difficulties one would expect on the basis of the foregoing analysis. John Witte Jr. draws attention to one such difficulty when he writes:

> The simple state vs. individual dialectic of modern human rights theories leaves it to the state to protect rights of all sorts—"first generation" civil and political rights, "second generation" social, cultural and economic rights, and "third generation" environmental and developmental rights. In reality, the state is not, and cannot be, so omni-competent—as the recently failed experiments in socialism have vividly shown. A vast plurality of "voluntary associations" or "mediating structures" stands between the state and the individual, religious institutions prominently among them. Religious institutions, among others, play a vital role in the cultivation and realization of all rights, including religious rights. They create the conditions (if not the prototypes) for the realization of first generation civil and political rights. They provide a critical (and sometimes the principal) means to meet second-generation rights of education, health care, childcare, labour organizations, employment, and artistic opportunities, among others. Religious institutions offer some of the deepest insights into norms of creation, stewardship, and servant-hood that lie at the heart of third generation rights.[32]

Carol S. Robb similarly draws attention to another difficulty, which has to do with the concept of group rights vis-à-vis individual rights, just as the earlier difficulty had to do with the state vis-à-vis the individual. She writes:

> It is common to speak of the development of arguments in the domain of human rights in terms of the first, second, and third generation of proposed rights. The first generation rights are the civil and political rights, the protections against coercion. The second-generation rights are group rights, which are hardly digestible in the United States legal tradition, which is

> heavily rooted in the first generation. Group rights tend to be associated with the claims of peoples claiming rights to land and culture. Such rights are focused largely on a people's right to self-development, which involves both claims for the positive provision of certain goods and also restraints on the conduct of economic relations between poor and rich countries. The two Covenants of the United Nations Declaration seem generally to discuss and protect, separately and respectively, rights of the first and second generations. However, since both Covenants have articles promoting the inherent right of all peoples to enjoy and use fully and freely their natural wealth and resources, there already exists the basis for group rights, though this generation is still developing.[33]

The point, then, is that on account of the original individualistic orientation of human rights, extensions of it to cover society or social groups and the environment are not achieved without struggle.

One may now turn to the Hindu view, which starts out not with the individual but from the cosmos. If the modern secular view takes the individual as the starting point and then expands beyond this point to embrace society and environment, the traditional Hindu view starts out from the cosmos and then zeroes in on the individual, through the intervening layer of society. A movement of this kind is also not without its problems, for while this ensures that such a perspective is relatively more at ease in dealing with ecological and social and cultural rights, it becomes a struggle to do full justice to the individual's rights, as distinguished from duties. This difficulty has been articulated as follows by an Indian scholar. He begins by raising the questions

> Is there a theory or doctrine of rights in the Indian tradition? How does one even begin to think of rights in the context of the ancient and classical Indian moral thinking? Would it be legitimate to speak of rights as some kind of entitlements without reference to the fundamental moral conceptions such as *ṛta, dharma* and *vidhi* or to scripturally sanctioned actions and so on? It would appear that just as in contemporary moral discourse it becomes extremely difficult to speak of duties without giving priority to rights, in the traditional Indian context, one cannot speak of rights—if one can speak of rights at all—without giving priority to duties. Duties, it would seem, are the primary concept in Indian social and ethical thought.

> Even so, there is almost no possibility of considering or determining the duties and obligations with regard simply to the natural entitlements of the individual, for a human being is only ever so conceived in the total context of the social order sanctioned by tradition (with the possible exception of the *sannyāsin*). An isomorphism is supposed between *ṛta* (the cosmic or natural order, later referred to as *sat*, "existence") and the right as righteousness (*satya*) and actions of human beings, which promote this harmony. This isomorphism is expressed in the comprehensive conception of dharma, which gradually becomes the touchstone of Indian life and the transcendental framework for determining the legitimacy or otherwise of the normative culture, of the gods, kings and subjects alike, at any point in time.[34]

Nevertheless, just as human rights discourse in the West has tried to overcome its individualistic orientation by evolving the concept of different generations of rights, dharma discourse in India is also trying to overcome the overshadowing of the individual and of his or her rights as a result of an emphasis on duties by reviving and moving the concept of *adhikāra* or entitlement from a ritualistic into a moral and legal realm, and the privileging of it. In this respect,

> The Indian Constitution (which as a whole is termed "*Adhikāra-patra*") . . . draws attention to what it calls "Fundamental Rights," reinforcing the view of the progressive realisation for all citizens of something to which they are each entitled. It was, however, Gandhi's strong influence which led to the inclusion of special rights for the "Harijans" and the extension of certain fundamental rights for all individuals, regardless of whether they are citizens of the nation or not. Several amendments have since been introduced or mooted to iron out certain deficiencies and inadequacies in the Constitution on issues of rights and their implementation, or to curtail certain rights and their implementation, or to curtail certain rights which the government (or rather elite) of the day felt were being misappropriated by one group or another.[35]

IV

This might be the right point to supplement the foregoing structural or functional parallel with a historical one.

The development of rights discourse in the West can be visualized as undergoing two phases. The first phase is distinguished by the emergence of the concept of rights itself, and the second phase is marked by the emergence of different kinds of rights.

Let us begin with the emergence of the concept of rights itself. It is widely held that with the spread of Western trade and commerce around the globe and the consequent increase in wealth, the need for the protection of the property and person of the individual against the arbitrary conduct of the state became a primary concern. The rise of capitalism thus marks the first step in what would ultimately become property rights in the thought of Locke. Enlightenment thinking marked the next step; the concept then acquired a *moral* and rational dimension, as distinguished from the legal. Finally, when over the centuries, these rights came to be shared by all through the rise of democracy, their *human* dimension came to the fore. All human beings came to be looked upon as possessing these rights by virtue of their moral nature. Once the concept of *human* rights had emerged in the twentieth century, their conception evolved further beyond the civil and political rights of the first generation to include the "second generation" social, cultural, and economic rights and the "third generation" environmental and developmental rights. It is worth remarking that the evolution starts with the individual dimension, then proceeds to embrace the social dimension, and finally envelops the environment. In the modern conception of rights, the impulse of the movement is outward: from the individual to the cosmos.

The ancient Hindu conception of dharma is also widely believed to have undergone three phases, as reflected in the corpus of the sacred literature in Hinduism called the Vedas. This body of literature, which according to most modern scholars began to take shape around 1500 B.C., contains three divisions, which also roughly correspond to three phases in the development of the tradition itself. The first division is referred to as the Saṁhitā or Mantra period, the second the Brāhmaṇa period, and the third the Upaniṣad period (the way one might refer to the Old Testament and the New Testament in the Bible). What is striking is the semantic change that the word "dharma" undergoes at each stage. Its primary meaning in the first or Saṁhitā (Mantra) period is cosmic order, otherwise called *ṛta*. In the second period, called the Brāhmaṇa period, the concept primarily comes to refer to orderliness of ritual activity in its social and sacrificial dimension. In the third period, called the Upaniṣadic period, the meaning of personal morality and salvation becomes important.

This transformation in the meaning of the word "dharma" follows a particular course: it is a movement from cosmos inward toward society and then to the individual. It should also be obvious that this movement is opposite to the one identified in the case of rights, where the movement was from the individual to the social and the cosmic.

There are, of course, pitfalls involved in comparing conceptual movements, which span two centuries of recent Western history, with those which range over a thousand years of ancient Indian history, but such are the risks a comparative religionist regularly takes as part of his or her profession!

This broad comparison renders two sets of conclusions possible. To arrive at the first it is useful to examine the word "right" and to recognize that the word can mean (1) righteousness or conformity to some norm or standard, as visiting someone who is sick or helping an old lady across the street; and (2) entitlement, such as the right to be left alone (the right to privacy) and certainly not to be arbitrarily picked up and imprisoned (right to liberty). As a next step, one might entertain the possibility that these meanings of the word can either merge or diverge in their usage. For instance, they merge when it is said that to keep one's promise is to do the right thing. Thus, it is "both right and a matter of right to keep a contractual promise." But the meaning could also diverge, as when we might say, "It is right (morally) to help others but others have no right to be helped (legally)."

We are now in a position to state the first conclusion, a conclusion anticipated earlier, which is that these two meanings separate in modern Western thought but are brought together in Hindu thought, with the result that Western discourse on rights tends to be legal and the Hindu discourse, moral.

The second conclusion is easier to state, as the ground for it has already been prepared. It only needs to be (re)iterated: the three aspects of dharma in Hinduism, in its chronological development from cosmic righteousness (defined primarily through order *ṛta*), to social righteousness (defined primarily through norms [dharma, specially as *varṇa* or "caste"]) to personal righteousness (or rules of conduct [*svadharma*]). These correspond broadly to the three generations of human rights. The priority in Vedic Hindu thought runs "order → norms → rules," while in modern Western thought it runs "rights → norms → order," as noted earlier.

V

We must now pause to consider the place that the right to family planning, contraception, and abortion, or what may collectively be referred to as reproductive rights, must be accorded in these developments.

Reproductive rights, at first blush, seem to readily qualify as individual rights. The exercise of such rights by the individual, however, has major implications for society. Reproduction is closely associated with demography and demography with democracy, which typically represents the political system within which such rights are exercised.[36] The assertion of cultural rights, for instance, assumes a critical mass of population to assert them. Similarly, reproductive rights have major implications for the environment, which come into play, for instance, through the phenomenon of overpopulation, which is tied directly to reproduction.[37] These dimensions of the problem have received less recognition in the West, perhaps because it does not face the problem of minorities or overpopulation the way India does. In the West, reproductive rights, at the level of the second generation, have been tied to the provision of certain goods for a group, as for instance, the right of all women to abortion; and, at the level of the third generation rights, with the biotic rights of other species.

In terms of the three levels of Hindu thought—of the cosmos, society, and individual—it is interesting that while there is a clear recognition of one's duties to the cosmic order (through the doctrine of the three debts), as well as at the social level (in the form of such doctrines as Strī-dharma, etc.), what was emphasized at the individual level was the duty to reproduce. It has the interesting consequence of implying the right to sex as a reproductive right for women vis-à-vis the husband, or even men in general. There also seems to be a clear recognition of the "right" to contraception on the part of the male. All this seems to justify the hope that "religions can provide, as the human rights idea does not adequately provide, for the tensions between rights and responsibilities, between individual and community, between material and the spirit."[38]

One must also at this point distinguish among three concepts: (1) the duty to reproduce; (2) the right to reproduce; and (3) reproductive rights. From the traditional Hindu perspective, women had the duty to reproduce, and also the right to reproduce (as well as the right to sex). We are, however, at the moment concerned with the reproductive rights rather than with the right to reproduce. And while reproductive rights include the right to reproduce, they also include much more, such as the right *not* to reproduce, if we acknowledge the right to family planning, contraception, and abortion. With the introduction of the modern concept of rights, through its incorporation in the revalorized locution of *adhikāra*,[39] these reproductive rights are now freely available to Hindus in modern India. Women in India have the right to family planning, to contraception, and to abortion. It is not often realized that India was the first country in the world to promote family planning as official policy, and this of course involved the adoption of contraception, despite Gandhi's opposition to all forms of family planning[40] (with the sole exception of abstinence).[41]

The situation regarding abortion may be summarized as follows:

> In the late 1980's, 3.9 million induced abortions were reported annually in India. Abortion has been legal in India since 1971, when the Medical Termination of Pregnancy Act was passed. It allowed for abortions when "the continuance of the pregnancy would involve a risk to the life of the pregnant woman or of grave injury to her physical or mental health" or when "there is substantial risk that, if the child were born, it would suffer such physical or mental abnormalities as to be seriously handicapped." Two appendices state that when a pregnancy is caused by rape or the failure of a birth control device, "grave injury" will be assumed.
>
> However, traditional Hinduism opposes abortion. The Vedic literature includes an incantation against whomever causes a pregnant woman to abort: "the blood-sucking demon and him that tries to rob health, Kanva, the devourer of our offspring, destroy, O Prisni-parni" (*Atharvaveda* 2.25.2). On the question of "When does life begin?" the Hindu manual on medicine, *Caraka Samhita*, says explicitly that life begins at conception, when the soul and mind enter the zygote formed by the union of the sperm and egg. This means that "a being with a human genetic code is indeed a human being." Thus, the fetus is inviolable and abortion is not an option, for it would be a violation of the moral principle of *ahimsa* (non-injury) to all living beings. . . .
>
> In the final analysis, however, Hinduism is a religion that recognizes that each person must make his or her own ethical decisions, because each person alone suffers or enjoys the *karmic* consequences.[42]

This last statement is significant. It tries to reconcile this modern development with Hinduism through the concept of karma. Karma is a highly individualistic concept, whereas our analysis had focused on the concept of dharma, which is a highly social and cosmic concept. Even the social and cosmic dimensions of karma in Hindu thought take a backseat in comparison with its individualistic orientation.

It was pointed out earlier that modern secular human rights discourse, despite its individualistic starting point, is in the process of incorporating social and environmental concerns within that discourse, through the concept of several generations of human rights. This raises a parallel question in the Hindu context: is Hindu dharmic discourse capable of accommodating the idea of reproductive rights (as distinguished from the right to reproduce)? The attempt to answer this question takes us into the next section.

VI

Is it possible to come to terms with reproductive rights in a dharmic way? The problematic may be spelled out more clearly before an answer is attempted. According to traditional Hindu thought, it is the dharma of the couple—and of women—to multiply. The concept of reproductive rights, however, could and does carry the opposite implication of restricting rather than promoting reproduction. Is it not then opposed to dharma, at least as traditionally conceived? How could what is anti-dharma, be reconciled with dharma? Similarly, Hindu traditional thought is opposed to abortion. How could it then possibly support or even condone abortion?

Traditional dharmic thinking no doubt distinguishes between dharma and *adharma*. It, however, also contains a provision that what is at one time dharma may, with the passage of time, become *adharma* and vice versa. An everyday illustration of the operation of this principle in Hinduism is provided by the fact that as a student one is supposed to remain a celibate. Celibacy is one's dharma as a student. Yet, as soon as one gets married, celibacy becomes *adharma*. Here biography recapitulates history; what is dharma in one age can similarly become *adharma* in another. S. Cromwell Crawford draws creatively on this principle when he writes:

> The concept of *dharma* or morality is a dynamic notion in Hindu ethics, open to processes of change as different situations arise. The *dharma* of *Vedas* was to beget "ten sons." That made sense in times when warfare, an agricultural economy, and high rate of infant mortality were the order of the day. For most of India's history, these exigencies have prevailed, and hence the practice of having large families has become part of a hallowed tradition. But today the same dharmic principle of welfare dictates a radical shift in attitude, both toward fertility and towards fertility as a requirement of *dharma*. Bluntly stated, yesterday's *dharma* is today's *adharma*. "The rules of *dharma* are the mortal flesh of immortal ideas and so are mutable."[43]

Next, abortion. In order to understand abortion in a dharmic context one needs to tap into another concept associated with dharma, namely, that what is dharma in any situation needs to be determined by an appeal to more than one factor. These factors are listed severally, but a list of four factors is fairly standard. According to this view, the following four serve as "sources" of dharma: (1) divine revelation or Veda; (2) traditional lore or *smṛti*; (3) exemplarily conduct; and (4) conscience.

This fourfold listing is also found in the Manusmṛti, widely regarded as a text of high authority in the matter of dharma. It places the Vedas or the revealed scriptures of Hinduism at the head of the list, but K. Satchidananda Murty, a distinguished contemporary Hindu thinker, notes that according to this text

> Even the entire Veda is not the sole source of dharma, . . . but a source along with (a) the smṛtis and (b) conduct of its knowers, as well as (c) the conduct of the good and (d) the glad satisfaction of oneself (ātmanastuṣṭi). It is important to note that in addition to the first two, it mentions two more factors, implying that the good may not be with the Veda-knowers only and that what is taken to be Vedic teaching must also appeal to and satisfy an individual. The good in the world or a country constitutes a much larger number than that of the Veda-knowers; the first includes the second.[44]

He goes on to say:

> This smṛti goes on to say that the character of dharma is fourfold: the Veda, the smṛti, the conduct of the good and what is pleasing to oneself (priyamātmanaḥ). It goes without saying that "the glad satisfaction of oneself" or "what is pleasing to oneself" cannot be also the exclusive source or character of dharma. Of course, for those inquiring about dharma, it ordains, the ultimate authority is śruti. But, another significant thing in this connection is that the chapter in which these verses occur begins with a definition of dharma, which does not refer to the Veda! Dharma is that which the wise and the good, without attachment and aversion, always practised, and which they acknowledged heartily (hṛdayenābhayanujñāta) as dharma. It is difficult to think of a more enlightening and progressive definition of dharma. As this is followed by the

> other verses already cited, one may venture to conclude that what is cumulatively defined by all these verses put together is the Vaidika dharma.[45]

How significant a point may be involved here will become clear from the fact that the Manusmṛti does not refer to the practice of suttee. It has been credibly argued that the Vedas also do not contain any unambiguous references to suttee. So the question naturally arises: how could a practice not vouched for either by *śruti* or *smṛti* (that is, revealed literature or traditional lore) acquire the status of dharma? The answer briefly is: through *ācāra* (custom). A modern Hindu scholar knows what he is talking about when he says that in premodern India, custom was king![46]

The distinction between theory and practice helps clarify the point. An intellectual approach to life tends to privilege theory over practice. Traditional Hindu thought, however, reverses the equation and seems to privilege practice over "theory" (i.e., what is propounded in texts is considered secondary to what is found in practice).

This principle contains a revolutionary implication, of which suttee provides a negative example. Practice can itself validate it and make something dharmic, strange as it might sound. This is one way in which we may wish to understand the statement that "*dharma* is not established by deduction but is radically empirical."[47]

VII

In this final section, one may now raise a difficult question. Modern secular human rights discourse is in the process of assimilating reproductive rights. Dharmic Hindu discourse is also in the process of assimilating them. We did, however, note that modern secular human rights discourse is rights-oriented and that traditional Hindu dharmic discourse is duty-oriented. Reproductive rights discourse is thus arguably consistent with *both* rights discourse and duty discourse. The sensitive question we might now wish to ask is: should we employ these modes of discourse in the context of reproduction at all? In order to understand the force of this question one must ask another. Why do we reproduce? Why do we bring children into the world?

Couples bring children into the world presumably because they love each other, and therefore make love, and thereby have children, whom they love. In other words, they do not bring children into the world by saying "O.K. Let us now exercise our right to reproduce" (except perhaps in jest). Nor do we bring children into the world by saying "O.K. Let us fulfill our duty to our race." Having children or sex does not belong properly to either rights discourse or even duty discourse; it is intrinsically a part of the discourse of affection. Martin Buber says somewhere that nothing becomes a person more than to deal with another person in justice, except if it be in love. I put to you that when we use either rights discourse or duty discourse, we are dealing with the other person in justice rather than in love.

I am not trying to be sentimental or romantic. What I am trying to do is to draw attention to the fact that, unlike many other areas of life, the area of life covered by reproduction is intrinsically more closely related to affection discourse, just as our professional life may be more closely related to duties discourse and our political life to rights discourse. Because affection discourse is not perfect—no discourse is—some vulnerable parties within it may need protection, and this is how the state comes into the picture. As the state steps in we may need to employ rights discourse, but we must be on our guard to ensure that such discourse only provides safeguards against deviations from affection discourse and does not usurp it. Duty discourse similarly contains elements of drudgery at the one end and dedication at the other, yet for someone to make love for motives other than that of love (even if it be out of a sense of duty or even dedication) must leave us feeling uncomfortable. It is true that by the very fact of referring to reproductive rights as rights we are assuming an entitlement in law rather than in affection, and accepting the proposition that law must step in where affection has failed. But we must not lose sight of the fact that we are dealing with the exception and not the rule. If confrontation is characteristic of rights discourse and obligation of duties discourse, then love is characteristic of affection discourse, in relation to which both confrontation and obligation constitute subtractions rather than additions.

Part III

15

Reciprocal Illumination within a Method

The purpose of this short chapter is to propose that some of the expressions used by Professor W. Brede Kristensen in his discussion of the phenomenology of religion reveal their true significance when read in the context of their use by G. van der Leeuw. In other words, reading Kristensen and van der Leeuw can be reciprocally illuminating in the context of the phenomenology of religion, as will become clear upon examining two expressions: (1) *ideal connection* and (2) *significance*.

Ideal Connection

Kristensen, in remarking on the phenomenological method, points out that this method of study brings together the similar facts and phenomena it encounters in different religions and studies them in groups.[1] One such group or category could be sacrifice.[2] Now the question arises: "How do we come to see what the religious significance of sacrifice is?"[3] In the course of answering this question, he remarks:

> It is difficult to give an answer on the basis of data from one particular religion. We must have a general view based on observations gathered from as many religions as possible in order that we may achieve certainty. Therefore we must compare them with one another, and it is the research undertaken in phenomenology, to consider the phenomena, not only in their historical context, but also in their *ideal connection*.[4]

What is the significance of the expression *ideal connection* here? Kristensen does not go on to say much about it. But the following passage from Van de Leeuw seems to shed light on it.

> The observance of what appears implies a *clarification* of what has been observed: all that belongs to the same order must be united, while what is different in type must be separated. These distinctions, however, should certainly not be decided by appealing to causal connections in the sense that A arises from B, while C has its own origin uniting it to D—but solely and simply by employing structural relations somewhat as the landscape painter combines his groups of objects, or separates them from one another. The juxtaposition, in other words, must not become internalization, but structural association; and this means that we seek the ideal *typical interrelation*. . . .[5]

Significance

Kristensen repeatedly uses the expression "religious significance," or just "significance." Thus, of "ritual purification" he asks: What is its religious significance?[6] Earlier, he had inquired into the religious significance of sacrifice.[7] What is the significance of this expression itself? W. Brede Kristensen does not tell us much about it, but G. van der Leeuw seems to. He writes that structure is "the sketching of an outline within a chaotic maze of so-called 'reality' "[8] and continues:

> Structure is a connection which is neither merely experienced directly, nor abstracted either logically or causally, but which is *understood*. It is an organic whole, which cannot be analyzed into its own constituents but which can from these be comprehended; or in other terms, a fabric of particulars, not to be compounded by the addition of those, nor the deduction of one from the others, but again only *understood* as a whole. In other words: structure is certainly experienced, but not immediately, it is indeed constructed, but not logically, causally and abstractly. Structure is reality significantly organized. But the *significance* in its own turn belongs in part to the "someone" who attempts to understand it.[9]

It is clear then that it is in the apposition with G. van der Leeuw that the full significance of some of the expressions used by Kristensen is revealed.[10] Kristensen pointed out that "data shed light upon one another" is one of the principles on which phenomenology works. Obviously phenomenologists shed light upon one another too!

16

The History of Religions

Buddhism and Judaism

The history of religions often makes use of typology to gain a deeper understanding of the religious traditions, whose study comprises its subject matter. One way in which it proceeds is by classifying religions as: living and dead religions; primitive and world religions; prophetic and wisdom religions; Eastern and Western religions; missionary and nonmissionary religions; theistic and nontheistic religions; and so forth. Erich Fromm has also attempted a classification of religions from a "psychological stand,"[1] and it is this classification that I intend to take up for further consideration.

Before one takes up the discussion of the classification suggested by him, however, the fact that his classification represents an interaction of *two* methods in the study of religion should be immediately recognized. In this case these two methods are the historical and the psychological methods. It may also be noted that the distinction between theistic and nontheistic religions represents a coupling of the historical and the theological methods as well, something that may not be apparent at first sight.

We now revert to a consideration of Erich Fromm's classification. He decides in the interest of economy to "deal with only one distinction, but one which in my opinion is the most important, and which cuts across theistic and non-theistic religions: that between *authoritarian* and *humanistic* religions."[2] According to Fromm, the "essential element in authoritarian religion and in the authoritarian religious experience is the surrender to a power transcending man. The main virtue of this type of religion is obedience, its cardinal sin disobedience."[3] Fromm cites Calvinism and Fascism as examples here, the latter as an example of "authoritarian secular religion."[4] By contrast, humanistic religion "is centered around man and his strength."[5] And inasmuch as "humanistic religions are theistic, God is a symbol of *man's own powers* which he tries to realize in his life, and is not a symbol of force and domination, having *power over man*."[6]

> Illustrations of humanistic religions are early Buddhism, Taoism, the teachings of Isaiah, Jesus, Socrates, Spinoza, certain trends in the Jewish and Christian religions (particularly mysticism), the religion of Reason of the French Revolution. It is evident from these that the distinction between authoritarian and humanistic religion cuts across the distinction between theistic and non-theistic, and between religions in the narrow sense of the word and philosophical systems of religious character. What matters in all such systems is not the thought system as such but the human attitude underlying their doctrines.[7]

Fromm then proceeds to cite examples from humanistic religions. We shall confine ourselves to two citations—one from early Buddhism and the other from Rabbinic Judaism. The one from early Buddhism I have chosen to cite deals with the Buddha's attitude toward authority.

> The Buddha once visited a small town called Kesaputta in the kingdom of Kosala. The inhabitants of this town were known by the common name Kālāma. When they heard that the Buddha was in their town, the Kālāmas paid him a visit, and they told him: "Sir, there are some recluses and brāhmaṇas who visit Kesaputta. They explain and illuminate only their own doctrines and despise, condemn and spurn others' doctrines. Then come other recluses and brāhmaṇas, and they, too, in their turn, explain and illumine only their own doctrines, and despise, condemn and spurn others' doctrines. But, for us, Sir, we have always doubt and perplexity as to who among these venerable recluses and brāhmaṇas spoke the truth, and who spoke falsehood."
>
> Then the Buddha gave them this advice, unique in the history of religions: "Yes, Kālāmas, it is proper that you have doubt, that you have perplexity, for a doubt has arisen in a matter which is doubtful. Now, look you Kālāmas, do not be led by reports, or tradition, or hearsay. Be not led by the

> authority of religious texts, nor by mere logic or inference, nor by considering appearances, nor by the delight in speculative opinions, nor by seeming possibilities, nor by the idea: 'this is our teacher.' But, O Kālāmas, when you know for yourselves that certain things are unwholesome (*akusala*), and wrong, and bad, then give them up. . . . And when you know for yourselves that certain things are wholesome (*kusala*) and good, then accept them and follow them."
>
> The Buddha went even further. He told the bhikkhus that a disciple should examine even the Tathāgata (Buddha) himself, so that he (the disciple) might be fully convinced of the true value of the teacher whom he followed.[8]

The other illustration from Rabbinic Judaism, translated from the original (Talmud, Baba Meziah, 59, b) by Fromm himself, runs as follows:

> A number of other famous rabbinical scholars disagreed with Rabbi Eliezar's views in regard to a point of ritual law. "Rabbi Eliezar said to them: 'If the law is as I think it is then this tree shall let us know,' Whereupon the tree jumped from its place a hundred yards (others say four hundred yards). His colleagues said to him, 'One does not prove anything from a tree.' He said, 'If I am right then this brook shall let us know,' whereupon the brook ran upstream. His colleagues said to him, 'One does not prove anything from a brook.' He continued and said, 'If the law is as I think then the walls of this house will tell.' Whereupon the walls began to fall. But Rabbi Joshua shouted at the walls and said, 'If scholars argue a point of law, what business have you to fall?' So the walls fell no further out of respect for Rabbi Joshua but out of respect for Rabbi Eliezar did not straighten up. And it is the way they still are.
>
> Rabbi Eliezar took up the argument again and said, 'If the law is as I think, they shall tell us from heaven.' Whereupon a voice from heaven said, 'What have you against Rabbi Eliezar, because the law is as he says.' Whereupon Rabbi Joshua got up and said, 'It is written in Bible: The law is not in heaven. What does this mean? According to Rabbi Jeremiah it means since the Torah has been given on Mount Sinai we no longer pay attention to voices from heaven because it is written: You make your decision according to the majority opinion.' It then happened that Rabbi Nathan (one of the participants in the

> discussion) met the Prophet Elijah (who had taken a stroll on earth) and he asked the Prophet, 'What did God himself say when we had this discussion?' The Prophet answered, 'God smiled and said, My children have won, my children have won.' "[9]

Fromm goes on to point out, after comparing the biblical accounts of the Fall and the Flood, that "both principles . . . the authoritarian and the humanistic . . . are present at the root of the Judaeo-Christian religion," and adds that, "in the development of Judaism as well as Christianity both principles have been preserved and their relative preponderance marks different trends in the two religions."[10]

How does the principle of reciprocal illumination shed further light on these points? To answer this question it is useful to focus on the Flood account, as it was after this, according to Fromm, that "the relationship between God and man changes fundamentally"[11]—with God promising to be, shall we say, more reasonable?

The exercises about to be undertaken may be clearly mapped out first. The methods involved are the historical, which classifies traditions,[12] and the psychological, which now provides a basis for classifying them à la Fromm. And now two traditions may be drawn on—one living, namely Judaism; and the other dead, namely Babylonian religion. Thus, two methods and traditions are in play.

It is widely believed that the Judaic account is borrowed from the more literary and elaborate Babylonian account contained in the Gilgamesh epic,[13] although the view that both may be adaptations of a prior account should not be discarded. Thus, now we have a monotheistic Hebraic account as well as a polytheistic Babylonian account to consider. The interesting point that emerges in terms of Fromm's typology is that, in terms of his distinction between authoritarian and humanistic orientations, the polytheistic account is relatively more humanistic when compared with the monotheistic. This raises the interesting historical point whether the humanization of Yahweh in Judaism, apparent in the Flood account, may not have been, at least in part, the result of the influence of the Babylonian account from which it may have been borrowed. Apparently in this borrowing the polytheism of the Babylonian account is pruned into monotheism, but in the process that one remaining god, it seems, may also have been humanized.

In any case, the contrast between the Babylonian and the Judaic account is marked both at the levels of gods and men. In terms of the god(s) involved, the contrast in part is between polytheism and monotheism but another part of the contrast consists in the self-sufficiency of the Judaic god and the human dependency of the Babylonian gods, who feel famished during the flood, as no sacrifices reach them. When Utanapishtim offers sacrificial thanks for having been saved, the Gilgamesh epic tells us (9.159):

> The Gods savoured the smell,
> The Gods savoured the sweet smell;
> The Gods foregathered, like flies,
> Above the maker of the offering.[14]

This gastronomic banquet of the gods is reduced to an olfactorily satisfying whiff of Yahweh in the biblical account (Gen. 8:21).

Thus despite the somewhat capricious behavior of the gods and tenuous links between morality and meteorology by comparison with the biblical account, human beings in the Babylonian version do have more clout with the gods. Similarly, unlike Noah being assisted by Yahweh in being saved from the flood, Utanapishtim makes it on his own. Unassisted by the gods he prepares the ark, closes the door, and even has a navigator to steer the course. After the flood recedes, Yahweh tells Noah what to do, but Utanapishtim acts on his own. In the Gilgamesh epic, even the gods are said to have been terrified by the destruction they had caused—a very human reaction; it could be that the Yahweh account caught the contagion of this sentiment. As A. Heidel remarks: "The Biblical story is pervaded by the spirit of complete submission to the will of God and complete dependence on him, while the Babylonian traditions reveal something of the spirit of self-determination and self-reliance."[15]

The point of illumination, then, is that when we borrow the form from another tradition to serve a function of our own, the manner in which the original form functioned may reappear with it as well.

17

The Phenomenology of Religion and Buddhism

An important aspect of the phenomenological method, specially as outlined by Kristensen, consists in placing oneself in the shoes of the believer of another tradition, on the grounds that if we are to understand a religion, it must be understood as the believer understands it. Thus, he wrote:

> Let us never forget that there exists no other religious reality than the faith of the believer. If we really want to understand religion, we must refer exclusively to the believer's testimony. What we believe, from our point of view, about the nature or value of other religions, is a reliable testimony to our own faith, or to our own understanding of religious faith; but if our opinion about another religion differs from the opinion and evaluation of the believers, then we are no longer talking about their religion. We have turned aside from historical reality, and are concerned only with ourselves.[1]

But is it possible to achieve a complete understanding of another person without becoming the other person and ceasing to be oneself? The logical corollary of this in the study of religion then would consist of a Christian becoming a Muslim, if the Christian really wants to understand Islam completely. This, however, is ruled out by Kristensen. He writes that while the scholar should adopt the standpoint of the believer,

> the historian cannot understand the absolute character of the religious data in the same way that the believer understands them. The historian's standpoint is a different one. There is a distance between him and the object of the research; he cannot identify himself with it as the believer does. We cannot become Mohammedans when we try to understand Islam, and if we could, our study would be at an end: we should ourselves then directly experience the reality. The historian seeks to understand, and he is able to do that in an approximate way, approximate, but no more.[2]

Thus, the study of religion must remain a second-order enterprise, and Kristensen's approach may thus best be described as one of empathetic approximation, for he goes on to explain:

> By means of empathy he tries to relive in his own experience that which is "alien," and that, too, he can only approximate. This imaginative re-experiencing of a situation strange to us is a form of representation, and not reality itself, for that always asserts itself with sovereign authority. We can even assume such an inheritance: we can form a more or less clear picture of our own national character, and we often do so. But then we always feel the shortcomings of our own formulation; the representation is always something else than the reality. The "existential" nature of the religious datum is never disclosed by research. That cannot be defined. Here we see the limit to the validity of historical research. But recognizing a limit of validity is not to deny the value of this research.[3]

This position in the phenomenological approach to the study of religion may be contrasted with that of Buddha's omniscience in Mahāyāna Buddhism, wherein the idea that knowing an object—whether animate or inanimate—entails completely becoming it is given free rein. Thus, Edward Conze writes that while even in pre-Mahāyāna Buddhism the Buddha was acknowledged as omniscient in the sense that "he knew everything necessary for salvation, his own and that of others, and therefore in matters spiritual is a sure and infallible guide,"[4] the understanding of Buddha's omniscience is more extensive and literal in Mahāyāna Buddhism.

> The Mahāyāna now claims that he knows also all other things, that he is omniscient in the full sense of the term. But since it

> is one of the peculiarities of a Buddha's gnosis that therein the subject is identical with the object, the fact that he knows everything there is, implies that he also *is* everything there is. In consequence the Buddha becomes identical either with the Absolute, or with the sum total of existence, with the totality of all things at all times. It is only because he has merged with everything that the Buddha has cast off all traces of a separate self and has attained complete and total self-extinction.[5]

The bodhisattva, however, forever approaches Buddhahood. It is on account of this that it was the ideal of the bodhisattva (as distinguished from the Buddha ideal) that caught on[6] in Mahāyāna Buddhism, and according to historians explains the remarkable speed with which this form of Buddhism actually spread.[7] The point to bear in mind here is that, like the phenomenologist or the historian in relation to the believer, the bodhisattva must only approximate but not achieve Buddhahood.[8] As a matter of fact, in both the cases the greater the approximation,[9] the greater their usefulness in their respective rôles, which comes to a sudden end at the moment when either achieves identity with the object of approximation.

Kristensen maintains that if a Christian, instead of empathetically approximating the experience of being a Muslim, himself becomes a Muslim, "our study would be at an end." But must this be so? It is not possible to identify oneself completely *but temporarily* with the object of one's knowledge? The suggestion has a clear implication for the study of religion: what if a scholar temporarily converts to another religion? Can the scholar then not revert to his (or her) original position, or even reflect on the tradition he had both embraced *and* is studying? It seems to me that such a procedure may be less problematical in the case of those religions in which entry and exit is easily allowed for than in those in which such is not the case. Thus, ethnic religions like Hinduism and Judaism are easy to leave but difficult to enter, as membership is usually linked to birth. Islam is easy to enter but difficult to leave if the penalty for apostasy, which is death, is imposed. The opinion may differ from country to country, however, on this point of the Sharī'ah. Buddhism in this respect is the least problematic, allowing both entrance and exit freely. In fact, it was to prevent such freedom from degenerating into a revolving door approach to the Order that a limit was set on the number of times one could rejoin the Order. It is not out of place to mention here that a man of religion—Rāmakṛṣṇa—apparently actually accomplished what is being discussed here regarding a student of religion. Rāmakṛṣṇa experimented with Christianity and Islam by "converting" to them.[10]

The Buddhist case, however, works out differently, and the difference is illuminating. Whereas the student of religion can revert to his or her parent tradition after temporary conversion, and whereas Rāmakṛṣṇa could revert to his ancestral Hinduism after experimenting with various faiths, no reversion from Buddhahood is possible.[11]

18

The Psychology of Religion and Buddhism

I

A strong case could be made in favor of studying Buddhism basically from a psychological perspective because of the nature of the tradition itself. This would involve matching method with subject matter. Such a suggestion has in fact been made by Fritz Staal in relation to the religions of India in general. He suggests that

> the religions of India provide the materials which one day may show that religion can be studied as a branch of psychology—a psychology, of course, which is an integrated science of the mind, the soul and the spirit, not just a discipline that confines itself just to the experimentation with a small selection of mental phenomena. I know that critics of Indian religion will readily adopt such an evaluation. But the same approach can be applied to the study of all religions. That India should provide such materials more easily is due to a variety of circumstances; for example, the free and unhampered complete development of religion, and the importance of mental approaches (e.g. mediation) in the area of religion.[1]

The suggestion, however, has particularly been made in relation to Buddhism. Edward Conze, while discussing Buddhism as a philosophy, remarks:

> Philosophy, as we understand it in Europe, is a creation of the Greeks. It is unknown to Buddhist tradition, which would

> regard the enquiry into reality, for the mere purpose of knowing more about it, as a waste of valuable time. The Buddha's teaching is exclusively concerned with showing the way to salvation. Any "philosophy" there may be in the works of Buddhist authors is quite incidental. In the ample vocabulary of Buddhism we find no word to correspond to our term "philosophy." An analogy may clarify the position. The Chinese language, as the Chinese understood it, did not contain any grammar, and it was taught in China without any grammatical instructions. Some European philologists, on the model of our Latin grammatical categories, have constructed a "grammar" for the Chinese language. It does not fit particularly well, and the Chinese continue to dispense with it. The Latin-style grammar, with its familiar categories, may, however, help some Europeans to learn the Chinese language more easily. In a similar way, an attempt to define Buddhist thought in philosophical terminology current in Europe may facilitate the approach to it. Buddhism, as a "philosophy" could then be described as a "dialectical pragmatism" with a "psychological" turn.[2]

Conze then proceeds to discuss dialectics, pragmatism, and psychology in relation to Buddhism. It is his remarks on the psychological dimension of Buddhism that concern us here. He writes:

> Meditation is in Buddhism easily the chief means of salvation. The stress is throughout far less on "doing something by overt action, than on contemplation and mental discipline." What one aims at is the control of mental processes by meditating on them. In consequence, Buddhist thought is impregnated with what we call *Psychology*. It mixes metaphysics and psychology in a way to which we have no parallel in the West.[3]

Edward Conze thus accords considerable importance to psychology in the study of Buddhism, and seems to place it on a par with philosophy. Lama Angarika Govinda takes a somewhat similar stance, with a slightly greater tilt toward psychology. He even declares: "[T]he distinction between religions of revelation and science on the one hand, and Buddhism on the other pertains to the domain of psychology."[4] However, the overall picture drawn is one in which both philosophy and psychology (as conceived in Buddhism) play their role in the study of Buddhism. He writes:

> From this it is clear that in Buddhism psychology and philosophy, as the process of knowing (cognition) and the formulation of the known, are indivisibly bound up with each other. The training of consciousness is the indispensable antecedent condition of higher knowledge, because consciousness is the vessel upon whose capacity depends the *extent* of what is to be received. Knowledge on the other hand is the antecedent condition required for the *selection* of the material to be received, and for the *direction* of the course to be pursued for its mastery. Without the presence of a tradition, in which the experiences and knowledge of former generations are formulated (philosophy), every individual would be compelled to master the entire domain of the psychic, and only a few favoured ones would attain the goal of knowledge. Just as little adequate, however, would be the mere acceptance or intellectual recognition of the results laid down as philosophy to the pioneer truth-seeker. Every individual must himself tread the path of realization, for only the knowledge that is won by experience has living, i.e. life-, value. It is here that the philosophy of Buddhism is distinguished from the intellectual philosophies of our time, which exhaust themselves in abstract thinking without exercising any influence on man. The same is the case with the purely scientific systems of psychology, especially when they have lost their spiritual background. It is the close interweaving of philosophy and psychology, which protects Buddhism from stagnation.[5]

The tilt toward psychology as a method of exploring at least such a key concept in Buddhism as *nirvāṇa,* if not Buddhism itself, is even more demonstrably a feature of Rune A. Johansson's approach. In fact, his tilt toward psychology is so strong that he is virtually willing to fall out of the philosophical armchair. He writes:

> Anybody with a good knowledge of psychology and its history who reads the Pali Nikayas must be struck by the fact that the psychological terminology is richer in this than in any other ancient literature and that more space is devoted to psychological analysis and explanations in this than in any other religious literature. A psychologist immediately finds that he can follow easily much of this literature, and if he knows Pali he quickly discovers that the English translators

> were badly at home in this field. This makes the psychologist feel generally hopeful: he can understand, he can do something. And if he, for instance, becomes interested in the meaning of nibbāna, he might put the question to himself: how far can I, with my special background, understand nibbāna? Nibbāna may not ultimately be a psychological concept, but there may be psychological aspects, or conditions or consequences. Exactly how far can I follow? And if I can follow at all, would it not be desirable to compare the ancient ways of expression with our modern ways? Human mind cannot have changed much; only ways of expression change. So would it not be interesting to try to understand and express the old experiences in modern terminology? And one consideration more. Psychology has recently helped semantics to develop methods for analyzing the exact contents of concepts and define their meanings. Quite possibly these methods could be helpful in studying a concept like nibbāna.[6]

His conclusion:

> These are then the pros and cons. We have no illusion that this investigation is the final one of nibbāna. But considering the many different explanations in contemporary literature, every serious study could be helpful. Why should not psychology enter and do its duty?[7]

In this context it is interesting to recall a conversation I had with David J. Kalupahana in Honolulu several years ago, in the course of which he expressed the view that Buddhism flourished in India so long as it remained a "psychology" and disappeared in India once it became a "philosophy."

At least four scholars have indicated how the discussion of at least some points of Buddhism could be easily moved in the direction of modern and especially depth psychology. The first instance is provided by Heinrich Zimmer. In his discussion of the Act of Truth in Indian religions, Zimmer switches at one point to an illustration from Buddhism, which he cites as follows:

> Even a shameful truth is better than a decent falsehood—as we shall learn from the following witty Buddhist tale.
>
> The youth Yaññadatta had been bitten by a poisonous snake. His parents carried him to the feet of an ascetic, laid

him down and said, "Reverend sir, monks know simples and charms; heal our son." "I know no simples; I am not a physician." "But you are a monk, therefore out of charity for this youth perform an Act of Truth." The ascetic replied, "Very well, I will perform an Act of Truth." He laid his hand on Yaññadatta's head and recited the following stanza:

For but a week I lived the holy life
With tranquil heart in quest of merit.

The life I've lived for fifty years
Since then, I've lived against my will.

By this truth, health!
Poison is struck down! Let Yaññadatta live!

Immediately the poison came out of Yaññadatta's breast and sank into the ground. The father then laid his hand on Yaññadatta's breast and recited the following stanza:

Never did I like to see a stranger
Come to stay. I never cared to give.

But my dislike, the monks and Brāhmans
Never knew, all learned as they were.

By this truth, health!
Poison is struck down! Let Yaññadatta live!

Immediately the poison came out of the small of Yaññadatta's back and sank into the ground. The father bade the mother perform an Act of Truth, but the mother replied, "I have a Truth, but I cannot recite it in your presence." The father answered, "Make my son whole anyhow!" So the mother recited the following stanza:

No more, my son, do I now hate this snake malignant
That out of a crevice came and bit you, than I do your father!

By this truth, health!
Poison is struck down! Let Yaññadatta live!

> Immediately the rest of the poison sank into the ground, and Yaññadatta got up and began to frisk about.[8]

After citing this incident, Zimmer immediately suggests an explanation in terms of depth psychology.

> This is a tale that could be taken as a text for psychoanalysis. The opening up of the repressed truth, deeply hidden beneath the years of lies and dead actions that have killed the son (i.e., have killed the future, the life, of this miserable, hypocritical, self-deceiving household), suffices, like magic, to clear the venom from the poor, paralysed body, and then all of that deadness (*asat*), "Non-existence," is truly non-existent. Life breaks forth anew, in strength, and the living is spliced back to what was living. The night of nonentity between is gone.[9]

A second scholar who adopts a similar approach is Erich Fromm. He first recounts the following Jātaka tale:

> Once a hare sat under a mango tree and slept. Suddenly he heard a loud noise. He thought the world was coming to an end and started to run. When the other hares saw him running they asked, "Why do you run so fast?" He replied, "The world is coming to an end." Upon hearing this they all joined him in his flight. When the deer saw the hares running they asked them, "Why do you run so fast?" and the hares answered, "We run because the world is coming to an end." Upon which the deer joined them in their flight. Thus one species after another joined the animals already running until the whole animal kingdom was in a panicky flight, which would have ended in its destruction. When Buddha, who at that time was living as a wise man, one of his many forms of existence, saw all the animals running in their panic he asked the last group that had joined the flight why they were running. "Because the world is coming to an end," they answered. "This cannot be true," Buddha said. "The world is not coming to an end. Let us find out why they think so." He then inquired of one species after another, tracing the rumour back to the deer and then at last to the hares. When the hares told him that they were running because the world was coming to an end, he asked which particular hare had told them so, they pointed to the one who had started the report, and Buddha turned to him and asked, "Where

> were you and what did you do when you thought the world was coming to an end?" The hare answered, "I was sitting under a mango tree and was asleep." "You probably heard a mango fruit fall," Buddha told him. "The noise awakened you, you got frightened and thought the world was coming to an end. Let us go back to the tree where you sat and find out whether this was so." They both went to the tree. They found that indeed a mango had fallen where the hare had sat. Thus Buddha saved the animal kingdom from destruction.

After narrating the story, Erich Fromm remarks:

> I quote this story not primarily because it is one of the earliest examples of analytic inquiry into the origins of fright and rumours but because it is so expressive of the Buddhistic spirit. It shows loving concern for the creatures of the animal world and at the same time penetrating, rational understanding and confidence in man's powers.[10]

This is more in the tradition perhaps of Adler than Freud.

The third scholar who refers to modern psychology—actually, to depth psychology and to Freudian psychology in particular—is James P. McDermott. He remarks, while describing the process of rebirth as explained by Vasubandhu, that the "Oedipal character of his analysis would do justice to Freud."[11] The process is actually described in detail in the Tibetan Book of the Dead in the following terms:

> If so far you have been deaf to the teaching, listen to it now! An overpowering craving will come over you for the sense-experiences, which you remember having had in the past, and which through your lack of sense organs you cannot have now. Your desire for rebirth becomes more and more urgent; it becomes a real torment to you. This desire now racks you; you do not, however, experience it for what it is, but feel it as a deep thirst which parches you as you wander along, harassed, among deserts of burning sands. Whenever you try to take some rest, monstrous forms rise up before you. Some have animal heads on human bodies; others are gigantic birds with huge wings and claws. Their howlings and their whips drive you on, and then a hurricane carries you along, with those demonic beings in hot pursuit. Greatly anxious, you will look for a safe place of refuge.

> Everywhere around you, you will see animals and humans in the act of sexual intercourse. You envy them, and the sight attracts you. If your karmic coefficients destine you to become a male, you feel attracted to the females and you hate the males you see. If you are destined to become female, you will feel love for the males and hatred for the females you see. Do not go near the couples you see, do not try to take the place of one of them! The feeling, which you would then experience, would make you faint away, just at the moment when egg and sperm are about to unite. And afterwards you will find that you have been conceived as a human or as an animal.[12]

A fourth scholar who brings depth psychology into a potentially fruitful relationship with Buddhism is K. N. Jayatilleke. In a posthumous work, edited by Ninian Smart, he writes:

> If we turn to the theory of reality, the Buddha's achievements were equally outstanding. Buddhism recognises the reality of the material world and its impact on experience. Conscious mental phenomena have a physical basis in one's body. Life (jīvitendriya) is a by-product (upādā-rūpa) of matter. The economic environment conditions human relationships and affects morality. Like modern psychologists, the Buddha discards the concept of a substantial soul and analyses the human personality into aspects of experience such as, impressions and ideas (sañña), feelings or hedonic tone (vedanā), conative activities (saṅkhārā) as well as cognitive or quasi-cognitive activities (viññaṇa). There is a dynamic conception of the mind and the stream of consciousness (viññaṇa-sota) is said to have two components, the conscious and the unconscious. The first explicit mention of unconscious mental processes and the unconscious (anusaya) motivation of human behaviour is in the Buddhist texts. *The Buddhist theory of motivation may be compared with that of Freud* although it is more adequate than the latter.[13]

These remarks are useful, although Freudians may not be happy with the parting shot, which makes them suffer by comparison with Buddhism. They may, however, have reason to be unhappy with Jayatilleke for more than just an affront to their amour propre when he says next: "Man is motivated to act out of greed, which consists of the desire to gratify our senses and sex (kāma-taṇhā, comparable with the *libido* of Freud) as well as the desire to gratify our egoistic impulses (bhava-taṇhā, comparable with the *ego-instincts* and *super-ego* of Freud), and also out of erroneous beliefs."[14]

There is apparently some problem here with making the right equations. *Kāma-taṇhā* is congruent with libido or the sex drive, but *bhava-taṇhā* is more like life instinct or eros rather than the superego. However, *vibhava-taṇhā*, may be properly equated with *thanatos* or the death instinct.

II

An interesting illustration of reciprocal illumination between a method and a tradition arises in this broad context of the psychological method and the Buddhist tradition.

The Buddhist tradition, like the Hindu, attaches considerable importance to verbal veracity. One of the five normal vows of the householder, and one of the ten vows of a monk, is phrased negatively as "abstention from false speech"[15] and constitutes an integral part of Buddhist ethics. Buddhaghosa explains in detail the significance of the two components of the vow—"false speech" and "abstention." He explains "false speech" as follows:

> "False"—this refers to actions of the voice, or actions of the body, which aim at deceiving others by obscuring the actual facts. "False speech" is the will to deceive others by words or deeds. One can also explain: "False" means something, which is not real, not true. "Speech" is the intimation that that is real or true. "False speech" is then the volition which leads to the deliberate intimation to someone else that something is so when it is not so. The seriousness of the offence depends on the circumstances. If a householder, unwilling to give something, says that he has not got it, that is a small offence; but to represent something one has seen with one's own eyes as other than one has seen it, that is a serious offence. If a mendicant has on his rounds got very little oil or ghee, and if he then exclaims, "What a magnificent river flows along here, my friends!," that is only a rather stale joke, and the offence is small; but to say that one has seen what one has not seen, that is a serious offence. Four factors are involved; something which is not so, the thought of deception, an effort to carry it out, the communication of the falsehood to someone else. There is only one way of doing it: with one's own body.[16]

"Abstention" is then explained thus:

> "To abstain from"—one crushes or forsakes sin. It means an abstention, which is associated with wholesome thoughts. And it is threefold: (1) one feels obligated to abstain, (2) one formally undertakes to do so, (3) one has lost all temptation not to do so.
>
> (1) Even those who have not formally undertaken to observe the precepts may have the conviction that it is not right to offend against them. So it was the Cakkana, a Ceylonese boy. His mother was ill, and the doctor prescribed fresh rabbit meat for her. His brother sent him into the field to catch a rabbit, and he went as he was bidden. Now a rabbit had run into a field to eat of her corn, but in its eagerness to get there had got entangled in a snare, and gave forth cries of distress. Cakkana followed the sound, and thought: "this rabbit has got caught there, and it will make a fine medicine for my mother!" But then he thought again: "it is not suitable for me that, in order to preserve my mother's life, I should deprive someone else of his life." And so he released the rabbit, and said to it: "Run off, play with the other rabbits in the woods, eat grass and drink water!" On his return he told the story to his brother, who scolded him. He then went to his mother, and said to her: "Even without having been told, I know quite clearly that I should not deliberately deprive any living being of life." He then fervently resolved that these truthful words of his might make his mother well again, and so it actually happened.[17]

I need to go no further with his explanation, as the point I wish to draw attention to has already surfaced by now. It is obvious from the edifying example of the Ceylonese boy, Cakkana, that although the telling of the truth is phrased *negatively* as "not telling falsehood," it possesses a *positive* force. By the power of his "truthful words" the mother became well again.

This leads one into a discussion of the Act of Truth (*saccakiriyā/satyakriyā*) through which this force is exercised. An example from the life of Angulimāla, the robber-turned-monk who was a contemporary of the Buddha, provides an interesting case of the exercise of this power of truth. The account runs as follows:

> Then the venerable Aṅgulimāla, having dressed in the morning, taking his bowl and robe, entered Sāvatthī for almsfood. And as the venerable Aṅgulimāla was walking in Sāvatthī on an uninterrupted round for almsfood, he saw a woman in difficult and dangerous labour. On seeing her, it occurred to him: "Beings are indeed impure, beings are indeed impure."
>
> Then the venerable Aṅgulimāla, having walked in Sāvatthī for almsfood, on returning from the alms gathering after the meal, approached the Lord; having approached, having greeted the Lord, he sat down at a respectful distance. As he was sitting down at a respectful distance, the venerable Aṅgulimāla spoke thus to the Lord: "Now, I, revered sir, having dressed in the morning. . . . And as I was walking in Sāvatthī . . . I saw a woman . . . it occurred to me: 'Beings are indeed impure, beings are indeed impure.' "
>
> "Well then, do you Aṅgulimāla, approach Sāvatthī; having approached, speak thus to that woman: "I, sister, am not aware of having intentionally deprived any living thing of life since I was born. By this truth may there be well-being for you, well-being for the unborn child.' "
>
> "But would not this be deliberate lying on my part, revered sir? For, revered sir, many living things have been intentionally deprived of life by me."
>
> "Well then, do you, Aṅgulimāla, approach Sāvatthī; having approached, speak thus to that woman: 'I, sister, am not aware of having intentionally deprived any living thing of life since I was born of the ariyan birth. By this truth may there be well-being for . . . the unborn child.' "
>
> "Yes, revered sir," and the venerable Aṅgulimāla, having answered the Lord in assent, approached Sāvatthī; having approached, he spoke thus to that woman: "I, sister, am not aware of having intentionally deprived any living thing of life since I was born of the ariyan birth. By this truth may there be well-being for . . . the unborn child."[18]

The procedure was apparently successful. The reference to the "Ariyan birth" refers to his entry into the Order. "The words uttered by him in this Act of Truth, 'Since I was born of the Ariyan birth' (*yato aham . . . ariyāya jātiyā jāto: M.II.163*) are considered as a protection (*paritta*) to avert dangers, and they constitute the *Aṅgulimālaparitta*. Even, the water that was used to wash the seat on which he sat in that woman's house came to be regarded as a panacea."[19] It would have been noticed that Angulimāla hesitates to say that he has not willfully deprived any creature of life because he *consciously* knows this not to be so. He therefore chooses to phrase his statement more accurately. In another example of the Act of Truth, cited earlier, as narrated by Heinrich Zimmer, [20] the subconscious was also involved.[21]

This narrative has obviously brought us to the frontiers of depth psychology and to the point where it can be shown how depth psychology can shed light on the word "truth" in such a way as might be meaningful for Buddhism. To see this, one needs to recognize with Erich Fromm that "*truth* is the basic aim of the psychoanalytic process."[22] Once one is armed with this realization it becomes clear that telling the truth is a much more complex business than might appear at first sight, as it involves knowing the truth about oneself.

Psychoanalysis has given the concept of truth a new dimension.

> In pre-analytic thinking, a person could be considered to speak the truth if he believed in what he was saying. Psychoanalysis has shown that subjective conviction is by no means a sufficient criterion of sincerity. A person can believe that he acts out of a sense of justice and yet to be motivated by cruelty. He can believe that he is motivated by love and yet be driven by a craving for masochistic dependence. A person can believe that duty is his guide though his main motivation is vanity. In fact most rationalizations are held to be true by the person who uses them. He not only wants others to believe his rationalizations but believes them himself, and the more he wants to protect himself from recognizing his true motivation the more ardently he must believe in them. Furthermore, in the psychoanalytic process a person learns to recognize which of his ideas have an emotional matrix and which are only conventional clichés without root in his character structure and therefore without substance and weight. The psychoanalytic process is in itself a search for truth. The object of this search is the truth about phenomena not outside of man but in man himself. It is based on the principle that mental health and happiness cannot be achieved unless we scrutinize our thinking and feeling to detect whether we rationalize and whether our beliefs are rooted in our feeling.[23]

Fromm himself goes on to say that such an approach results in the "ability to discern between genuine and false experience" and illustrates his point by quoting from Tibetan Buddhist sources on the need to distinguish desire from faith, attachment from compassion and so on. The glimmer of reciprocal illumination can be detected in his remark. The point I would like to single out for emphasis in this context, however, is simply this: that the Act of Truth seems to imply not merely verbal accuracy but heartfelt conviction; and that conviction is more likely to be effective—not necessarily in a magical way, but perhaps in a charismatic one—if our truth-statements are free from self-deception.

Psychoanalysis also prompts reflection on another aspect of Buddhism—specially early Buddhism—namely, that of memory. Herein reciprocal illumination does not so much bring illumination as lead to the recognition of the need for illumination. Let me explain. The Buddhist denial of the existence of a self naturally raises the question: How is the phenomenon of memory to be explained in the absence of an abiding self? P. S. Jaini has noted the textual tardiness within Theravāda Buddhism in addressing the issue.[24] This contrasts with the great emphasis placed on the role of memory in psychoanalysis.

It is therefore at first sight a significant divergence. But in another respect there is an interesting parallel. For it is not the case that the issue of the recovery of memory does not figure in Theravāda Buddhism at all. In fact the recovery of the memory of past lives (*pubbenivāsānussatiñāṇa*) is listed as one of the six higher knowledges.[25] But such knowledge is also one of the three knowledges, which, according to certain texts,[26] constituted the content of Buddha's enlightenment; it is not entirely clear in them whether such knowledge was the result of enlightenment or a contributing factor in its attainment.[27] If retrocognition is an aid to attaining enlightenment, then the recovery of memory might even be said to play a role in enlightenment analogous to its role in effecting a cure in psychoanalysis,[28] except that in the former case it is the memory of previous lives that is retrieved, while in the latter case it is only memory within a lifetime. Even here the contrast between a single life and several lives may have to be toned down, if two items are admitted as possessing probative value. First, at least some psychoanalysts have been led to the verge of the rebirth hypothesis by their experience with patients. Second, a meditational exercise in Buddhism is specially geared toward the recovery of the memory of past lives—*including* that of the segment of one's life already past in this present life. Buddhaghosa describes the practice as follows:

> A monk who is still a beginner, and who wants to learn how to remember his previous lives, should in the afternoon, after

> he has finished his meal, go to a solitary and secluded spot, and enter successively into the four trances. He should then emerge from the fourth trance, which is the basis of the Superknowledges, and think of the last thing he did before his meditation, which was the act of sitting down. After that he should, in reverse order, think of everything he did during the day and night, i.e. how he spread the seat on which he sat down, how he entered his lodging, got ready his robe and alms bowl, the time when he ate, when he came back from the village, when he went to the village for his alms, when he entered the village for his alms round, when he departed from the monastery, when he saluted the shrine, the time when he washed his alms bowl, when he took hold of his alms bowl, and from there whatever he did after the washing of the mouth, everything he did early in the day, everything he did in the last and everything he did in the first watch of the night.
>
> All this becomes manifest to the ordinary mind already, but to the mind, which is prepared by trance it stands out most distinctly. But if anything should not be obvious to him, he should once more enter into the fourth basic trance, and, on emerging from it, should direct his mind unto it. In that way these things become as clear to him as if lit up by a lamp. He should furthermore think back in reverse order on what he did two days ago, three, four, and five days ago, ten days ago, half a month ago, one month ago, up to one year ago. In this manner he goes on for ten years, twenty years, and so on, until he comes to the time of his birth in this becoming, and then he should also direct his mind on the mental and physical processes which took place at the moment of his decease in his immediately preceding existence.[29]

In this section we first discussed a case in which the psychological method deepened our understanding of an aspect of Buddhism, namely, that of speaking the truth and the phenomenon of the Act of Truth. Then we examined the role of memory to illustrate how it raises important questions for both psychoanalysis and Buddhism. In the next illustration I will demonstrate how our appreciation of psychoanalysis is advanced through the light shed on it by Buddhism.

The oedipal complex is a key concept in Freudian psychoanalysis and basically refers to the desire on the part of the male child for the mother and the related hostility toward the father. In Freudian psychology this complex originates in *childhood*, though its consequences may ramify through the rest of life. The importance of this concept in Freudian psychology can hardly be overestimated.[30] The fact, therefore, that this phenomenon is referred to in Buddhist texts is of some relevance. What renders it even more relevant is the fact that it is referred to as occurring not in childhood but in the very process of birth, or more properly, rebirth, in Buddhist terms. The Pali word *gandhabba* (Sanskrit, *gandharva*) is of special relevance here, as it stands for a being in "the intermediate stage (between death and birth)."[31]

> Given the existence of such an intermediate-state being, Vasubandhu proceeds to an explanation of how rebirth (*pratisaṃdhi*) takes place. The Oedipal character of his analysis would do justice to Freud: driven by karma, the intermediate-state being goes to the location where rebirth is to take place. Possessing the divine eye by virtue of its karma, it is able to see the place of its birth, no matter how distant. There it sees its father and its mother to be, united in intercourse. Finding the scene hospitable, its passions are stirred. If male, it is smitten with desire for its mother. If female, it is seized with desire for its father. And inversely, it hates either mother or father, which it comes to regard as a rival. Concupiscence and hatred thus arise in the *gandharva* as its driving passions. Stirred by these wrong thoughts, it attaches itself to the place where the sexual organs of the parents are united, imagining that it is there joined with the object of its passion. Taking pleasure in the impurity of the semen and blood in the womb, the *antarā bhava* establishes itself there. Thus do *skandhas* arise in the womb. They harden; and the intermediate-state being perishes, to be replaced immediately by the birth existence (*pratisaṃdhi*).[32]

The process of rebirth is referred to in similar terms in the Tibetan Book of the Dead, as mentioned earlier.

This coincidence between the Freudian and Buddhist versions of oedipal behavior must be considered remarkable.[33] The Buddhist example expands the horizon of its operation considerably. What seems to be even more remarkable is the fact that this correspondence defies normal expectation. The rejection of the rebirth idea in Freudian psychology and its axiomatic acceptance in the Buddhist *Weltbild* would seem to constitute a virtually insuperable barrier between the two—and yet the wall has been breached, in a manner of speaking, in a most unlikely place to let in some fresh light.

19

The Psychology of Religion and Hinduism

I

The 1960s were the golden age of the drug culture, and since then interest in drugs has waned, although there are now reports of some revival of interest. Even in its heyday, however, although psychedelic experience was closely associated with mysticism and mysticism with Hinduism, no scholarly effort seems to have been made to study psychedelic experiences in relation to Hinduism. I am aware of only two efforts, one more specific than the other. These were made by Huston Smith and Walter Huston Clark, respectively. Huston Smith wrote, while reviewing the book on *Soma* by Wasson, about the results his "own first ingestion of mescaline" produced:

> Another phrase came to me: "empirical metaphysics." The emanation theory and elaborately delineated layers of Indian cosmology and psychology had hitherto been concepts and inferences. Now they were objects of direct, immediate perception. I saw that theories such as these were required by the experience I was having.
>
> I found myself amused, thinking how duped historians of philosophy had been in crediting those who formulated such worldviews with being speculative geniuses. Had they had experiences such as mine they need have been no more than hack reporters.[1]

Walter Huston Clark, in his book *Chemical Ecstasy*, tried to show how, through a proper understanding of the nature of mystical experience, the idea of nonviolence might make sense in mystical terms for someone who has been exposed to psychedelic experience. He wrote:

> It is important, therefore, that we be as clear as possible about this elusive state of mind, this "mystical consciousness." It is usually thought of as a state of considerable vagueness, if not confusion, an emotion that addles the brain, deludes the subject and confounds any business influenced by it. In academic circles there is hardly a more cutting comment than to brand an opponent "mystical."
>
> I have already, by referring to the studies of W. T. Stace, given a phenomenological description of the mystical state. But it is necessary to emphasize that the mystical consciousness is not primarily an emotion; it is a perception. Furthermore, this perception is not hazy, vague or confused. It is, particularly in its most distinguished exponents, remarkably simple, cogent and clear.
>
> What does one mean when he speaks of a "perception"? It may help to present a simple series of illustrations to bring the word into context and so illuminate further the term "mysticism."
>
> One enters a dimly lit room and notices a coiled object in the corner. One sees it to be a coiled rope. This recognition is a "perception," probably to be dismissed with little or no response as one goes about his business. But this perception may change with closer scrutiny, and one may see the object as a coiled cobra. Immediately the perceiver's emotions are aroused. The emotion is closely associated with the perception, and yet is distinct from it. The emotion might disorganize the observer leading him, in his fright, to confused and even foolish acts. But it would be the very cogency and clarity of the initial perception that would lead to his sharp and disorganized reactions as he seeks either to flee from or to kill the snake.
>
> Let us take the illustration another stage and suppose the perceiver a truly pious Hindu, informed not only by the letter of his beliefs but by actual and immediate perception of the eternal Unity, the experience to which mystics universally testify. He will perceive not only a cobra. Even in his terror and dread, he will perceive a fellow creature with which he must dwell despite mortal danger. He will no more think of killing this creature than he would consider cutting off one of his own hands. In a peculiarly cogent sense this would

> be a religious or mystical perception, and the encounter with the cobra would be transformed from a frightening trauma into a religious experience. To us, this reaction from the Hindu may seem like the merest folly. But it illustrates how the strange alchemy of mystical experience may enable an individual to "love his enemy." It also shows that the essential principle of mysticism is perception, even though usually accompanied by strong emotion, which the uninformed may mistake for the perception itself. With a marvellous Franciscan cogency and clarity often combined with a startling suddenness, the mystic perceives all things as one, all men as his brothers, all creatures as his fellows and all matter holy. It is no wonder that a mystical vision marks a sharp change in behaviour.[2]

The material presented by R. E. L. Masters and Jean Houston in this respect, in their pioneering work *The Varieties of Psychedelic Experience,* seems to have gone largely unnoticed. This is all the more intriguing in view of the following comment found in the book itself:

> Do the psychedelic drugs in fact pose a threat that a significant number of presently productive individuals will, if exposed, abandon their posts as bank presidents, manufacturers, clergy-men, engineers, physicists, educators, in favour of writing blank verse or pondering the riddle of the cosmos? And, if so, do the presumed interests of the state and society transcend and override the rights of individuals to dedicate themselves to aesthetic or spiritual endeavours? What is really best for the person himself? And is he discovering where his true genius lies or is he succumbing to suggestions owing their exceptional potency to chemical effects and yielding subsequent self-delusion? *We will not attempt to answer those latter questions, but think it extremely improbable that the psychedelic drug experience could ever make another India of a country whose citizens are so overwhelmingly rooted in Western traditions.*[3]

The purpose of this chapter therefore is threefold: (1) to identify descriptions in the book suggestive of the Indic, that is, primarily Hindu-Buddhist roots; (2) to compare the psychedelic with the Hindu or Buddhist experiences of a similar nature; and (3) to indicate where the recognition of a connection with the Indic religious tradition may shed light upon or advance some of the conclusions reached in the book.

There are, first of all, experiences described by the subjects, which are highly suggestive of the Hindu belief in rebirth. To be sure, this may not be the only possible explanation of them; but it is bound to be considered as one of them. Consider, for instance, the following passage:

> In many of the images that came to me I saw myself, sometimes with my wife, more often alone. I was a fur-capped Mongol huntsman, cold-eyed and cruel, bow in hand, striking down a running rabbit from the back of a racing, gaunt half-wild stallion. I was a stark black-robed figure, protected by an amulet from a heavy gold chain that was worn about my neck, sombrely wandering, lost in bitter ascetic reflection, among the crumbling walls of old temples overgrown by thick, twisted and gnarled vines. At another times there were legions of warriors, darkening deserts or in ranks that extended across immense bone-littered plains. There were brown-cowled monks, pacing cloisters in silent, shared but unadmitted desperation. Image after image, flowing in succession more rapid than I would have wished, but all exquisitely detailed and with colours richer and more brilliant than those either nature or the artist has yet managed to create.[4]

The experience of the subject as Example #3 has more of Indic content in it than many others. For that reason it seems worthy of being reported in full.

> Example #3. S., a twenty-four-year-old university instructor, was given 225 mg. of LSD. (She had had one previous LSD experience with a 100 mg dose). Her account is as follows:
>
> The experience began in my fourth floor walk-up in Greenwich Village. After the initial physical sensations (a very mild nausea and stiffness of the neck) had passed, I began to notice that the wooden floor had started to ripple. I walked across the floor, climbing up its steep waves and sliding down its inclines. Occasionally, I would catch one of its oaken crests and ride it to the wall in much the same way that a surf rider travels on the waves.
>
> I looked first at my guide, whose appearance was unchanged, and then at my co-subject R, *who was sitting in the lotus position*. His well-fringed face was alternately shifting from Christ to satyr, then back to Christ again, and he opened

his eyes and came out of his private Nirvana for a moment to say to me: "Well, this is it! What more is there to say?"

I directed my attention towards the room and suddenly everything was holy. The stove, and the pottery and the chairs and the record player and the soup ladles and the old bottles—all were touched with sacrality, and I bowed to each of them in turn and worshipped. One pot in particular was so well endowed with divinity I dared not come closer to it than four or five feet lest I be burned to ashes for my unclean lips and impure heart. But a godly peach proved friendlier and accepted my adoration with kindly beneficence, radiating on me the preternatural light of its numinous fuzz. I vowed to gratitude and moved on, transfigured by the deity of things.

I remember looking at a finely detailed photograph of the Swiss Alps. I had admired this photograph before, in my pre-LSD days an hour or an aeon ago, but now its precision became reality and the temperature plunged and fine crystals of snow whipped across my face and I circled like an eagle above the crags and snowy summits of the mountaintop. An expedition of climbers waved up at me and I lifted one talon to wave back.

I was called back to Greenwich Village by obscenity. A sound, a chant, lascivious and brutal, a whining pornography assaulted my ears and left me furious with moral indignation. "How dare you say things like that to me!" said I to the disembodied chant. It suddenly ended, as quickly as it had begun, and I saw R *removing a record, which he explained to me, was a recording of fertility mantras directed to the goddess Kali*. A Bach toccata then was put on the phonograph and the music of the spheres left their archetypal abode and took up residence in the walk-up on —— Street.

It was at this time that I closed my eyes and experienced a vision of the future that unfolded in vivid colours before my closed eyes and was accompanied by voices that were audible, however, only inside my head. I found myself and the rest of mankind standing together on the foothills of the earth, being addressed by two splendid and luminous figures many hundreds of miles high. They told us that they were the elders of this particular part of the cosmos and lost their patience with the human creatures of this earth. The recalcitrance of greedy, warring, barbarous mankind had overexceeded itself and now that nuclear power had been discovered the

> outrageous breed evolved on our plane might yet attempt to subvert the whole cosmos. And so it had been decided in the Council of Elders that unless mankind could find something in its creations with which to justify itself it would have to be destroyed.
>
> Having heard this message, we earthlings scattered and searched our libraries, museums, histories and parliaments for some achievement that might be seen as justification for our being. We brought forth our greatest art objects, our Leonardos, Michelangelos, Praxiteles—But the elders only shook their heads and said solemnly: "It is not sufficient." We brought forth our great masterpieces of literature, the works of Shakespeare, Milton, Goethe, and Dante. But these also were deemed insufficient. *We searched in our religious literature and offered the figures of the religious geniuses—Jesus, Buddha. Moses, St. Francis,* but the elders only laughed and said: "Not sufficient."
>
> It was then, when destruction seemed imminent and all had given themselves up to their fate, that I came forward and offered to the elders the music of Johann Sebastian Bach. They listened to the entire corpus and great silver tears of incredible brilliance shimmered and trickled down the length of their luminous bodies, after which they were silent. On and on this silence extended, until they broke it to say only: "It is sufficient. You of the earth are justified." And then they went away.[5]

Now that the account has been read, several points need to be made about it.

1. The experience of the holiness of *everything* is a very important component of Tantra, both in Hinduism and Buddhism. From this point of view the paragraph beginning with "I directed my attention towards the room and suddenly everything was holy" is significant.[6]

2. Paradoxically, in a subsequent paragraph, the charge of obscenity is laid and the records dealing with mantras of Kālī had to be removed. And Kālī is a key figure in Tantra.[7] This confusion, however, has antecedents in Western perceptions of India.[8]

3. There is confusion in the account between Indra and Śiva. The cosmic dance is associated with *Śiva,*[9] not Indra.

4. The iconoclastic experience with the Buddhas is interesting. Is it a case against image-worship? This would be more curious were it so, as the valorization of eidetic images by psychedelic experience is an important theme of the book.[10]

5. The appearance of the people like animated waxworks is remotely reminiscent of the cosmic vision of Arjuna in the Bhagavadgītā, and directly reminiscent of the following experience of Rāmakṛṣṇa:

> Master (to the devotees): "Do you know what I see right now? I see that it is God Himself who has become all this. It seems to me that men and other living beings are made of leather, and that it is God himself who, dwelling inside these leather cases, moves the hands, the feet, and the heads. I had a similar vision once before, when I saw houses, gardens, roads, men, cattle—all made of One Substance; it was as if they were all made of wax.
>
> "I see that it is God Himself who has become the block, the executioner, and the victim for the sacrifice."
>
> As he describes this staggering experience, in which he realizes in full the identity of all within the One Being, he is overwhelmed with emotion and exclaims, "Ah! What a vision."[11]

6. The experience of aging—forward and backward—is a curious one, but often pictured in books on Hinduism as a series of shots of a person progressing, in blurred outlines, from childhood to youth and old age.[12]

7. The experience of seeing all of Manhattan in a rough square of pavement, or the world in a grain of sand, is recorded by some people in their encounter with mystics.[13]

III

Even the experience of other subjects (apart from those of No. 3, recounted above in detail) has a familiar ring for the student of Indic religions at certain points. For instance, the following description is bound to intrigue the student of Hindu and Buddhist art by virtue of its affinity to the figure of Gaṇeśa:[14]

> A great face with the trunk of an elephant that is blowing liquid on the face of a demon whose body has been trampled into the ground. The elephant is blowing liquid on the face of the demon either in an attempt to revive him or as a gesture of contempt. A herculean male figure rises next to the elephantine face. He is trapped to the waist in stone and this marbled stone looks like sea foam, it is so delicate and lacy. Everything blends into everything else. The herculean figure is also the ear of a face and the elephant-like trunk is the bridge of the nose of another larger, still more complicated figure.[15]

Śiva and Pārvatī are well-known figures of Hindu mythology.

> Their son, the elephant-headed god Ganesha, "The Lord and Leader of the Hosts of Shiva," called also "The Lord and Master of Obstacles" (*vighneśvara*), sits above a rat. Ganesha forges ahead through obstacles as an elephant through the jungle, but the rat, too, is an overcomer of obstacles, and, as such, an appropriate, even though physically incongruous, mount for the gigantic pot-bellied divinity of the elephant head. The elephant passes through the wilderness, treading shrubs, bending and uprooting trees, fording rivers and lakes easily; the rat can gain access to the bolted granary. The two represent the power of this god to vanquish every obstacle of the Way.[16]

It is, however, the mystical rather than the mythic parallels that continue to be more striking. In the case of No. 3, the universe had seemed as if made of wax. The strong parallel between this and Rāmakṛṣṇa's experience has been noticed. It is, therefore, a matter of considerable interest that another subject, No. 2, should report a similar experience:

> When I opened my eyes and looked at the objects around me, it was as if they were made of tallow and were melting. There was a drippiness of colours, and it also seemed that these things might be made of waxen candy. It occurred to me that this was probably due not only to my heightened awareness of objects, but also to the liquid in my eyes now imparting to everything a liquid coating. Along with these perceptions there was the sense of the intense sensuality of oneself, an extremely luxurious sensuality.[17]

From the point of view of the parallels afforded by the mystical experiences of Rāmakṛṣṇa, the following experience of the same subject is equally if not more significant.

> The world is experienced as a physical extension of oneself, of one's own nervous system. Consequently I felt the blows of pick axes wielded by construction men tearing up the street. One possessed a kinaesthetic identity with the street, and yet the blows did not hurt. For the street knows in its own being that it is being broken up and yet does not experience the judgement of pleasure or pain. Related to this was an acute awareness of energy in the world. One felt one's body to be supercharged with "energy," a word that was variously associated with "nervous" and "spirit." Or it could be associated with tension of the spirit. The other, when it is person, is super-charged with energy like neonized electric generators, sizzling firecrackers as distinguished from the other when it is object and is perceived as static electricity. Only water fountains, among things, have energy. Other objects are frozen.[18]

Rāmakṛṣṇa reported similar experiences, but they were more intense in two ways. Even the damage done to the "street" would probably have been experienced by him. In the account that follows, he felt physically hurt by footfalls on earth. What happened to other human beings also seemed to affect him directly.

> At one time a particular spot of the garden of the Kali temple was covered with newly grown Durva grass and was beautiful to look at. While he was looking at it, the Master transcended the normal consciousness and was feeling identified with that spot when a man just happened to walk across that field at which he became very restless, feeling unbearable pain in his chest. Mentioning that event, he said to us later, "I then felt just that kind of pain which is felt when anybody tramples on one's chest. That state of Bhavasamadhi is very painful. Although I had it for only six hours, it became quite unbearable."
>
> One day the Master while in Bhavasamadhi was looking on the Ganga, standing at the spacious Ghat with the open portico. Two boats were at anchor at the Ghat and the boatmen were quarrelling over some matter. The quarrel became gradually bitter and the stronger man gave a severe slap on

> the back of the weaker. At that, the Master cried out suddenly with pain. Hriday heard it from the Kali temple, went there quickly and saw that the Master's back had become red and swollen. Impatient with anger, Hriday said repeatedly, "Uncle, show me the man who has beaten you; I'll tear off his head." When afterwards the Master quietened [*sic*] down a little, Hriday was astonished to hear of the event and thought, "Is it ever possible?" Girish Chandra Ghosh heard the event from the Master's lips and narrated it to us. Innumerable events of this nature regarding the Master may be mentioned but we refrain from doing so to avoid superfluity.[19]

The same subject reported a heightened desire to know God. The aspiration in his case is disclosed aesthetically:

> And along with this there was the sense that one must speak to beauty and commune with beauty in all of its forms, including persons. This included not just pretty girls, but also trees: the obedient benevolence of trees. One was obliged to commune with them, and with statues. This imperative was part of a larger imperative that seemed to stand out absolutely from all other thought as the one overriding imperative statement: *That one must seek God.* The beautiful is a part of the imperative that one must approach the Godhead. This was the ultimate procedural prescription. All of the rest of thought was dispensable and this prescription alone could guide one. Related to this was the falling away of all the normal power and authority sanctions and seeming rightness of familiar social and prescriptive forms of behaviour and purpose and attitude. These melted away with awareness of what was truly important, valid and authoritative. Since there was no reason not to, I sat down in the middle of a busy sidewalk and let people pass around me.[20]

In the case of Rāmakṛṣṇa the intense desire was not merely revealed but seems to have been actually felt as well.

> Again, impatient on account of the separation from the divine Lord, I rubbed my face against the ground so vehemently that it got cut and bruised and bled in many places. I had no consciousness of how the whole day slipped away in prayer, meditation, devotional exercises, offering of the self, and so

> on. When afterwards, at the approach of the evening, conch-shells were blown and bells rung, I remembered that the day was at an end. Another day passed in vain; and I had not yet seen the Mother. Intense sorrow seized me and made the heart so restless that I could no longer remain calm. I threw myself violently on the ground saying, "Mother, Thou hast not shown Thyself to me even yet." I filled the quarters with wailing and struggled on account of pain. People said, "He has got colic pain and that is why he is crying so much."[21]

A disregard for normal conventions also characterized Rāmakṛṣṇa's life, especially during the ecstatic phases.[22]

III

One particular experience of subject No. 2 needs to be discussed in some detail. But it must be related first:

> All people seemed to me to be no more than simply different forms of oneself, different masks of oneself. They were all of the different lives that one has, or that one is to live. And there was the sense that the world has no greater claim to substance than does a *dream;* that all authority, all validity rests with oneself and the world is entirely one's possession. Later, when I went out, this resulted in a total unconcern for social forms, such as not sitting down on the sidewalk or in the street; for now one knew that the sidewalk was a part of one's brain and one could do with it what one liked.
>
> My solipsism was accompanied by delusions of grandeur not logically consistent with it, yet reconcilable for the reason that they had a logic of their own. Although I was the All, I participated in the test of living that somehow was connected with the training of the future of God. I was awed by the stereoscopic solidity of reality, the sheer substantiality of it all. Yet reality was my own thought and I was struck with wonder that one's thoughts could suddenly become so substantive and stereoscopic. I congratulated myself upon being able to create reality so well. I felt that others should be grateful to me for supporting their existence. I was holding them up, containing them, giving them air. I was benevolent and did not kick them.[23]

This existential realization of solipsism is a striking example of how philosophically marginal ideas can become mystically significant by virtue of the fact that they are experienced. It also serves to illustrate how analysis must accompany experience.

Mystics often describe the sensation of feeling one with the universe—of being part of it, rather than the universe being part of them and at the disposal of their imagination. Thus, the above case does not quite fit *pantheism*.[24] On the other hand, in the mystical experience of *monism*,[25] oneness, the ego usually dissolves. Here we have a case that fits neither of these categories, and is appropriately described as *solipsism*. This extreme form of subjective idealism has parallels in Indic thought, but it does not typically seem to assume the form it has acquired here, except in a few late Advaitic texts. But even there one is said to create not *the* universe but one's *own* universe. Perhaps one is groping here for a distinction between psychedelic and religious experience. These lines are hard to draw, but the following comments seem to provide a good starting point:

> The most important of the experiences reported by William James in *The Varieties of Religious Experience* are of this type in which the person seems to be encountered on the most profound level of his being by the Ground of Being. Religious experience can be defined, then, as that experience which occurs when the "depths of one's being" are touched or confronted by the "Depth of Being." Mystical experience differs from this in degree, not in kind. This latter occurs when one's personal depths dissolve into the "transpersonal" depths—when one is unified at one's deepest level with the source level of reality.[26]

IV

A few points scattered through Masters and Houston's book by way of reflections resonate with the Indic worldview in an interesting way. For instance, the view that "the forest, then, is a place where individuation is restored"[27] can hardly be overlooked in a culture that attaches such significance to *āśramas* or forest retreats, and even includes residence in a hermitage (*vānaprastha*) as a stage of life. In Buddhism, too, the retreat is emphasized, and in Thailand the Order (or Sangha) itself distinguishes between forest and other monasteries.

The use of symbols is, of course, characteristic of Hinduism and Buddhism. Herein psychedelic experience provides a significant insight in insisting that they can be personal. Hinduism does have the concept of a chosen deity (*iṣṭa-devatā*), but perhaps it needs to enlarge the category to include self-made ones.

> Subjects reaching the *symbolic* level of the psychedelic experience do not concern themselves exclusively with traditional or essential symbolisms. In a number of cases symbols hitherto unrecognized as "symbolic" have emerged spontaneously, pregnant with personal meaning, and have provided the subject with a living reality and a directional frame of reference previously unknown. These symbols, novel at least to the subject, would seem to be as effective as their better-known counterparts and like them provide psychic energy for the formation of new attitudes and for the development of more extended and mature states of consciousness. *Examples of such emerging symbols have included a personal totemic animal* (eagle, tiger, lion), whose idealized symbolic characteristics the subject seeks to realize in himself; geometric configurations (spirals, circles within circles); microcosm-macrocosm analogies; organic growth processes (especially as they occur in trees and flowers); and mandalas.[28]

As in this context, the significance of the *maṇḍala* can also be repossessed.

> The mandala is, after all, a highly personal symbolic form; in fact, the symbolic condensation of the thematics and dynamics of the person's own nature. It is the coded formula of the subject's personal mythos. The significant percentage of mandala imagery then may be testimony to one of the key phenomena of the psychedelic experience; the discovery and creative utilization of personal patterns of being against the backdrop of universal structures and sanctions.[29]

Two more distinct points need to be made here. One would be the possibility of relating the "polytheism" of Hinduism and Buddhism to the recognition of the role of eidetic images in psychic life. Thus, their polytheism may pose the same challenge to the historian of religion as the profusion of the eidetic images of the subject poses to the psychologist.[30] The other would be to suggest that since these traditions, despite their polytheism, favor the *via negativa* to start with anyway, the following conclusion of Masters and Houston may be entertained with some caution:

While it is impossible at this time to make comparative qualitative judgements concerning psychedelic and traditional mysticism, it appears to us evident that the process leading toward Mystical Culmination is *far richer* in the case of the psychedelic subject than is the *via negativa* or path of obliteration of the traditional mystic. This is an area which our conclusions have not yet crystallized and to the consideration of which we plan to give much further attention.

However, we do feel it possible to suggest that the disparate processes involved in these two mysticisms may do much to explain the withdrawal from life of many of the traditional mystics as compared to the psychedelic mystic's oft-observed tendency to move towards a fullness of experience.[31]

V

It is now time to bring the discussion to a conclusion. The first step toward it can be taken by emphasizing the fact that the psychedelic experience enables us to experience *more* than we normally experience. As one subject put it so dramatically:

> The mind is able to contain, at any given moment, MORE. Within consciousness, MORE simultaneous mental processes operate without any one of them interfering with the awareness of the others. Awareness has MORE levels, is many dimensions. Awareness is of MORE shades of meaning contained in words and ideas.
>
> One feels, or responds emotionally with MORE intensity, MORE depth, MORE comprehensiveness.
>
> There is MORE of time, or within any clock-measured unit of time, vastly MORE occurs than can under normal conditions.
>
> There is MORE empathy, MORE unity with people and things.
>
> There is MORE insight into oneself, MORE self-knowledge.
>
> There are MORE alternatives when a particular problem is considered, MORE choices available when a particular decision is to be made. There are MORE ways of "looking at" a thing, an idea or a person. . . .[32]

It is, however, not easy to define the nature of this *extra* element. There has been considerable discussion of the relationship between psychedelic and mystical states, which need not be recapitulated here, but it seems that at least one simple and straightforward point can be made in the light of these comparisons.

It is this. Most mystics have been known to alternate between what we might call "mystical consciousness" and what we would ordinarily call "ordinary experience." It is as if these are two vantage points from which one can view the world and one's experience of the world. Without implying anything about the comparability of psychedelic and mystical experiences, it is clear that psychedelic experiences disclose another "vision" of the universe. The point of convergence here between Hinduism and the varieties of psychedelic experience is provided by the fact that according to Hinduism our normal way of experiencing may be only one way of experiencing the universe and also not the only way of experiencing the universe. Ralph Waldo Emerson said: "Consciousness ever moves along a graded plane." Our normal experience of the universe reveals one grade of it and psychedelic experience another.[33]

20

The Sociology of Religion and Hinduism

I

As is well known to students of Hinduism and the history of religions, classical Hinduism[1] contains the doctrine of the four stages of life called *āśramas*.[2] According to this view, a person, especially if he is a male and belongs to the higher castes,[3] is ideally supposed to go through four stages in life. As the full span of life is taken to consist of a hundred years, the first quarter of it is meant to be spent as a celibate student, the next quarter as a householder, the third quarter as a forest dweller, and the fourth quarter as a renunciant or *sannyāsin*, without the need of being too dogmatic about this notional allocation. This chapter will be confined to a discussion of the mode of life recommended for the last quarter of one's life, the stage technically known *sannyāsa*. It might be added that the discussion of *sannyāsa* as a mode of life here does not include those renunciants who reside in a monastery,[4] or those renunciants who are married.[5] Nor does it take into account the special sense in which the word occurs in the Bhagavadgītā.[6] It is taken here in the sense it is described, say, in the law book of Manu and other similar texts:

> SAṀNYĀSA (or *sannyāsa*, "renunciation"), the stage of the sannyāsī (or *–nyāsin*), when the man renounces all of his possessions except his loincloth, begging-bowl, and water-pot, and subsisting on *food obtained by begging* is regarded as free from all duties, obligations and observances. The Vedas are consigned by a ritual act to fire or water, and the implements of Vedic sacrifice disposed of. Contact with cities, towns and even

villages is, as far as possible, avoided. Human contact and speech are reduced to the absolute minimum. As Manu says, "He thinks of the body as a temporary shack. The bones are the beams, flesh and blood the mortar, and the skin the thatching. It is foul-smelling, filled with urine and ordure, infested with decay, harrowing by pain, wrecked with passion and altogether perishable." So meditating he acquires an unruffled, philosophical equanimity, and as his body dissolves into its material elements so his soul slowly dissolves into the Universal Spirit.[7]

II

The point that needs to be singled out now is that the renunciant or *sannyāsin* lives by begging alms. P. V. Kane, the author of the authoritative *History of Dharmaśāstra*, a work generally regarded as a masterly survey of ancient and medieval Hindu religious and civil law, identifies twenty-two salient features of this institution in his discussion on *sannyāsa*. Almost half of these features contain a direct or indirect reference to begging. Numerous texts could be cited to establish the fact that the *sannyāsin* does not prepare his food; he lives on food offered by others. Thus, one text says: "there are only four proper actions for an ascetic" or renunciant "and no fifth viz. contemplation, purity, begging, always staying alone."[8] The locus classicus of *sannyāsa*, the Jābālopaniṣad, "declares that the ascetic (parivrāṭ)"—whom we have been referring to as the renunciant—"wears discoloured (not white) garments, has a tonsured head, has no possessions, is pure, hates (or injures) no one, begs for alms and thereby attains to non-difference from *brahman*."[9] The word "Brahman" represents the ultimate reality in Hinduism—whether viewed in absolutistic or theistic terms or in impersonal or personal terms; in the former sense it is referred to as *nirguṇa brahma* and in the latter sense as *saguṇa brahma*.[10] It should be further added that ideally the *sannyāsin* should not ask for food; it should be offered to him.[11]

III

Now that the *sannyasin* has no ostensible means of livelihood, if we were to ask him who supports him, more often than not he is likely to say "God."[12] The fact that *sannyāsa* has been institutionalized in Hinduism so that the Hindus are socialized to offer alms to the *sannyāsin* should not blind one to this aspect of the situation.[13] The *sannyāsin* relies on God. Practices differ, but here is one account of how one might proceed when begging alms or what is called *bhikṣā*:[14]

> There are two methods of obtaining *bhikṣā* for the day. One may select a hut at random, the less orthodox and, to my taste, the less appropriate way. The other method has the approval of orthodox monastic convention, and it is to take from each donor just about one morsel of rice, or just one *roṭī*, according to whether the region's staple diet is rice or wheat. Here again, the prescribed way seems to me the most elegant one, and I insist that such judgments on the border between ethics and aesthetics apply to many monastic actions. As the monk enters the village boundary he stands still and calls out loudly but without shouting: *om namo nārāyaṇāya*. The villagers hear him, and then usually half a dozen village women, or some men peep out and ask him if he would have some food.[15]

Note that the words *om namo nārāyaṇāya* mean: Salutation to God. The renunciant does not literally ask for food, he only takes the name of God.[16]

IV

How can this phenomenon, that a renunciant asks for food by offering salutation to God, be explained in Durkheimian terms?[17] It is apparent that it is society that is supporting the renunciant, rather than God. The theology of *sannyāsa* can easily be converted into the sociology of Hinduism if we invoke the Durkheimian equation of God with society. The general thesis of Emile Durkheim's famous work *Les formes élémentaires de la vie religieuse* is well known. It is presented below in a very general form in the words of Durkheim himself:

> The general conclusion of the book, which the reader has before him, is that religion is something eminently social. Religious representations are collective representations, which express collective realities; the rites are a manner of acting which take rise in the midst of the assembled groups and which are destined to excite, maintain or recreate certain mental states in these groups. So if the categories are of religious origin, they ought to participate in this nature common to all religious facts; they too should be social affairs and the product of

> collective thought. At least—for in the actual condition of our knowledge of these matters, one should be careful to avoid all radical and exclusive statements—it is allowable to suppose that they are rich in social elements.[18]

This may be followed up by a more comprehensive yet brief recapitulation of the general outline of his theory to assist subsequent analysis.

> Durkheim wished to lay bare the fundamental basis of religion, to find religion in the purest form unobscured by "popular mythologies and subtle theologies." He found this elementary form of the religious life in the totemism of Australian aborigines, members of the society, which, he felt, was surpassed by no other in its simplicity. He assumed that among these clans it was possible to explain their religion without reference to any other forms of religion. Here, Durkheim argued, rituals and ritual attitudes were directed towards the totem, a representation of some species ascribed to all members of a given clan and the source of that clan's identity. This was not a case of animal-worship; animals and plants derived their sacredness from the fact that they were used as totemic objects rather than totems deriving their sacred character from the totemic species.
>
> The totem was a representation of something else, a power greater than itself which Durkheim calls the totemic principle or god. In worshipping the totem and observing taboos concerning the totemic object, the clansmen were reaffirming their collective sense of belonging. Society, Durkheim stressed here as elsewhere, is essentially a moral force; it is external to us and instils in each a sense of obligation. To Durkheim, society, morality, and religion were the three major elements of a closed and interacting system. The circularity in Durkheim's analysis was not seen as a weakness in his argument; rather, it emphasized that religion was not being reduced "to the merely social," for the "social" was the most fundamental reality of all.[19]

V

There is further evidence that reinforces this application of Durkheim's thesis to the institution of *sannyāsa*, both negatively and positively.

There are cases of *sannyāsins* that either clearly realized that it was society and not God who was providing for them, or whose actual situation clearly reflected this fact to a degree. However, there are cases of non-*sannyāsins* who claimed to rely on God for support in the manner of the *sannyāsin*, when the facts of the situation demonstrate that it was society that actually supported them.

Let us first look at the *sannyāsins*. One well-known religious figure of India in the nineteenth century is Swami Dayānanda Sarasvatī (1824–83), who was a *sannyāsin*. The circumstances in which he took *sannyāsa* are recounted by a recent biographer as follows:

> The future Dayānanda had already that great ability to concentrate on his work and sweep aside obstructions: "during my time as a brahmachārin, I sometimes had to prepare my own meals. I felt this constituted an obstacle to my studies. *There I felt that it would be a good thing to enter into the order of sannyāsa." As a member of that order he would then be entitled to be fed by the Hindu lay folk.* However, perhaps because this motive did not seem good enough, and also because he was still too young, he was at first refused ordination by the two monks he approached. But his insistence soon bore fruit: Pūrṇānanda Sarasvatī from the Shringeri Math of the South initiated him as a *sannyāsī* in the order of the Daṇḍīs, and gave him the name he would make famous, Dayānanda Sarasvatī.[20]

By contrast, when another major religious figure of the nineteenth century, Swami Vivekananda (1869–1902) took *sannyāsa,* he did so along with two other disciples of his late Master Rāmakṛṣṇa (1836–86). At the "end of December 1886, . . . there was a regular ceremony in which the young devotees took the vow of leading a life of renunciation, celibacy, and poverty, with a view to the realization of God."[21] It was indicated earlier how *sannyāsins* are meant to wander alone, but the disciples of Rāmakṛṣṇa lived together in a dilapidated house at this time, and thus by not conforming to the rules of *sannyāsa* as recognized by society they did not fare very well, at least to begin with. Vivekananda's own account of those days is revealing.

> There have been days when the Math was without a grain of food. If some rice was collected by begging, there was no salt to take it with! On some days there would be only rice and salt, but nobody cared for it in the least. We were then being carried away by a tidal wave of spiritual practice. Boiled Bimba leaves, rice and salt—this was the menu for a month at a

> stretch. Oh, those wonderful days! The austerities of that period were enough to dismay supernatural beings, not to speak of men.[22]

VI

Further pieces of evidence from Hinduism on the point under investigation serve to thicken the plot, as it were. They are also connected to the life of Swami Vivekananda (1863–1902) and pertain to the mendicant phase of his life. The first few incidents, described below, are less significant than the ones to follow, but serve to illustrate the unconscious identification of society with God in an almost Durkheimian manner.

> Once, while observing the vow not to ask for, or take food that was not offered to him, he was very hungry, and went on and on through a forest when he heard a man shouting from behind that he had brought food for him. Resolved, it is said, "to test this apparent act of Providence," he ran and the man ran also, finally overtaking him and insisting on his taking the food that he had brought for him.[23]

Another similar incident, which also has a lighter side to it, may also be narrated.

> On another occasion, after bathing in a tank, he came back to the place where he had taken off his *kaupin* (loincloth) and after washing it had left it for drying. When he came back, he found to his consternation—for he had only one kaupin—that it was gone! A monkey had lifted it and, seated comfortably on a high branch of a tree with it in his hands, made faces at him as he appealed to it to give it back to him. Unable in his condition of nudity to return to a human location, the Swami resolved to enter into the deepest recesses of the forest, even if it meant that he was to starve to death. But Providence in the guise of a man who had seen him and probably divined his intention came to his rescue once again. As he was advancing into the forest, the man came up with a new *gerua* (saffron-robe) and some food, which so overwhelmed him with a sense of gratefulness to him and to God who, he felt, was watching him, that he accepted them.[24]

It is the next account, however, which is crucial, because it seems to confirm Durkheim and yet goes beyond his analysis. The account is somewhat detailed, but the details are necessary to develop the point. In the first extract, it should be noted that the householder criticizes the Swami for being a social parasite. The householder, in this sense, represents the profane world by which the sacred, in the form of the swami, is challenged. We must remember here the "clear evidence in *The Elementary Forms of Religious Life* (1964), that Durkheim saw the social order as continuously threatened by individual, profane interests,"[25] as well as the fact that the system of āśramas is clearly an attempt to establish a social order within Hinduism. It helps to assess the full significance of the following incident if the incident is read bearing these considerations in mind. Here is Dhar's description of this incident:

> Another time (perhaps an earlier journey), while travelling in a railway carriage on one of the hottest days of summer season in U.P., hungry and thirsty, he had, as a fellow-passenger, a *bania* (small businessman) who, with almost unbelievable perversity, brought water with which he quenched his own thirst, while lecturing to the Swami on the life of a householder as contrasted with the life of a *sannyasin* who renounced both money and the world. Lest his precious thoughts happen to be above the Swami's intelligence, he pointedly referred to the present case. He, who earned money by the sweat of his brow, was drinking nice, cool, water while the Swami, who did not work for his bread and was a social parasite, was going without it. Detraining at Taraghat station, the Swami repaired to the third-class passenger's waiting-shed, but being turned out of it by a porter, sat on the ground outside it leaning against one of its posts. Meanwhile the *bania* who had also alighted at the same station came and seated himself in the shade inside the waiting-shed and near enough to be able to talk with him. (It was a one-sided affair, because the Swami was completely silent, now as before). Resuming his "pleasantries" the little man took out *puris* (bread) and *laddus* (sweetmeats) and began to eat them as he went on lecturing to the Swami in the vein he was doing during their railway journey together. Then a miracle happened.

The miracle that follows is indeed curious, as it seems to indicate that not only may the "collective consciousness" be involved in generating "religion," as Durkheim argues,[26] the "collective consciousness" à la Jung may also be involved, though the point cannot be pursued further within the limits of this chapter. Now the miracle.

> A man appeared on the scene carrying a bundle and a tumbler in his right hand, a *dhurry* (carpet) under his left arm, and a *surahi* (earthen water jug) in his left hand. He hastily spread out the *dhurry* in a clean spot, put on it the things that he was carrying and in a gentle and earnest voice invited the Swami to come and partake of the food which, he said, he had brought for him. The Swami was surprised and thinking that there was some mistake, told him that it must be some other man for whom he had brought the food, for they had not seen each other before this. "You are the man," insisted the newcomer, in tones bespeaking both conviction and reverence, and then narrated his story. He said he was a *haluikar* (sweetmeat manufacturer) of this city and after finishing his morning's business and his midday meal was having a nap. He had an extraordinary dream; Sri Ramachandra was standing before him and, pointing him (the Swami) out to him, said He was pained that he was going without food since the previous day and asked him immediately to get up, prepare some *puris* and run to the railway station for feeding him. Awaking and recollecting his nice dream—which he thought was only a dream—he went back to his nap. But Shri Ramji, out of His infinite kindness for His humble servant, again appeared before him and asked him post-haste to carry out His instructions. There was no mistaking about it this time; and there were no doubts in his mind that he was the Sadhu the Lord had pointed out to him. "It is all the will of Shri Ramji," he concluded. The Swami acknowledged it. The jeering *bania,* who was listening to the conversation, was struck with awe, and after taking the dust of the Swami's feet, departed.[27]

VII

Although it is the *sannyāsī* who is formally required to depend on God alone for his sustenance, non-*sannyāsins* are not debarred from experimenting with this great theological—and, in the present context, sociological—insight. In fact, the other evidence on this point comes from non-*sannyāsins*. One such piece of evidence relates to Paramhansa

Yogananda (died 1952) *before he became a sannyāsin*.[28] He entered into a bet with his brother as a young lad that he would survive in Vṛndāvana without a penny in his pocket and without asking for help. His adventures are described in chapter 2 of his autobiography. He succeeded, along with a penniless friend, in this mission presumably because Vṛndāvana is a famous center of pilgrimage[29] and social life in the city is almost unconsciously so organized as to take care of travelers and pilgrims from distant lands. The claim was made that they had put their faith in God and God responded; the explanation seems to lie more in the nature of the social rather than spiritual reality. Another illustration is provided by the life of Mahatma Gandhi (1869–1948). In a chapter of his autobiography, Mahatma Gandhi, who never became a formal *sannyāsin* in the technical sense but adopted a generally ascetic mode of life, narrates how he decided to discontinue his life insurance and to rely on God. Mahatma Gandhi's study of the Bhagavadgītā had produced a great effect on him:

> There words like *aparigraha* (non-possession) and *samabhava* (equability) gripped me. How to cultivate and preserve that equability was the question. What was the meaning of making no distinction between insulting, insolent, and corrupt officials, co-workers of yesterday raising meaningless opposition, and men who had always been good to one? And how was one to divest oneself of all possessions? Was not the body itself possession enough? Were not the wife and children possessions? Was I to destroy all the cupboards of books I had? Was I to burn my boats, give up all I had and follow Him? Straight came the answer: I could not follow Him unless I gave up all I had.[30]

It is well known that Mahatma Gandhi was actually supported by the Indian community in South Africa during his public ministry, and by other Indians later.[31] "His image was that of an ascetic in sandals and loincloth eating only fruits, nuts and goat milk. But the maintenance of that image was not easy. 'It takes a great deal of money to keep Bapu[32] living in poverty' reported Sarojini Naidu, one of his secretaries. During one period twelve men were hired to collect the simple fruits and nuts Gandhi demanded."[33] Even when due allowance is made for rhetorical flourish in the above statement, it can hardly be denied that Mahatma Gandhi lived on the support provided by his admirers (who may have admired his devotion to and reliance on God) rather than by God as such.

VIII

In conclusion, let me say that at least when the Hindu institution of *sannyāsa* or the mode of living associated with it is analyzed, Durkheim's equation of society with God is uncannily applicable. Although Durkheim arrived at his conclusion in the context of primal religion, it is perhaps of more than passing interest that his insight should be applicable to such a prominent aspect of the religious life of Hinduism as *sannyāsa*.

If the principle of reciprocal illumination is adopted, additional observations become possible. First of all, the Hindu example sheds this light on the sociology of religion: that certain social constructs can function both as modes and as institutions. Or to express the same point in terms of function and form, the sociological insights although arrived in the context of one may be applicable to both. For instance, in the course of our analysis of *sannyāsa* as an institution or form, we were led into identifying cases of people who had not actually taken *sannyāsa* or embraced the "form" but nevertheless tried it out temporarily as a mode of existence, testing the premise whether the general principle on which the form was based ("God provides") functioned independently of it or not. However, the method of sociology also sheds light on the institution of *sannyāsa*. *Sannyāsins* have often been accused of being social parasites. The sociological analysis lends credence to this charge. *Sannyāsa* allegedly has also been used as an escape mechanism. It has been argued, for instance, that it sustained the caste system by providing a safety valve: an institutionalized escape from it at an individual level. There are limits to this explanation, since it was members of the higher castes that typically took *sannyāsa*, whereas it is the lower castes that are generally believed to have been at the receiving end of the system. Nevertheless, the argument may have individualistic as distinguished from systemic relevance.

However, as Durkheimian analysis tends to view society as a whole, the interaction of tradition and method seems to raise illuminating questions, even if answers are hard to come by. For instance, during the period of the Delhi Sultanate, which followed the establishment of Muslim rule in India, the ranks of *sannyāsins* are believed to have swelled. Supposing this was indeed so, what are the factors responsible for it? Was it the result of the failure of society to continue to provide cohesion—either ideologically or economically? The fact that Sikhism, a movement that rose around this time, is opposed to *sannyāsa* becomes significant here. During the period between the suppression of the so-called Mutiny in India in 1858, and the partition of Bengal in 1905, a large number of distinguished *sannyāsins* tried to reform Hinduism. Was this because during this period, as British paramountcy choked off all avenues of political self-expression, *sannyāsa* alone provided a viable option for potential leaders? How do these speculations fare in a Durkheimian context?

Scholars have long noted the elements of "antistructure" in relation to *sannyāsa*. This could shed some light on the equation of religion and society, for it forms part of the broader problem raised by Durkheimian analysis: if religion integrates society, then how are religious divisions to be explained? Moreover, the fact that Durkheim's explanation should so successfully illustrate a particular social institution rather than society as a whole, and then too that part of it which really relates to the renunciation of society rather than integration with it, seems to offer modest evidence of its continuing relevance—in unexpected ways.

21

Reciprocal Illumination and the Dialogue of World Religions

Christianity and Islam

One of the main theological obstacles to an appreciation of Christianity on the part of the Muslims is the doctrine of the Trinity. It smacks of *shirk*, or assigning partners to God, than which no greater *kufr* is possible.

For Christians there is a perhaps equally strong obstacle to appreciating Islam, inasmuch as, according to Christians, Islam misrepresents (apart from misunderstanding) the Christian doctrine of the Trinity. The misunderstanding seems to arise from the fact that Muslims interpret the doctrine of the Trinity as one of tritheism, which Christianity also rejects. W. Montgomery Watt points out that although "there are considerable differences between the Qur'an and the New Testament," yet it should be noted

> that so far as the actual statements of the Qur'an are concerned, the differences are not so great as they are sometimes supposed to be. Modern scholars, Christian and Muslim, tend to read later controversies into the wording of the Qur'an. Thus the rejection of the doctrine that "God is one of three" (5. 73/7) is usually taken to be a denial of the Christian doctrine of the Trinity, yet strictly speaking what is rejected is a doctrine of tritheism which orthodox Christianity also rejects. Similarly, the rejection of the fatherhood of God the Father, and the sonship of God the Son, is strictly speaking a rejection

> of fatherhood and sonship in a physical sense; and this Christianity would also reject. The Virgin Birth is taught (19. 16-33/4), but is interpreted simply as a miracle. The denial that Jesus died on the cross (4.157/6–159/7) is primarily a denial that the crucifixion was a Jewish victory; but, in line with the absence of the conception of sacrifice, it means that the Qur'an never speaks of the atonement or saving work of Jesus.[1]

One is, however, still left with the misrepresentation of the Trinity as consisting not of God, Jesus, and the Holy Spirit, but of Mary, Jesus, and God.[2] Though this may make more biological sense, it makes less soteriological sense,[3] at least in terms of Christianity. So the question arises: How did Mary come to be considered part of the Trinity?[4]

The historical explanation offered in this case is that the Greek Orthodox Church did not approve of having the Chalcedonian formula imposed on it, and one of the ways in which it resisted the imposition was through Mariolatry. It must have been an important feature of Christianity for Muḥammad to be aware of it.

I would like to dwell here only on one historical fact: that the three persons of the Trinity as conceived in Islam are God, Jesus, and Mary. Historical criticism has of course provided many useful insights, and demonstrates that the virgin birth of Jesus, though accepted in Islam as in Christianity, is *understood* differently. Hans Küng explains:

> The position of Jesus in the Qur'an is unambiguous. Dialogue is therefore not aided by contemporary well-meaning Christians who read more into the Qur'an than it contains, claiming that in the Qur'an Jesus is called the "Word" of God. For the Qur'an, however, he is not the Word of God in the sense of the prologue of John's Gospel, in which the pre-existent divine *logos* became flesh. If the Qur'an acknowledges the virgin birth of Jesus, it is a sign of God's omnipotence, but emphatically not a sign of the deity of Jesus.
>
> In other words, for the Qur'an, Jesus is a prophet, a greater prophet than Abraham, Noah, and Moses—but certainly not more than a prophet. Further, just as in the New Testament John the Baptist is the forerunner of Jesus, so in the Qur'an Jesus is the forerunner of, and undoubtedly the encouraging example for, Muhammad.
>
> According to the Qur'an, Jesus was created directly by God as a second Adam (this is the meaning of the virgin birth), unlike the Prophet.[5]

There is, then, a *historical* explanation of how the components of the Trinity got shuffled.

From the Muslim perspective, one can better appreciate the need for the doctrine in terms of the situation faced by the church. When the Christian doctrine is now approached from a *historical* rather than a doctrinal standpoint, it is apparent, first of all, that Christianity arose in a Jewish environment permeated with monotheism. Then early Christianity had this extraordinary experience with the person of Jesus, which had to be brought into relationship to one God, as his person became the focus of devotion. Finally, the early church underwent the remarkable Pentecostal experience with the Holy Spirit. All these profound beliefs and experiences had to be integrated within the unity of God—hence the Trinitarian doctrine.

The point being pressed here is that if both the Christians and the Muslims begin to appreciate the historical situations, which crystallized into doctrinal positions, it might become possible to take a "softer" view of the alleged misrepresentations.

Christianity and Hinduism

The Christian doctrine of heaven appears simpleminded to the Hindus, while Hindu cosmological computations appear bizarre to the Christians. If, however, both sides develop a historical appreciation of the factors underlying these developments, each may be able to take a gentler view of the other's position.

It will now be proposed that apocalyptic expectation might provide a useful link between Christian eschatology and Hindu cosmology, notwithstanding the improbable nature of the suggestion. It is well known that in early Christianity the Second Coming was considered imminent.[6]

As a matter of fact, the first major crisis the church had to face arose when it became clear that it was not going to occur as soon as had been expected. R. J. Zwi Werblowsky summarizes the consensus on the point as follows:

> The message and teachings of the "historical Jesus" (as distinct from those of the Christ of the early church) are considered by most historians as beyond recovery. There has been, however, a wide scholarly consensus, especially at the turn of the century, that Jesus can be interpreted correctly only in terms of the eschatological beliefs and expectations current

> in the Judaism of his time. The Qumran sect (also known as the Dead Sea sect) was perhaps one of the most eschatologically radical groups at the time. In other words, he preached and expected the end of this world and age, and its replacement in the immediate future, after judgement, by the "kingdom of God." Early Christianity was thus presented as an eschatological message of judgment and salvation that, after the crucifixion and resurrection, emphasized the expectation of the imminent Second Coming. The subsequent history of the church was explained by these scholars as a result of the crisis of eschatology caused by the continued delay of the Second Coming.[7]

Thus gradually the church shifted the vision of its followers from the earth (where it was to materialize) to heaven (where it was dematerialized).

An apocalyptic expectation similar to Christianity—interestingly, more or less around the same time—is also vouched for in Puranic literature in the history of Hinduism. Most historians think that this is connected with foreign invasions of India during the centuries preceding and succeeding the Christian era, which made the Hindus feel threatened and generated both the despair of the collapse of the established order of things and the hope of its reestablishment through a savior figure—the Kalkī Avatāra.

> The end of the Kali-yuga, according to many epic passages, is marked by confusion of classes, the overthrow of established standards, the cessation of all religious rites, and the rule of cruel and alien kings. Soon after this the world is destroyed by flood and fire. This view is propounded strongly in texts, which date from about the beginning of the Christian era, when alien kings did in fact rule much of India, and established practices were shaken by heresies such as Buddhism and Jainism. An earlier tradition would place the Mahābhārata War c. 900 B.C., according to which the 1,200 years of the Kali-yuga, if read as human years and not as "years of the gods," would at this time be nearing their end. Evidently some pious Hindus thought that the dissolution of the cosmos was imminent. Perhaps it is to the departure of this fear in later times that we must attribute the devising of the "years of the gods," which made the dissolution of the world comfortably distant. Most medieval texts state that the cosmic dissolution occurs only after the last cycle of the kalpa, and that the transition

> from one aeon to the next takes place rapidly and calmly; the expectation of the Kalkin, who will not destroy but regenerate the world, could not otherwise be harmonized with the scheme of the yugas. In this, its final form, the Hindu system of world-cycles is clearly an imperfect synthesis of more than one independent doctrine; the manvantaras, especially, do not fit tidily into the scheme, and must surely be derived from a source different from that of the mahāyugas.[8]

It is illuminating that the end of the age was millenarian in both the cases, preceded by a cosmic accounting either through resurrection or destruction. In both cases the temporal contours were extended. In this context A. L. Basham provides an unexpected moment of reciprocal illumination when he writes "that many simple Hindus have taken the Kalkin very seriously, and long for his arrival just as old-fashioned Christians look forward to the second coming of Christ."[9]

The alert reader would have noted some overlap in the preceding discussion of Hinduism and Christianity in the context of dialogue with a similar (but not identical) discussion toward the end of the first part of the book. The discussion there involved a comparison of Hindu and Christian eschatologies, as embodied in the concepts of the Kali Yuga and the Apocalypse. The content here is comparable to that of the earlier discussion, but the intent is different. The first comparison was only meant to demonstrate how each case promotes a better understanding of the other; here it is accompanied by the hope that the comparison might help the Christian take a more indulgent view of the mind-numbing figures involved in Hindu calculations of the ages, since these might have arisen in response to a problem with which Christianity is not unfamiliar.

In other words, there is a recognition here that the study of religion, which is a human enterprise, might also possess a certain humanistic implication—not as a goal, to be sure, but as a consequence.

Conclusion

Comparison is the hallmark of the study of religion and the raison d'être of that form of it called comparative religion, and as such calls for a closer look.

An attempt was made to undertake such an examination in the preceding pages. It was prompted by the perception that whenever two items are compared in religious studies, there is an incipient tendency to assimilate one item of comparison into the other. Thus, if Christianity is compared to Hinduism, there is a tendency to understand Hinduism in terms of Christianity and vice versa. This tendency could be described as a tendency toward "theological" reductionism. Similarly, when a religious tradition is studied in the light of a method, there is a tendency to understand elements that mirror the method in terms of that method. This tendency could be described as a tendency toward "methodological" reductionism.

Both these forms of reductionism are varieties of epistemological reductionism. There is also a reductionism of a deeper dye, which may be called ontological reductionism. In this form of comparison, one item of comparison is considered just an incomplete version or illustration of the other. Thus theological reductionism of the ontological variety would claim that Christianity was the crown of Hinduism. Similarly, methodological reductionism of the ontological variety might claim, for example, that any element of a religious tradition that offered solace merely served as the opium of the masses.

The present study is a prolonged answer to the short question: what if one compares things not in order to judge one item in terms of another, but to see how our understanding of the items themselves is enhanced in the process, or even in some other dimension of religious life that one did not have in mind to begin with. This approach to comparison, which I have called reciprocal illumination, is what this book is all about. Whether the book has succeeded in demonstrating the viability of such an approach is for the reader to judge.

In evaluating this approach, the reader might find it helpful to take into account some of the recent developments in the comparative study of religion, which have occurred in an intellectual climate in which many charges have been brought against the comparative method. It has been charged with promoting "intellectual imperialism, universalism, theological foundationalism, and anti-contextualism." In this atmosphere "in particular the work of Mircea Eliade, the late doyen of the history of religions, is held to be unredeemable."[1] All of these developments are directly or indirectly connected with the great paradox of the field: that comparison is perhaps the most important but at the same time in many ways the least understood concept in the study of religion. Some of the scholars whose theories of comparison have attracted scholarly attention in this connection in recent times are Benson Saler, Jonathan Z. Smith, Robert Cummings Neville, Ninian Smart, William Paden, and Dale Cannon.

Benson Saler has invoked prototype theory as a way of approaching the very definition of religion,[2] with the interesting consequence that comparison is woven into the very fabric of the definition of religion. He summarizes his argument as follows:

> My suggestion for conceptualizing religion is this: Religion is an abstraction. For analytical purposes we may conceptualize it in terms of a pool of elements that more or less tend to occur together in the best exemplars of the category. While all of the elements that we deem to pertain to the category religion are predicable of that category, not all of them are predicable of the phenomena that various scholars regard as instantiations of religion. Those instantiations, called religions, include the Western monotheisms, our most prototypical cases of religion. They also include whatever else we deem to participate in the pool of elements to the extent of resembling the Western monotheisms in significant respects. And how do we establish what is significant? By cogent analytical arguments about elements that we deem analogous to those that we associate with our reference religions, the Western monotheisms.[3]

Although Western monotheism is circumspectly not considered the "prototype," yet religions representing it—Judaism, Christianity, and Islam—are to be taken as "among the most prototypical" examples of what we mean by it;[4] and although (again, circumspectly) other religious phenomena are not graded in terms of it and are to be dealt with in a "contingency sensitive" manner[5] as "particular instantiations of the category,"[6] the prototypical examples remain the point of reference:

> Predications of theism, in short are contingency sensitive. For most Westerners, however, certain cases that prominently include theism (e.g., "Judaism," "Christianity") are likely to seem better exemplars of the category religion than those that do not (e.g., "communism") or that do not accord it crucial cosmogenic and soteriologicial significance (e.g., "canonical Theravāda Buddhism").[7]

Thus the approach developed by Benson Saler seems to virtually define religion itself in terms of reciprocal differentiation; however, such reciprocal differentiation is quite distinct from reciprocal illumination, inasmuch as it uses a prototype as the reference for such comparison notwithstanding all the caveats. No such prototypicality is usually associated with what we have described as reciprocal illumination. Flashes of reciprocal illumination nevertheless do light up the intellectual terrain covered by Saler, as when he writes: "[O]ne might say that 'Islam' and 'Communism' both exemplify the same two categories, 'religion' and 'political movement,' while also deeming Islam to be a clearer or better example of religion than communism, and communism to be a better example of a political movement than Islam."[8]

While Saler infused comparison into the definition of religion itself, Jonathan Z. Smith has infused it into the "comparative" component of the expression "comparative religion." This might seem like carrying coal to Newcastle, but his point is that it might impart some rigor to the amorphous field of comparative religion if we learnt to say that "A is more comparable to B than to C"—as an exercise in, shall we say, comparative comparison. Perhaps this might prove liberatory for a field in which hitherto "the perception of similarity has been construed as the chief purpose of comparison," and in which "contiguity, expressed as historical 'influence' or filiation, has provided the explanation."[9]

Apart from this innovative suggestion, Smith has this to say on the "ends" of comparison. The passage is somewhat long, but upon reading it the reader will realize why no apology is offered for its inclusion.

> The "end" of comparison cannot be the act of comparison itself. I would distinguish four moments in the comparative

> enterprise: description, comparison, redescription, and rectification. Description is a double process which comprises the historical or anthropological dimensions of the work: First, the requirement that we locate a given example within the rich texture of its social, historical and cultural environments that invest it with its local significance. The second task of description is that of reception-history, a careful account of how our second-order scholarly tradition has intersected with the exemplum. That is to say, we need to describe how the datum has been accepted as significant for the purpose of argument. Only when such a double contextualization is completed does one move on to the description of a second example undertaken in the same double fashion. With at least two exempla in view, we are prepared to undertake their comparison both in terms of aspects and relations held to be significant, and with respect to some category, question, theory, or model of interest to us. The aim of such a comparison is the redescription of the exempla (each in light of the other) and a rectification of the academic categories in relation to which they have been imagined.[10]

The concept of reciprocal illumination as canvassed in the present book is based on a concept of the "end" of comparison rather different in its aim. One aim of comparison, according to Smith, is a "redescription of the exempla (each in the light of the other." In reciprocal illumination no such redescription is involved; only a deeper understanding is achieved. But this difference is merely semantic in the popular sense of the word, for the enhanced understanding, if spelled out, could count as redescription. In the sense of the aim of comparison as visualized by Smith, reciprocal illumination could be considered as involving "redescription." However, in the case of reciprocal illumination, such redescription may not apply to the exempla: illumination of either exemplum may suffice; that of both (prescribed by Smith) is welcome but not required. Similarly, while the rectification of the academic category in the light of the exercise may be desirable, this is not the end sought by reciprocal illumination, although reciprocal illumination may serve as a means for it. Finally, although reciprocal illumination is achieved through comparison, it does not assess the comparative difference involved in terms of degrees of comparison, for it does not go in for prototypicality.

Robert Cummings Neville has edited three volumes as the director of the Comparative Religious Ideas Project. They embody the work of the project, which was motivated by two purposes: "To develop and test a theory concerning the comparison of religious ideas and to make some important comparisons about religious ideas of the human condition, ultimate realities, and religious truth."[11] It is the idea of comparison as utilized in the project that is relevant here.

> The shortest possible version of our conception of comparison is the following. In any comparison, the things compared are compared in some respect. The "respect of comparison" is a vague category. So, for instance, to compare religious traditions or texts in respect of what they say about the human condition is to treat the human condition as a vague category that is made specific in different ways by what the traditions of their representatives say about it. The same is true in regard to comparing traditions and their ideas with respect to what they take to be religious truth. Comparative categories, then, need to be identified in three ways; in their vague form that applies neutrally to all the things under comparison, as specified variously by the things compared, and summarily so that it is possible to see just what the category is as integrating the comparisons. In the *Human Condition* we clearly understand the first two moments of identification, distinguishing the vague categories from their various specifications. But there we did not get very far past the listing of different specifications in the direction of full-blown comparison. We attempted to remedy that in the conclusions to *Ultimate Realities* and again in this volume.

Reciprocal illumination as developed in the pages of the present book is not against the formation of categories, but it typically operates at a level a step below—that of phenomena themselves, even if they have been categorized.

The contemporary theories of comparison examined so far had a bearing on the conception of reciprocal illumination; the theories that now follow have a bearing on its application. In the body of the book I took the several religious traditions and the various methods of studying them as my points of comparison, sometimes mediated by the typologies usually employed in such study. Various proposals made of late in the field would have the effect, if accepted, of enlarging these configurations. Ninian Smart, for instance, has proposed that the word "religion" be replaced by "worldviews," transforming "the comparative study of religion" into the "comparative study of worldviews."[12] This has the merit of allowing those phenomena which exhibit many features of religion, but are often excluded from consideration for formal reasons, to be brought within the ambit of study. His favored example is nationalism.[13] He also identifies seven dimensions of such worldviews: (1) the ritual or practical dimension; (2) the doctrinal or philosophical dimension; (3) the myth or narrative dimension; (4) the experiential or emotional dimension; (5) the ethical or legal dimension; (6) the organizational or social dimension; and (7) the material or artistic dimension.[14] Smart then proposes a dialectical phenomenology as a way of approaching the study.

> By dialectical phenomenology I mean more particularly the relationship between different dimensions of religion and worldviews. In general we can say about any system or scheme that one element in it is in principle affected by all others. An organism functions as a whole, so that an injury to one part affects the whole to a greater or lesser degree. A set of religious doctrines, for instance the teachings of Eastern Orthodoxy, is a sort of loose organism. It is not necessarily a consistent whole, but one doctrine, such as the creation, is affected by others, such as the incarnation of Christ (so Christ becomes Creator) or the definition of the sacraments (so the created world is viewed as sacramental). We can therefore see items in this field in the context of the scheme in which they are embedded. But more than this, we can view the items in one dimension (in this case the doctrinal dimension) in their interaction with items in other dimensions, for instance the practical (or ritual) dimension. The idea that the world is created out of nothing should be seen in the light of the intensity of Christian worship: no limitation should be set on the glory of God. The idea that there is an ineffable aspect of God or Brahman should be related to the mystical path, as well as to other factors, such as the performative analysis of indescribability in the context of supreme praise (in other words, seeing how the language of ineffability actually performs the act of praising: you get something like this in "I cannot say how grateful I am" which conveys how grateful I am).[15]

He goes on to say:

> Again we can see dialectical phenomenology at work in relation to a secular worldview. It is part of the doctrine of the

> United States that it favours and incarnates democratic values: this in turn has effects on the style of the Presidency. Its rituals include the practice of the President's going out and among the people and being populist in his actions (displaying himself as a "man of the people").[16]

I have quoted him at some length, as it is quite clear that here we have another goal of reciprocal illumination, a principle he seems to obliquely accept when he writes: "[A]ny real similarity between the piety of one tradition and that of another poses obvious questions for each."[17] If we extend the term "religion" to include worldviews and compare material not only across the seven dimensions among them but among the dimensions themselves as well, then the frontiers of reciprocal illumination are recalibrated and perhaps enlarged as well.

A comparatively more holistic way of viewing and then comparing religions has been proposed by William Paden.[18] Paden emphasizes the "habitative" role of religion, that is, how it helps create the world we inhabit. Moreover, one inhabits not one but several worlds. Within such a context, "Paden endeavours to investigate distinctive life-categories of the 'insider' across the lines of different religious traditions while specifically examining religious myth, ritual, deity, and systems of purity."[19]

Paden's work, then—somewhat in the manner of Smart but in a richer context—would be particularly fruitful for moments of reciprocal illumination experienced by the "insiders" to the tradition, who are insiders either by way of commitment to the tradition or by way of commitment to the study of the tradition. We do confront here the question of distinguishing religion from the study of religion, but with that warning in mind, the possibilities of such interiorized reciprocal illumination are intriguing.

The manner in which Dale Cannon carries out comparisons is closer to the enterprise of this work.[20] Cannon works with a template of six hermeneutical orientations: (1) sacred rite; (2) right action; (3) devotion; (4) shamanic meditation; (5) mystical quest; and (6) reasoned inquiry.[21] He builds on the template of the four yogas of Hinduism: Karma Yoga, Bhakti Yoga, Dhyāna Yoga and Jñāna Yoga.[22] Like Smart and Paden, Cannon provides another framework within which the phenomenon of reciprocal illumination could be located. Not only could the six dimensions themselves be compared, à la Smart, within the same tradition; each could be used as a vector for comparing traditions as well. Cannon explores this possibility specifically in the context of Buddhism and Christianity.[23]

The ease with which reciprocal illumination can be applied in a given context might create the impression that the concept must lack clarity if it produces such a potpourri of results going in so many directions. It could be argued, however, that it is the clarity of the central idea rather than its ambiguity that accounts for the versatility of its applicability. The central idea is in some ways close to that of the earliest phenomenological writings that brought similar phenomena close together. In doing so they had their eye on the category to which they belonged, but reciprocal illumination seeks to see how one datum may shed light on another, or two data on each other, rather than on a common or transcendent category, and further seeks to show that apparently different phenomena may also unexpectedly shed similar light. The word "reciprocal" is not limited to a single set of data; it is primarily reciprocal in the sense that if in one case data from tradition A shed light on B, then in another case data from tradition B may shed light on A. The reader may have noted a certain skittishness on my part to apply reciprocal illumination to category formation. It was precisely in the interest of retaining this focus on the items, items that may enhance our understanding of one tradition and/or of another through reciprocal illumination. It is through the achievement of this enhanced understanding in terms of such religious intelligibility that the method as espoused here insists on local knowledge.

To sum up: the study of religion today may be characterized as multitraditional and polymethodic in nature. That is to say, it involves the study of many different religious traditions, such as Hinduism, Buddhism, Judaism, and Christianity; and this study is carried on with the help of a number of methods, such as the historical, the phenomenological, the sociological, and the psychological.

Both the multitraditional and polymethodic components of the study of religion make extensive use of comparison. When a particular religious tradition, such as Confucianism, is being examined, comparisons from other traditions are often brought to bear on it. Similarly, a particular method in the study of religion, such as the sociological, extensively utilizes comparative religious data.

In both these cases, however, comparative material is used to serve some end other than itself—that of understanding a tradition or applying a method. This book has tried to develop a new approach to comparable data in which comparison is not meant to serve some other end, but is used to clarify the items under comparison themselves. Because these data are not used in this method to illuminate anything other than the data themselves, it has been described as reciprocal illumination.

Notes

Chapter 1

1. Charles Elliott Vernoff, "Naming the Game: A Question of the Field," *Council on the Study of Religion Bulletin* 14, no. 4 (October 1983): 111.

2. See Wendy Doniger O'Flaherty, ed., *Karma and Rebirth in Classical Indian Traditions* (Berkeley and Los Angeles: University of California Press, 1980); but also Charles F. Keyes and E. Valentine Daniel, eds., *Karma: An Anthropological Inquiry* (Berkeley and Los Angeles: University of California Press, 1983), p. 10.

3. Yoga-Vāsiṣṭha Rāmāyaṇa 2.4–9.

4. Adhyātma-Rāmāyaṇa 2.6.14–16.

5. T. M. P. Mahadevan, *Outlines of Hinduism* (Bombay: Chetana, 1971), pp. 60–61.

6. David A. Stewart, *The Adventure of Sobriety* (East Lansing: Michigan State University Press, 1976), p. 76.

7. Edward Conze, "Buddhism: The Mahāyāna" in *The Concise Encyclopaedia of Living Faiths*, ed. R. C. Zaehner (Boston: Beacon Press, 1959), p. 298; Har Dayal, *The Bodhisattva Doctrine in Buddhist Sanscrit Literature* (Delhi: Motilal Banarsidass, 1970).

8. Ibid., p. 17; A. L. Basham, *The Wonder That Was India* (New York: Taplinger Publishing Company, 1967), pp. 277, 548.

9. See Edward Conze in R. C. Zaehner, *Concise Encyclopedia*, pp. 300–301.

10. Arthur Waley, trans., *The Analects of Confucius* (New York: Vintage Books, n.d.), p. 189.

11. Wm. Theodore de Bary et al., eds., *Sources of Chinese Tradition* (New York: Columbia University Press, 1960), p.49.

12. Waley, *Analects of Confucius*, pp. 177–78.

13. James Legge, trans., *The Texts of Taoism* (London: Oxford University Press, 1927), p. 49.

14. Personal communication from Janice Reid, University of Sydney.

15. This is a simplification. See Jacob Neusner, *Early Rabbinic Judaism* (Leiden: E. J. Brill, 1975), pt. I, chap. 2; Robert Goldenberg "The Broken Axis: Rabbinic Judaism and the Fall of Jerusalem," *Journal of the American Academy of Religion* 45, no. 3 (September 1977): supp. F: 869–82.

16. I am still in the process of tracing it to its primary source, although it is not infrequently attested.

17. Huston Smith, *The Religion of Man* (New York: Perennial, 1965), p. 330.

18. Qur'ān 7.157–58 in *The Meaning of the Glorious Qur'ān,* trans. M. M. Pickthall (New York: World Muslim League, 1977). Also see A. Guillaume, trans., *The Life of Muhammad* (New York: Oxford University Press, 1955), p. 252 n. 1; Maulana Muhammad Ali, *A Manual of Hadith* (London: Curzon Press, 1983), p. 35.

19. Qur'ān, 96.4–5.

20. Willard G. Oxtoby, ed., *Religious Diversity: Essays by Wilfred Cantwell Smith* (New York: Harper & Row, 1976), p. 24.

21. H. A. R. Gibb and J. H. Kramers, *Shorter Encyclopaedia of Islam* (Leiden: E. J. Brill, 1953), p. 200.

22. See W. Montgomery Watt, *Free Will and Predestination in Early Islam* (London: Luzac & Company, 1948), passim; *Bell's Introduction to the Qur'ān* (Edinburgh: Edinburgh University Press, 1970), pp. 150–53.

23. Frederick J. Streng, *Emptiness: A Study in Religious Meaning* (Nashville, TN: Abingdon Press, 1969), pp. 39–40 and passim.

Chapter 2

1. "If, in this way, the truth of the void and absolute reality necessarily reveals itself in our empirical world by means of the teaching, our actual, empirical world will be flooded with and cherished by the light of the void and absolute reality. The revelation of the void and absolute reality in the empirical world means the realization in the empirical world of that perfect wisdom which has reached the World of Awakening by destroying illusions (*prajñāpāramitā*)—that is, it means the salvation of this world. Therefore, according to Mahāyāna Buddhism the revelation in the empirical world of the void and absolute reality is called mercy (*karuṇā*). It is also called *upāya,* which means 'the way' or 'the means,' to show how the void and absolute reality reaches the empirical world so that, on its impulse and by its means, the empirical world may be enabled to approach the void and absolute reality. The word *upāya,* the way, clearly expresses the character of the mercy which takes the form of the revelation in the empirical world of the void and absolute reality." Susumu Yamaguchi, "Development of Mahāyāna Buddhist Beliefs," in *The Path of the Buddha,* ed. Kenneth W. Morgan (New York: Ronald Press Company, 1956), pp. 172–73).

2. "The becoming conscious of this śūnyatā (Tib. stong-panyid) is prajñā (Tib. shes-rab), or highest knowledge. The realization of this highest knowl-

edge in life is enlightenment (bodhi; Tib. byang-chhub), i.e., if prajñā (or śūnyatā), the passive, all embracing female principle, from which everything proceeds and into which everything recedes, is united with the dynamic male principle of active universal love and compassion, which represents the means (upāya; Tib. thabs) for the realization of prajñā and śūnyatā, then perfect Buddhahood is attained. Intellect without feeling, knowledge without love, and reason without compassion lead to pure negation, to rigidity, to spiritual death, to mere vacuity, while feeling without reason, love without knowledge (blind love), compassion without understanding, lead to confusion and dissolution; but where both are united, where the great synthesis of heart and head, feeling and intellect, highest love and deepest knowledge have taken place, completeness is re-established, and perfect enlightenment is attained.

The process of enlightenment is therefore represented by the most obvious, the most human and at the same time the most universal symbol imaginable; the union of male and female in the ecstasy of love, in which the active element (upāya) is represented as a male, the passive (prajñā) by a female figure, in contrast to the Hindu Tantras, in which the female aspect is represented as Śakti, i.e., the active principle, and the male aspect as Śiva, the pure state of divine consciousness or 'being,' i.e., the passive principle, or the 'resting in its own nature.'

In Buddhist symbolism, the Knower (Buddha) becomes one with his knowledge (prajñā), just as man and wife become one in the embrace of love, and this becoming one is the highest indescribable happiness, mahāsukha (Tib. bde-mchhog). The Dhyānī Buddhas (i.e., the ideal Buddhas visualized in meditation) and the Dhyānī Bodhisattvas, as embodiments of the active urge of enlightenment which finds its expression in upāya, the all-embracing love and compassion, are therefore represented in the embrace of their prajñā, symbolized by a female deity, the embodiment of highest knowledge.

This is not the arbitrary reversal of Hindu symbology, in which 'the poles of the male and the female as symbols of the divine and its unfoldment have to be exchanged apparently, as otherwise the gender of the concepts which they were intended to embody in Buddhism would not have been in harmony with them' but the consequent application of a principle which is of fundamental importance for the entire Buddhist Tantric system." Anagarika Govinda, "Principles of Tantric Buddhism," in *2500 Years of Buddhism,* ed. P. V. Bapat (New Delhi: Publications Division of the Government of India, 1963), pp. 364–65.

3. "In the early Mahāyāna *sūtras,* known as the Prajñāpāramitā ('perfection of wisdom') literature, the notion of skill in means is closely linked to that of *prajñā,* that is, to wisdom or insight into the true character of things. Such insight implies a recognition of the metaphysical voidness or insubstantiality of all phenomena and all factors of experience *(dharmas).* Insight and skill in means are two of the perfections in which a *bodhisattva* has to school himself. Hence, this usage (especially in the *Aṣṭasāhasrikaprajñāpāramitā Sūtra)* complements that of the Lotus. As an adept in training, the *bodhisattva* must manage the various features of practical religion that articulate his path, but

without becoming attached to them in any way. He must, for example, practice *dhyāna* ('meditation, trance') without being subject to its karmic consequences, that is, without rebirth in the various *deva* heavens that such meditation entails. These heavens, the teaching holds, are pleasant but religiously irrelevant existences; attachment to them is an impediment to the religious life: But what is the skill in means of a Bodhisattva? It is just this perfection of wisdom. And he applies himself to this skill in means in such a way that, endowed with it, the Bodhisattva enters into the trances without being reborn through the influence of the trances." Michael Pye, "Upāya" in *The Encyclopedia of Religion,* ed. Mircea Eliade (New York: Macmillan, 1987), 15: 153–54.

4. Ibid., 15: 152–53.

5. Ibid., p. 182. For more on *upāya* see Michael Pye, *Skilful Means: A Concept in Mahāyāna Buddhism* (London: Gerald Duckworth, 1970); idem, "Assimilation and Skilful Means," *Religion* 1, nos. 152–56 (1971). Also see Daigan and Alicia Matsunaga "The Concept of Upāya in Mahāyāna Buddhist Philosophy," *Japanese Journal of Religious Studies* 1, nos. 151–72 (1974), for its role in Mahāyāna; Walpola Rahula, *What the Buddha Taught* (New York: Grove Press, 1974), p. 62ff., for its role in Theravāda Buddhism. For the use of the term in Hinduism see T. M. P. Mahadevan, *Outlines of Hinduism* (Bombay: Chetana, 1971), p. 195.

6. S. Radhakrishnan, ed., *The Principal Upaniṣads* (London: George Allen & Unwin, 1953), p. 679.

7. Mahadevan, *Outlines of Hinduism* (1971), p. 21. N. K. Devaraja seems to come close to making a connection between the two concepts but doesn't quite seem to make it when he writes: "The Mahayanists believe that Buddha's teaching about *dharmas* was a concession to the popular mind, or the mind of the common man, who cannot comprehend the higher truth of the Śūnyatā or voidness of all things. Here we may allude to a notion widely current among Indian religious thinkers. They believe that there are different grades of persons as regards their intellectual ability and spiritual competence. Consequently, all human beings are not fitted to receive and appreciate all sorts of doctrines and spiritual teachings; nor can they usefully pursue the same pathway to God or liberation. This view is technically known as the doctrine of grades of spiritual competence (*Adhikāribheda*); it tends to make the Indian mind hospitable to variety of religious doctrines and forms of worship. Shri D. S. Sarma refers to another such doctrine as characteristic of the Hindus, namely the doctrine of the chosen deity (*Ishṭa-devatā*), which means 'that, out of the numerous forms of Supreme Being conceived by the heart of man in the past and recorded by the scriptures, the worshipper should be taught to choose that which satisfies his spiritual longing and to make it the object of his love and adoration.' " *Hinduism and Christianity* (New York: Asia Publishing House, 1969), p. 26.

8. Krishna Chandra Bhattacharyya, "The Advaita and Its Spiritual Significance" in *The Cultural Heritage of India,* ed. Haridas Bhattacharyya (Calcutta: Ramakrishna Mission Institute of Culture, 1953), 3: 252.

9. G. P. Malalasekera, *Dictionary of Pali Proper Names* (London: Pali Text Society, 1960), 1: 609–10.

10. Pye, "Upāya," p. 153.

11. Sri Ramanananda Sarasvathi, trans., *Advaita Bodha Deepika* [Lamp of Nondual Knowledge] (Tiruvannamalai: Sri Ramanasramam, 1967), pp. 19–20.

12. See Shrinivas Tilak, *Religion and Aging in the Indian Tradition* (Albany: State University of New York Press, 1989), p. 166, n. 18.

13. Edward Conze, I. B. Horner, David Snellgrove, and Arthur Waley, eds., *Buddhist Texts Through the Ages* (New York: Philosophical Library, 1954), p. 34, emphasis added.

14. D. S. Sarma, *Hinduism Through the Ages* (Bombay: Bharatiya Vidya Bhavan, 1956), p. 1.

15. Henry Clarke Warren, *Buddhism in Translations* (Cambridge, MA: Harvard University Press, 1915), p. xiv.

16. Edward Conze, *Buddhism: Its Essence and Development* (New York: Harper & Row, 1959), p. 175. Italics as per original text.

17. P. Sankaranarayanan, *What Is Advaita?* (Bombay: Bharatiya Vidya Bhavan, 1970), p. 238.

18. To a comparative religionist like N. K. Devaraja, the future of *upāya-kauśalya* as a concept would seem more promising than that of *adhikāra-bheda*. "While Christianity laid exclusive emphasis on faith as the instrument of religious knowledge and salvation, Indian religious teachers propounded the undemocratic but psychologically sound theory of grades of spiritual competence (*adhikāri-bheda*) thus recommending ritualistic religion for the lower grade people and reserving the higher forms of philosophic religion for the upper castes or the intellectual aristocracy. In the present age of growth of individuals and unbelief it does not seem possible to apply the principle of spiritual or even intellectual gradation either to persons or to groups. The expansion of higher education and man's increasing acquaintance with science and scientific methodology are other factors that militate against the acceptance of religious teachings by men as a matter of simple faith. Moreover, once a large section of the intelligentsia have learnt to discard authority and to test all sorts of pronouncements by reason and experience, the common people too tend to develop questioning attitudes towards authority. For these reasons I do not envisage an easy and secure future for such faith-centred creeds as Christianity and Vaishnavism. The only religions that seem to me to have a future are such rational creeds as Buddhism and philosophic Hinduism." Devaraja, *Hinduism and Christianity*, pp. 118–119.

Chapter 3

1. Eric J. Sharpe, *Comparative Religion; A History*, 2d ed. (London: Duckworth, 1986), chap. 1.

2. Ibid, chap. 2.

3. Ibid., p. 31.

4. Mircea Eliade, *From Primitives to Zen: A Thematic Sourcebook of the History of Religions* (New York: Harper & Row Brothers, 1967), contents.

5. G. van der Leeuw, *Religion in Essence and Manifestation*, trans. J. E. Turner (New York: Harper & Row, 1960), vols. 1 and 2, contents.

6. W. Brede Kristensen, *The Meaning of Religion*, trans. John B. Carman (The Hague: Martinus Nijhoff, 1960), table of contents.

7. Jean Holm, *The Study of Religions* (New York: Crossroad, 1977), pp. 83–90 and passim.

8. S. Radhakrishnan, *The Hindu View of Life* (New York: Macmillan, 1927), p. 39.

9. A. L. Basham, *The Wonder That Was India* (New York: Grove Press, 1954), p. 138.

10. Ibid., pp. 85–86. Also see Manusmṛti 8.4–8.

11. Mahābhārata (critical edition) 3.297.30, 32.

12. See Arvind Sharma, *Classical Hindu Thought: An Introduction* (Delhi: Oxford University Press, 2000), chap. 19.

13. The question may be asked why only priests and kings claimed divinity and not the other *varṇas*. The explanation may lie in part in the Indo-European background of Hinduism. "Kingship has a double aspect in all Indo-European traditions. This is shown most lucidly in the Indian divine pair Mitra-Varuna, who are almost always mentioned together in a grammatical dual form. Corresponding to these are the Roman Jupiter and Dius Fidius and the Germanic Tiwaz and Wodan. This pair represent the highest authority, which was twofold. In many respects the two gods present contrasts. Mitra is the god of agreements and contracts; he is a friend of men. Varuna the magician is violent and pitiless with anyone who has transgressed. Mitra is the guardian of law, prosperity, and peace, and Varuna is the patron of war and conquest. Although they contrast, Dumézil interprets them as the two faces of authority, protecting and preserving the social order and maintaining the law, but also as a revolutionary power, erupting through a fossilized order and creating new forms. While Varuna incorporates authority in a secular sense, Mitra does so spiritually. For that reason, in the Indian texts the *brahman* or priest and the *ksatra* or warrior often play their parts side by side." Jan de Vries, *The Study of Religion: A Historical Approach* (New York: Harcourt, Brace & World, 1967), p. 184.

14. W. Y. Evans-Wentz, ed., *Tibet's Great Yogi Milarepa*, 2d ed. (Oxford: Oxford University Press, 1969), p. 273.

15. Ibid., p. 281.

16. Ibid., p. 283.

17. Ibid., pp. 283–84.

18. Ibid.

19. Ibid., p. 288.

20. Ibid., p. 289.

21. Ibid., p. 268.

22. Ibid., p. 287. These are the Tibetan names for "Hevajra, Shamvara, Guhya-Kāla, and Vajra-Varāhī" (ibid.).

23. Ibid., p. 270.

24. Ibid.

25. Ibid., p. 266.

26. Ibid.

27. Ibid., p. 249.

28. Ibid., p. 302.

29. Ibid., p. 267.

30. Ibid., p. 286

31. G. van der Leeuw, *Religion in Essence and Manifestation*, trans. J. E. Turner (New York: Harper & Row Publishers, 1963), vol. 1, chap. 12.

32. I. B. Horner, trans., *The Book of Discipline* (London: Luzac & Company, 1962), 4: 14.

33. Malalasekera, *Dictionary of Pali Proper Names*, 1: 385–86.

34. Ibid., 2: 237.

35. Edward Conze, *Buddhism: Its Essence and Development* (New York: Harper & Row, 1959), pp. 89–90.

Chapter 4

1. Wilfred Cantwell Smith, *Towards a World Theology* (Philadelphia: Westminster Press, 1981), p. 90.

2. See Aelred Graham, *Contemplative Christianity* (New York: Crossroad, 1974), chap. 3.

3. D. G. Tendulkar, *Mahatma: Life of Mohandas Karamchand Gandhi* (New Delhi: Publications Division of the Government of India, 1961) 2: 230. The preceding remarks may also interest the reader: "I hold that it is the duty of every cultured man or woman, to read sympathetically the scriptures of the world. If we are to respect others' religions, as we would have them to respect our own, a study of the world's religions is a sacred duty. We need not dread upon our grown-up children, the influence of scriptures other than our own. We liberalize their outlook upon life by encouraging them to study freely all that is clean. Fear there would be when someone reads his own scriptures to young people with the intention, secretly or openly, of converting them. He must then be biased in favour of his own scriptures. For myself, I regard my study of and reverence for the Bible, the Koran, and all the other scriptures to be wholly consistent with my claim to be a staunch sanatani Hindu. He is no sanatani Hindu who is bigoted, and who considers evil to be good if it has the sanction of antiquity and is to be found supported in a Sanskrit book. I claim to be a staunch sanatani Hindu because, though I reject all that offends my moral sense, I find the Hindu scriptures to satisfy the needs of the soul."

Two questions naturally arise at this point: (1) whether Gandhi provides an instance when he was actually enabled to understand more clearly an obscure passage in Hindu scriptures by the reading of other scriptures; and (2) whether he instantiates cases when Hindu scriptures helped him to achieve a better understanding of the scriptures of other religions.

I have not been able to identify a case as yet where Gandhi directly refers to his understanding of a passage of a Hindu scripture being clarified by his reading of the scripture of another religion, but some suggestive hints in that direction can be identified. Mahatma Gandhi was much inspired by the first verse of the Īśāvāsyopaniṣad. When a correspondent suggested that the expression *tena tyaktena bhuñjīthāḥ* meant renouncing what one held dear, Gandhi replied that "his interpretation is only the well-worn doctrine of self-sacrifice," whereas "to live up to the verse means the new birth enunciated in the New Testament or Brahma-samarpana (dedication to God) as taught in Hinduism." (M. K. Gandhi, *In Search of the Supreme*, ed. V. B. Kher [Ahmedabad: Navajivan Publishing House, 1962] 1: 3). Nine years earlier he had remarked in connection with the same verse, "[S]o when a person who calls himself a Hindu goes through the process of regeneration or second birth, as Christians would call it, he has to perform a dedication or renunciation of all that he has in ignorance called his own property." Ibid., p. 108. Here Gandhi seems to be revalorizing the concept of *dvija* within Hinduism not only by connecting the idea with the first verse of the Īśa Upanishad rather than the Gāyatrī, but making it more meaningful for himself by seeing an analogy with the idea of being born again in Christianity. The second point is also difficult to instantiate specifically, but Gandhi does say that the "Gita has become for me the key to the scriptures of the world. It unravels for me the deepest mysteries to be found in them." Ibid., p. 333.

4. For a discussion of the evolution of the Christian positions on this and subsequent points, see Eric J. Sharpe, *Comparative Religion; A History*. 2d ed. (London: Duckworth, 1986), chap. 7. Islam presents the interesting example of a religion that freely accepts the fact of being connected to preceding traditions but only through God; see H. A. R. Gibb and J. H. Kramers, eds., *Shorter Encyclopedia of Islam* (Leiden: E. J. Brill, 1953), p. 391ff.

5. Hendrik Kraemer, *World Cultures and World Religions: The Coming Dialogue* (London: Lutterworth Press, 1960), p. 62.

6. See K. M. Munshi and R. R. Diwakar, eds., *Radhakrishnan Reader: An Anthology* (Bombay: Bharatiya Vidya Bhavan, 1969) pp. 4, 21; Gandhi, *In Search of the Supreme*, 3: 339–40.

7. Heinrich Zimmer, *Myths and Symbols in Indian Art and Civilization*, ed. Joseph Campbell (New York: Harper Torchbooks, 1962), p. 219.

8. Ibid., pp. 220–21.

9. Ibid., p. 221, emphasis added.

10. S. Radhakrishnan, however, comes close to endorsing his position at least in part in the sentiments he expresses at his appointment to the Spalding Chair of Eastern Religions and Ethics at Oxford University: "The great periods of human history are marked by a widespread access of spiritual vitality derived from the fusion of national cultures with foreign influences. If we take

Judaism we find that Abraham came from Mesopotamia and Joseph and Moses from Egypt. Later, Judaism shows the influence of Hellenism. Asia Minor and Egypt exercised considerable influence over the Greek development. The creative genius of the mediaeval world came from Palestine. The transition to the modern world was marked by the recovery of the ancient. In times of trouble we draw the profoundest inspiration from sources outside us, from the newly recovered past or the achievement of men under different skies. So, perhaps, the civilizations of the East, their religions and ethics, may offer us some help in negotiating difficulties that we are up against." Quoted in Munshi and Diwakar, *Radhakrishnan Reader*, p. 400.

11. Cited by Jolande Jacobi, *Complex/Archetype/Symbol in the Psychology of C. G. Jung*, trans. Ralph Manheim (Princeton, NJ: Princeton University Press, 1974), pp. 101–2. An interpretation parallel to this bimodal interpretation of dreams by Jung is provided in the interpretation of karma within Hinduism, in which *phala* or the external result of karma corresponds to the object level, and the impression it leaves on the psyche, the *saṁskāra*, corresponds to subject level. (See M. Hiriyanna, *The Essentials of Indian Philosophy* [London: Allen & Unwin, 1949], p. 49.) For the possible indebtedness of Jung to the doctrine of karma for his ideas about archetypes, see Harold G. Coward, "Karma and Rebirth in Western Psychology," in *Karma and Rebirth: Post Classical Developments*, ed. Ronald W. Neufeldt (Albany: State University of New York Press, 1986), p. 260. For more on Jung and Asian psychology in general, see Philip Novak, "C. G. Jung in the Light of Asian Psychology," *Religious Traditions* 14, nos. 66–87 (1991).

12. Jacobi, *Complex/Archteype/Symbol*, p. 102.

13. Ibid.

14. Ibid., pp. 71 and 114.

15. The use of the "collective" should be clarified here. Its association with the collective unconscious of Jung has prompted me to use the word "community," where I mean the society as a collective unit. I have avoided using the word "collective" here to prevent any subliminal confusion on account of the semantic ambience it possesses in Jungian psychology. A community as a collective unit possesses myths as the homologue of the individual's dream. An individual, however, in his dream may access the "collective unconscious" of which the myths of the community may also be expressions.

16. Zimmer, *Myths and Symbols*, p. 221.

17. A. Devaraja Mudaliar, comp., *Gems from Bhagvan* (Triuvannamalai: Sri Ramanasramam, 1978) pp. 34–35. Herewith another instance of the use of dream by Ramana (quoted in ibid., pp. 24–25): "All that we see is a dream, whether we see it in the dream state or waking state. On account of some arbitrary standards about the duration of the experience and so on, we call one experience a dream and another waking experience. With reference to reality both the experiences are unreal. A man might have such an experience as getting anugraha (grace) in his dream and the effects and influence of it on his entire subsequent life may be so profound and so abiding that one cannot

call it unreal, while calling real some trifling incident in the waking life that just flits by, is casual and of no moment and is soon forgotten. Once I had an experience, a vision or a dream, whatever you may call it. I and some others, including Chadwick, had a walk on the hill. Returning we were walking along a huge street with buildings, I asked Chadwick and others whether anybody could say that what we were seeing was dream and they all replied, 'Which fool will say so?' and we walked along and entered the hall and the vision or dream ceased, or woke up. What are we to call this?" After this point divergence emerges between Zimmer and Ramana. For Zimmer the revelation "*must* come through a stranger," while Ramana's emphasis rests elsewhere. However, curiously enough, Ramana also uses the metaphor of digging in the context of self-realization: "Make effort. Just as water is got by boring a well, so also you realize the Self by investigation." *Talks with Sri Ramana Maharshi* (Triuvannamalai: Sri Ramanasramam, 1984), p. 193.

18. Mudaliar, p. 41 (also see p. 42).

Chapter 5

1. M. Hiriyanna, *The Essentials of Indian Philosophy* (London: George Allen & Unwin, 1949), p. 137.

2. Paul Brunton, *A Search in Secret India* (New York: E. P. Dutton & Co., 1935), p. 140.

3. Ibid., p. 159. The contrast between this and the "I-Thou" position of Martin Buber is fairly obvious. As it well known, his "*I and Thou* has penetrated far beyond the bounds of Judaism!" J. F. Seurnarine, *Reconversion to Hinduism Through Śuddhi* (Bangalore: Christian Institute for the Study of Religion and Society, 1977), p. 3 n. 10.

4. Brunton, *Search*, pp. 159–60. Italics in original.

5. Ibid., pp. 299–300.

6. Ibid., p. 300, emphasis added.

7. Frank Whaling, "The Study of Religion in a Global Context," in *Contemporary Approaches to the Study of Religions*, ed. Frank Whaling (Amsterdam: Mouton, 1984), 1: 429.

8. Jean Holm, *The Study of Religions* (New York: Seabury Press, 1977), p. 6.

9. Ugo Bianchi, *The History of Religions* (Leiden: E. J. Brill, 1975), p. 32.

10. J. E. Barnhart, *The Study of Religion and its Meaning* (The Hague: Mouton, 1977), p. 17. Parentheses removed, emphasis added.

11. Bianchi, *History of Religions*, p. 30.

12. Ibid., p. 32. For some problems associated with the distinction between world religions and primitive religion see Holm, *Study of Religions*, pp. 3–7.

13. Wilfred Cantwell Smith, *Faith and Belief* (Princeton, NJ: Princeton University Press, 1979), p. 132.

14. Alfred Guillaume, trans. *The Life of Muhammad: A Translation of Ibn Isḥāq's "Sírat Rasúl Allah"* (London: Oxford University Press, 1955), p. 106. T. stands for Tabarí.

15. See Swami Saradananda, *Sri Ramakrishna: The Great Master*, trans. Swami Jagadananda (Madras: Sri Ramakrshna Math, 1952), p. 140.

16. Ibid. For background material see Christopher Isherwood, *Ramakrishna and His Disciples* (Calcutta: Advaita Ashrama, 1965), chap. 6.

17. For similar cases involving, however, the finding of a teacher see Paul Brunton, *A Search in Secret India* (New York: E. P. Dutton & Co., 1952), p. 242; Reginald Ray, "Na-ro-pa," in *The Encyclopedia of Religion*, ed. Mircea Eliade (New York: Macmillan, 1987), 1: 311.

18. The following remarks may be of some interest here: "While it is in this way possible with the help of the Ḳur'ān and Tradition to get an on the whole satisfactory picture of Muḥammad's development and his condition when prophesying, he himself gives in the Ḳur'ān quite a different interpretation of a peculiar theory which he apparently did not invent himself but adopted from others. The fundamental idea in it is the conception of a divine book existing in heaven, *al-kitāb*, a well guarded book, which only the pure may touch (lvi. 79), a well guarded tablet (lxxxv. 21 *sq*.), the mother of the book (xliii. 3 *sq*.), on honourable leaves, exalted and pure, by the hands of noble and pious scribes (lxxx. 13 *sqq*.). He himself did not read this book, as E. Meyer erroneously thinks, but it was communicated to him orally piece by piece, not in its original form but in an Arabic version intelligible to him and his countrymen (cf. xii. 1; xiii. 37; xx. 113; xxvi. 192 *sqq*.; xli. 3; xliv. 58, and especially xli. 44: 'If we had made it a Ḳur'ān in a foreign tongue, they would say: Why are its *āyāt* ['signs,' from the small sections of the text] not expounded intelligibly?, a foreign text and an Arab reader!'). In addition there is the fact that Muḥammad was aware that the complete contents of the book were not communicated to him, as he expressly states, e.g. of the stories of the prophets, not all of which were related to him (x. 78; iv. 164). He received the communications orally, Allāh rehearsing to him the substance of the separate sections (lxxv. 16 *sqq*. etc.), while in several passages it is stated more precisely that the revelations were communicated through the Spirit (xxvi. 192 sq.; xvi. 102; xiii. 52) or the Angel (xvi. 2; xv. 8; cf. liii. 5 *sqq*.; lxxxi. 23 *sqq*.); a late passage of the Madīna period (ii. 97) is even more precise in saying that they were communicated by Gabriel. References to visions are rare (e.g. the encouraging apparitions in Sūra viii. 43; xvliii. 27; the night journey must also have been a vision) and even in such cases the main thing is not what he heard (liii. 10; lxxxi. 19). These communications were the great miracle that was granted him, while he expressly and repeatedly says that the ability to perform miracles in the usual sense was denied to him (unlike Jesus)." H. A. R. Gibb and J. H. Kramers, eds., *Shorter Encyclopedia of Islam* (Leiden: E. J. Brill, 1953), p. 394.

19. W. Montgomery Watt, "Muḥammad," in Eliade, *Encyclopedia of Religion*, 10: 144.

20. This seems to be clearly the implication of the remark about Rāmakṛṣṇa made by J. N. Farquhar, *Modern Religious Movements in India* (Delhi: Munshiran Manoharlalm 1967), p. 189. For more on Kālī and Rāmakṛṣṇa, see Carl Olson, *The Mysterious Play of Kālī: An Interpretive Study of Ramakrishna* (Atlanta, GA: Scholars Press, 1990). Also see Jeffrey J. Kripal, *Kālī's Child: The Mystical and the Erotic in the Life and Teachings of Ramakrishna* (Chicago: University of Chicago Press, 1995).

21. John Hick, *Philosophy of Religion*, 4th ed. (Englewood Cliffs, NJ: Prentice-Hall, 1990), p. 91.

22. Ibid., p. 93.

23. Ibid.

24. Eric J. Sharpe, *Comparative Religion: A History*. 2d ed. (London: Duckworth, 1986), pp. 27–28.

25. Ibid.

26. Ibid., p. 31.

27. Ibid., pp. 31–32.

28. Marmaduke Pickthall, *The Meaning of the Glorious Koran* (London: George Allen & Unwin, 1948), p. 92.

29. W. Montgomery Watt, "Muḥammad," in Eliade, *The Encyclopedia of Religion*, 10: 143.

30. *The Holy Bible* (London: Collins' Clear-Type Press, n.d.) pp. 8–9. Authorized King James Version.

31. Paul Ricoeur, "The Symbol Gives Rise to Thought," in *Ways of Understanding Religion*, ed. Walter H. Capps (New York: Macmillan, 1972), p. 316.

32. S. Radhakrishnan, ed., *The Principal Upaniṣads* (London: George Allen & Unwin, 1953), p. 628.

33. Ibid.

34. Ibid.

35. Mircea Eliade, "Methodological Remarks on the Study of Religious Symbolism" in *The History of Religions: Essays in Methodology*, ed. Mircea Eliade and Joseph M. Kitagawa (Chicago: University of Chicago Press, 1959), p. 101.

36. Ibid. (emphasis added).

37. Ibid., p. 94.

38. Ibid., pp. 94–95.

39. Kees W. Bolle, *The Bhagavadgītā: A New Translation* (Berkeley and Los Angeles: University of California Press, 1979), p. 171. Barnett's explanation cited by Richard Gotshalk (*Bhagavad Gita: Translation and Commentary* [Delhi: Motilal Banarsidass, 1985], p. 203) is helpful here: "The sacred Fig-tree (see X. 26) typifies the eternal *saṁsāra*, the physical existence in which souls are bound to successive bodies. Its upper roots, which rise above the level of the earth, typify *avyakta*, primal matter; its branches typify *Buddhi*, *Ahaṁkāra*, the subtle elements, and other forms of physical being evolved from primal matter; they spread upward and downward, that is, they fill the whole of conditioned life. From them issue as leaves the Vedas, the divine rules for the

works of the world (ii. 42, etc.), and as fruits issue works. The general influence of the latter informing a sequence of fetters to the Soul (passion, hate, etc.), and thus maintaining physical being, is typified by the lower roots clinging deep in the earth."

40. W. Douglas P. Hill, *The Bhagavadgītā*, 2nd abridged ed. (London: University Press, 1966), p. 184.

41. Ibid., pp. 184–85.

42. R. C. Zaehner, *The Bhagavad-Gītā* (Oxford: Clarendon Press, 1969), p. 362, emphasis added. The ladder plays an important role in the shamanic versions of the Cosmic Tree.

43. Hill, *Bhagavadgītā*, p. 185 n. 1. For more on this, see Arvind Sharma, "The Appropriateness of Aśvattha Tree as a Symbol of Saṁsāra," *Aryan Path* 47, no. 4 (1976): 166–69. Also see J. G. Arapura, "The Upside Down Tree of the Bhagavadgītā Ch. XV," *Numen* 22 (1975): 131–44. The inverted tree has also been taken by some scholars as a representation of the nervous system, an imaginative but perhaps implausible suggestion; see M. Hiriyanna, *Reviews* (Mysore: Kavyalaya Publishers, 1970), p. 36.

Chapter 6

1. Wilfred Cantwell Smith, *Towards a World Theology* (Philadelphia: Westminster Press, 1981), p. 90.

2. *The Collected Works of Mahatma Gandhi* (New Delhi: Publications Division of the Government of India, 1969), 32: 588.

3. As cited in A. L. Basham, *The Wonder That Was India* (New York: Grove Press, 1954), p. 275, emphasis added.

4. Ibid., p. 276.

5. Wilfred Cantwell Smith, *The Faith of Other Men* (New York: Harper Torchbook, 1963), p. 6.

6. P. V. Kane, *History of Dharmaśāstra* (Poona: Bhandarkar Oriental Research Institute, 1962), vol. 5 (pt. 2), p. 1009 n. 1644a; M. Hiriyanna, *Outlines of Indian Philosophy* (London: George Allen & Unwin, 1932), p. 312–13; S. Radhakrishnan, *Indian Philosophy* (London: George Allen & Unwin, 1962), 2: 877 n. 1.

7. Smith, *Towards a World Theology*, p. 103.

8. Smith, *Faith of Other Men*, p. 49.

9. Wilfred Cantwell Smith, *Questions of Religious Truth* (New York: Scribner, 1967), p. 123.

10. The theological component of Smith's method has drawn fire from scholars. Patrick Olivelle's remarks made in the course of reviewing Tom Coburn's book *Devī-Māhātmya: The Crystallization of the Goddess Tradition* (Delhi: Motilal Banarsidass, 1984) are relevant here: "One aspect, however, of Coburn's method, which is based on the works of W. C. Smith, is cause for concern. He states that 'we must proceed with care, for while critical historical study is not

intrinsically antipathetic to the concerns of faith, the point at which the former begins to encroach upon the latter may vary from individual to individual' [p. 40], and that 'The conclusions emerging from this investigation . . . need not . . . violate the Puranic spirit, nor be destructive of individual faith' [p. 45]. That scholars, be they historians or social-anthropologists, have a duty to respect the people they study and not to offend their sensibilities needlessly, is obvious. That scholars should conduct their studies in ways that would not undermine the beliefs or practices of those people compromises scholarly investigation. It is not the business of scholars to discover how individual faith and the conclusions of scholarship can be reconciled, as it is not the duty of scientists to reconcile the discoveries of science with religious beliefs. These endeavors are best left in the hands of theologians of each faith; indeed, some religious people may not even feel the need to bring about such reconciliations. Another remark of Coburn is even more disturbing: 'That the Purāṇas have developed from an early nucleus to their present extent is historically verifiable, according to academic criteria. Whether that nucleus was of human or divine origin is obviously beyond the range of these criteria . . . It is a matter of personal faith. Before it, academic inquiry must remain silent' (38). This silence—or is it tacit acceptance?—strikes at the very foundation of scholarly inquiry, which presupposes the human origin of the objects of that inquiry, be they texts, beliefs, or institutions. Furthermore, personal faith does not assert that only the nucleus of a sacred text is of divine origin; it dictates that the text is entirely sacred and, therefore, that the entire text has a divine origin. Preserving just a nucleus of sacrality, it appears to me, is a greater offense to religious faith than letting the faithful deal with such matters on their own. A quote from W. C. Smith used by Coburn to show that historical study is compatible with faith, illustrates this problem well: 'history is not a closed system, since as agent within it stands man, his spirit in some degree open to the transcendent' [pp. 43–44]. This is clearly a theological assertion and not the conclusion of scholarship, what historical or other evidence is there to support either the existence of a 'transcendent' or of the openness of the human spirit to it? Religions have gods, goddesses, and similar divine beings; they do not have a 'transcendent.' This type of generic religion is not good scholarship. It is probably not even good theology." *Journal of the American Oriental Society* 107, no. 4 (October–December 1987), p. 774.

11. Wayne Proudfoot, *Religious Experience* (Berkeley and Los Angeles: University of California Press, 1985), p. 199.

12. Ibid., pp. 191–93.

13. Wilfred Cantwell Smith, "Comparative Religion: Whither—And Why?" in *The History of Religions: Essays in Methodology,* ed. Mircea Eliade and Joseph M. Kitagawa (Chicago: University of Chicago Press, 1959), p. 39 n. 17.

14. Ibid., p. 43.

15. See Bryan Rennie, ed., *Changing Religious Worlds: The Meaning and End of Mircea Eliade* (Albany: State University of New York Press, 2001); Douglas Allen, *Structure and Creativity in Religion: Hermeneutics in Mircea Eliade's Phenomenology and New Directions* (The Hague: Mouton, 1978).

16. Mircea Eliade preferred to regard himself as a hermeneut; personal communication from Professor Frederick J. Streng.

17. Frank Whaling, ed., *Contemporary Approaches to the Study of Religion* (Amsterdam: Mouton, 1984), 1: 215–16.

18. Franklin Edgerton, trans., *The Bhagavadgītā* (Cambridge, MA: Harvard University Press, 1952), pt. 1, pp. 81, 83, emphases added.

19. Mircea Eliade, *The Two and the One*, trans. J. M. Cohen (London: Harvill Press, 1962), chap. 1.

20. Mircea Eliade, *Birth and Rebirth*, trans. Willard R. Trask (New York: Harper & Brothers, 1958).

21. Johannes Maringer, *Gods of Prehistoric Men*, ed. and trans. Mary Elford (New York: Alfred A. Knopf, 1960), pp. 102–3.

22. Quoted by Ursula King, "Historical and Phenomenological Approaches," in Whaling, *Contemporary Approaches*, 1: 113.

23. Tamaru Noriyoshi, "Some Reflections on Contemporary Theories of Religion," *Japanese Journal of Religious Studies* 2, no. 1 (March 1976): 93.

24. R. C. Zaehner, "Conclusion," in *The Concise Encyclopedia of Living Faiths*, ed. R. C. Zaehner (Boston: Beacon Press, 1967), p. 416.

25. Ibid. Italics added.

26. Mircea Eliade, *The Sacred and the Profane*, trans. Willard R. Trask (New York: Harcourt, Brace & Co., 1959), p. 97, emphasis added.

27. M. Hiriyanna, *The Essentials of Indian Philosophy* (London: Allen & Unwin, 1949), p. 189.

28. Frank Whaling, "Comparative Approaches," in Whaling, *Contemporary Approaches to the Study of Religion*, 1: 218–19.

29. Reynold A. Nicholson, *The Mystics of Islam* (London: Routledge and Kegan Paul, 1963), pp. 91–92.

30. John Alden Williams, ed., *Islam* (New York: George Braziller, 1962), p. 150.

Chapter 7

1. The point has more force than may be obvious at first sight. In earlier times when "historia" was contrasted with "mythos," it is easy to see how history stood for facts as opposed to what was story. This understanding is reflected even in English usage perhaps up to the eighteenth century, before science became an independent discipline. Thus, as late as the time of Newton, geology could be referred to as natural history. (I am indebted for this last point to Adrian Snodgrass.)

2. See Peter Singer, *Hegel* (Oxford: Oxford University Press, 1983), passim.

3. Robert Ackerman, "James G. Frazer (1854–1941)" in *The Encyclopedia of Religion*, ed. Mircea Eliade (New York: Macmillan, 1987), 5: 416.

4. Jan de Vries, *The Study of Religion: A Historical Approach*, trans. Kees Bolle (New York: Harcourt, Brace & World., 1967), p. 62.

5. J. McBride Sterret, *Studies in Hegel's Philosophy of Religion* (London: D. Appleton and Company, 1890). Similar procedures have been adopted elsewhere as well, for instance in India. "There have been historians of Indian philosophy in our country who looked upon India's philosophic thought as a continuity in which it progressed rationally from one conception to another, where systems succeeded each other in intelligible order until it culminated in their own thought. All that was past was a progress towards their own present thinking. Mādhava's *Sarvadarśanasaṁgraha* is a well-known instance of the treatment of the history of thought as a continuous progress of Advaita Vedānta. In the West, Hegel related the past history of thought as a collection of errors over and against which stood out of his own idealism of truth. Intellectual unselfishness or humility is the mother of all writing, even though that writing may relate to the history of philosophy." K. M. Munshi and R. R. Diwakar, eds., *Radhakrishnan Reader: An Anthology* (Bombay: Bharatiya Vidya Bhavan, 1969), p. 25.

6. Wilfred Cantwell Smith, *On Understanding Islam: Selected Studies* (The Hague: Mouton, 1981), p. 288.

7. Hendrik Kraemer, *World Religions and World Cultures, The Coming Dialogue* (London: Lutterworth Press, 1960); J. N. Farquhar, *The Crown of Hinduism* (London: Oxford University Press, 1913).

8. Walter G. Neeval, Jr. "The Transformation of Sri Ramakrishna," in *Hinduism: New Essays in the History of Religions*, ed. Bardwell L. Smith (Leiden: E. J. Brill, 1976), p. 96.

9. How easy it is to move from reciprocal illumination between traditions to the hermeneutics of tradition may be demonstrated here. If it is pointed out that revelation in Judaism has been extended more in the temporal direction and in Islam in the spatial direction, then the time-span contrast is still reciprocally illuminating. But if this perspective is carried over into Hinduism, it can provide a clue for the hermeneutics of the tradition. It could be suggested that, given its primeval revelation, Hinduism has so far functioned in the temporal dimension by ensuring its survival and persistence and that it now stands poised to embrace the spatial dimension and is ready to spread its universalizing message over the globe, freed from its ethnic contingency.

10. *Talks with Sri Ramana Maharshi*, 3 vols. in one (Tiruvannamalai: Sri Ramanasramam, 1984, p. 318, emphasis added). The relationship between Girish Chandra Ghosh and Rāmakṛṣṇa Paramahaṁsa seems to confirm this interpretation; see Christopher Isherwood, *Ramakrishna and His Disciples* (Calcutta: Advaita Ashrama, 1965), pp. 253–54. Also see p. 200.

11. This surrender is very different from the obedience enjoined in 2 Corinthians, or that the wife should be "listening" in relation to the husband as part of the five cardinal relationships in Confucianism.

12. The context provides the occasion for offering a reflection in the history of religions. Religions have often been accused, perhaps not unjustly, of perpetuating exploitation and oppression by condoning or even actively encouraging practices like slavery, subjection of women, and so on. Is one not entitled to ask in good conscience, however, if instead of always perpetuating

oppressive social situations it was at least sometimes the case that when for various historical, political, or socioeconomic reasons the religions were confronted with desperate situations, they did their best to confer on them a redemptive role? May it not be that it is not so much the case that women were subjugated by religions but that the religions, finding them in a subjugated condition, sought to bring their situation within the range of salvation by offering a genuinely spiritual interpretation of their situation? After all, given the Christian doctrine of predetermination and a particular understanding of the doctrine of karma, this may be all that could probably be accomplished by the respective religions despite all goodwill.

13. Wilfred Cantwell Smith, *Towards a World Theology* (Philadelphia: Westminster Press, 1981), p. 7.

14. *The Collected Works of Mahatma Gandhi* (New Delhi: Publications Division of the Government of India, 1969), 32: 4: "Three persons have influenced me deeply, Tolstoy, Ruskin and Raychandbhai: Tolstoy through one of his books and through a little correspondence with him, Ruskin through one book of his, *Unto the Last*—which in Gujarati I have called Sarvodaya,—and Raychandbhai through intimate personal contact." The book by Tolstoy, not mentioned by name here, is *The Kingdom of God is Within You* (see Robert Payne, *The Life and Death of Mahatma Ghandi* [New York: E. P. Dutton & Co., 1969], pp. 81, 213–14, 217–18, etc.). Gandhi also named his farm in South Africa after Tolstoy (ibid., pp. 230ff.).

15. Payne, *Life and Death of Mahatma Gandhi*, p. 239.

16. Ibid., pp. 239–40.

17. Ibid., p. 240.

18. Mahābhārata, 11.5–6. (critical edition).

19. A. L. Basham cites it as a typical example of "the Jain outlook" as follows: "A traveller was journeying through a dense and wild forest when he encountered a mad elephant which charged him with upraised trunk. As he turned to flee, a terrible demoness with a naked sword in her hand appeared before him and barred his path. There was a great tree near the track, and he ran up to it, hoping to find safety in its branches, but he could find no foothold in its smooth trunk. His only refuge was an old well, covered with grass and weeds, at the foot of the tree, and into this he leapt. As he fell he managed to catch hold of a clump of reeds which grew from the wall, and there he hung, midway between the mouth of the well and its bottom. Looking down, he saw that the bottom did not contain water, but was surrounded by snakes, which hissed at him as he hung above them. In their midst was a mighty python, its mouth agape, waiting to catch him when he fell. Raising his head again, the man saw on the clump of reeds two mice, one white and the other black, busily gnawing away at the roots. Meanwhile the wild elephant ran up to the well, and, enraged at losing its victim, began charging at the trunk of the tree. Thus he dislodged a honeycomb which hung from a branch above the well, and it fell upon the man hanging there so precariously. Angry bees swarmed round his head and tormented him with their stings. But one drop of honey fell on his brow, rolled down his face and reached his lips. Immediately he forgot

his peril and thought of nothing more than of obtaining another drop of honey.

The main purpose of this story is quite obvious, but the Jain finds a parallel to each of the many horrors which beset the unfortunate traveller. The man, of course, is the soul, and his journey through the forest is *saṁsāra*. The elephant represents death; the demoness, old age. The tree is the way to salvation, which the ordinary man cannot climb. The well is human life, the snakes are passions, the python is hell. The tuft of reed is man's allotted span, and the black and white mice are the dark and bright halves of the month. The bees are diseases and troubles, while the honey, of course, represents the trivial pleasures of our earthly existence (*Samaraicca-Kahā*, ii. 55–80). Whether or not he taste a few more drops of honey, at last the mice will do their work and the man will fall down, for the python of hell must sooner or later disgorge the man and return him to the forest of the world, only to suffer further terrors of a like kind." A. L. Basham, "Jainism," in *The Concise Encyclopedia of Living Faiths*, ed. R. C. Zaehner (Boston: Beacon Press, 1959), p. 263. For the original story in translation see Wm. Theodore de Bary, et al., *Sources of Indian Tradition* (New York: Columbia University Press, 1958), pp. 56–58.

20. Smith, *Towards a World Theology*, pp. 9–196.

21. Ibid., p. 11: "We should seem then to have come full circle: from India to India via Sogdiana, Baghdad, Georgia, Mt. Athos, Kiev, Geneva, London and Durban. The circle does not stop spinning, however. Gandhi's most important twentieth-century disciple, it has been suggested, is perhaps Martin Luther King, whose non-violence both as a formulated ideal and as a deep character orientation he learned in substantial part from Gandhi."

22. Payne, *Life and Death of Mahatma Gandhi*, p. 239.

23. Quoted by Smith, *Towards a World Theology*, p. 7. It is interesting to be reminded of the Eliadean thesis that myth is sacred fact. It is apparent, however, that in the case of Smith, myth here represents an existential, fideistic fact, while for Eliade myth represents a ritual and celestial fact.

Chapter 8

1. Jacques Waardenburg, *Classical Approaches to the Study of Religion* (The Hague: Mouton, 1973), 1: 641.

2. W. Brede Kristensen, *The Meaning of Religion*, trans. John B. Carman (The Hague: Martinus Nijhoff, 1960), pp. 1–9.

3. Eric J. Sharpe, *Comparative Religion: A History*, 2d ed. (London: Duckworth, 1986), p. 249.

4. Ibid., p. 237.

5. George Widengren, "An Introduction to the Phenomenology of Religion" in *Ways of Understanding Religion*, ed. Walter H. Capps (New York: Macmillan, 1972), p. 149.

6. G. van der Leeuw, *Religion in Essence and Manifestation*, trans. J. E. Turner (New York: Harper & Row, 1963), 2: 672.

7. Ibid., p. 673.

8. Ibid., 1: 107.

9. Ibid., 1: 113.

10. Ronald M. Green, "Morality and Religion" in *The Encyclopedia of Religion*, ed. Mircea Eliade (New York: Macmillan, 1987), 10: 94.

11. Widengren, "Introduction," p. 144.

12. Kenneth K. S. Ch'en, *Buddhism: The Light of Asia* (New York: Woodbury, 1968), p. 148.

13. See Bardwell L. Smith, ed., *The Two Wheels of Dhamma* (Chambersburg, PA: American Academy of Religion, 1972).

14. See Henry Clarke Warren, *Buddhism in Translations* (Cambridge, MA: Harvard University Press, 1915), pp. 39, 41, 53, 52, 100–1.

15. A. Foucher, *The Life of the Buddha According to the Ancient Texts and Monuments of India*, trans. Simone Bvangier Boar (abridged) (Middletown, CT: Wesleyan University Press, 1963), p. 41.

16. Richard H. Robinson and Willard L. Johnson, *The Buddhist Religion: A Historical Introduction* (Belmont, CA: Wadsworth Publishing Company, 1982), p. 162.

17. Ibid., p. 163. Also see Ch'en, *Buddhism*, pp. 138–39.

18. Mahmoud A. Ayoub, "The Islamic Tradition," in *World Religions: Western Traditions*, ed. Willard G. Oxtoby, 2d ed. (Toronto: Oxford University Press, 2002), p. 168.

19. See Willard Cantwell Smith, *On Understanding Islam: Selected Studies* (The Hague: Mouton, 1981), chap. 12, for the process that may be involved.

20. K. A. Nilakanta Sastri, *A History of South India from Prehistoric Times to the Fall of Vijayanagar*, 3d ed. (London: Oxford University Press, 1966), pp. 271–72.

21. Frank Whaling, ed., *Contemporary Approaches to the Study of Religion* (Amsterdam: Mouton, 1984), 1: 219.

Chapter 9

1. See Sakuntala Narasimhan, *Sati: Widow Burning in India* (New York: Doubleday, 1990), "A Note by the Author," n.p.

2. There is a considerable and growing mass of literature on the subject, which may be consulted with profit. Some of the more recent publications include: Lata Mani, *Contentious Traditions: The Debate on Satī in Colonial India* (Berkeley and Los Angeles: University of California Press, 1998); and Catherine Weinberger-Thomas, *Ashes of Immortality: Widow Burning In India*, trans. Jeffrey Mehlman and David Gordon White (Chicago: University of Chicago Press, 1999).

3. *Good News Bible* (Toronto: Canadian Bible Society, 1976), New Testament, p. 261.

4. A. L. Basham, *The Wonder That Was India*, (New York: Grove Press, 1954), pp. 240–41.

5. Robert Payne, *The Life and Death of Mahatma Gandhi* (New York: E. P. Dutton & Co., 1969), p. 34.

6. *Good News Bible*, New Testament, p. 92, emphasis added.

7. Basham, *Wonder That Was India*, p. 239.

8. P. V. Kane, *History of Dharmaśāstra* (Poona: Bhandarkar Oriental Research Institute, 1974), vol. 2, pt. 1, pp. 165–67.

9. S. Radhakrishnan, ed., *The Principal Upaniṣads* (London: George Allen & Unwin, 1953), pp. 466–67.

10. *Good News Bible*, New Testament, p. 108, emphasis added.

11. Heinrich Zimmer, *Philosophies of India*, ed. Joseph Campbell (New York: Pantheon Books, 1951), p. 167.

12. *Good News Bible*, New Testament, p. 129, emphasis added.

13. *Talks with Sri Ramana Maharshi* (Tiruvannamalai: Sri Ramanasramam, 1984), p. 423.

14. K. N. Devaraja, *Hinduism and Christianity* (New York: Asia Publishing House, 1969), p. 99.

15. Mahadev Desai, trans., *Gandhi's Autobiography* (Washington, DC: Public Affairs Press, 1948), p. 155.

16. Ibid., pp. 155–56.

17. Ibid., p. 156.

18. Devaraja, *Hinduism and Christianity*, p. 80.

19. R. C. Zaehner, *Hindu Scriptures* (New York: Dutton, 1966), p. 112.

20. R. C. Zaehner, ed., *The Concise Encyclopedia of Living Faiths* (Boston: Beacon Press, 1959), p. 415; S. Radhakrishnan, *Brahma Sūtra: The Philosophy of Spiritual Life* (London: George Allen & Unwin, 1960), p. 185ff.

21. Ramchandra Gandhi, *I Am Thou* (Poona: Indian Philosophical Quarterly Publications No. 8, 1984), pp. 40–45.

22. John B. Noss, *Man's Religion*, 3rd ed. (New York: Macmillan, 1963), p. 616.

23. Ibid.

24. Ibid., note.

25. A. L. Basham, *The Origins and Development of Classical Hinduism*, ed. Kenneth G. Zysk (Boston: Beacon Press, 1989), pp. 43–44.

26. Radhakrishnan, *The Principal Upaniṣads*, p. 179, emphasis added.

27. Noss, *Men's Religion*, p. 629.

28. Ibid.

29. Ibid., p. 634.

30. Ibid., p. 640.

31. Mahatma Gandhi, *Hindu Dharma*, ed. Bharatan Kumarappa (Ahmedabad: Navajivan Press, 1950), pp. 263–64.

32. K. Satchidananda Murty, *Rashtriya Sri Shankaracharya Jayanti Mahotsava: Inauguration Address* (New Delhi: Vigyan Bhavan, 1989), pp. 6–7.

33. Ibid., p. 7.

34. Ibid., p. 8.

35. J. G. Davies, "Christianity: The Early Church," in Zaehner, *The Concise Encyclopedia of Living Faiths*, pp. 54–55.

36. Basham, *Origin and Development of Classical Hinduism*, p. 321.

37. See D. Flusser, "Salvation Present and Future," *Numen* 16, no. 2 (1969): 139–55; but also see Uri Wernik, "Frustrated Beliefs and Early Christianity," *Numen* 22, no. 2 (1975): 96–130.

38. Basham, *The Wonder That Was India*, p. 321.

39. Michel Meslin, "Baptism," in *The Encyclopedia of Religion*, ed. Mircea Eliade (New York: Macmillan, 1987), 2: 61.

40. Swami Nikhilananda, trans., *The Gospel of Sri Ramakrishna* (New York: Ramakrishna-Vivekananda Center, 1952), p. 674.

41. Devaraja, *Hinduism and Christianity*, p. 74.

42. A. Devaraja Mudalier, *Gems from Bhagavan* (Tiruvannamalai: Sri Ramanasramam, 1978), p. 15.

Chapter 10

1. T. M. P. Madadevan, *Outlines of Hinduism* (Bombay: Chetana, 1971), p. 141. Italics in the original. But also see S. Radhakrishnan, *The Hindu View of Life* (New York: Macmillan, 1927), p. 48.

2. Edward J. Thomas, *The History of Buddhist Thought* (New York: Barnes & Noble, 1971), p. 236. Whether the one fact can be considered an abstraction will be disputed by some Advaitins (see M. Hiriyanna, *The Essentials of Indian Philosophy* [London: George Allen & Unwin, 1948], p. 162).

3. S. Radhakrishnan, *The Hindu View of Life* (New Delhi: Harper Collins Publishers India Put, 1993), p. 34.

4. Ibid., p. 35.

5. K. Satchidananda Murty, *Revelation and Reason in Advaita Vedānta* (New York: Columbia University Press, 1959), p. 219.

6. M. Hiriyanna, *The Essentials of Indian Philosophy* (London: George Allen & Unwin, 1949), p. 173.

7. J. L. Brockington, *The Sacred Thread* (Edinburgh: Edinburgh University Press, 1981), p. 7.

8. Alain Danielou, *Hindu Polytheism* (New York: Pantheon Books, 1964).

9. Radkakrishnan, *Hindu View of Life*, p. 40.

10. Ibid., p. 30.

11. S. Radhakrishnan, *The Brahma Sūtra: The Philosophy of Spiritual Life* (London: George Allen & Unwin, 1960), p. 156.

Chapter 11

1. See R. C. Zaehner, ed., *The Concise Encyclopedia of Living Faiths* (Boston: Beacon Press, 1959), pp. 267, 365.

2. G. P. Malalasekera, ed., *Encyclopedia of Buddhism* (Colombo: Government of Ceylon, 1966), 2: 464.

3. Lama Anagarika Govinda, *The Psychological Attitude of Early Buddhist Philosophy* (London: Rider & Company, 1961), p. 43.

4. Malalasekera, *Encyclopedia of Buddhism*, p. 465 n. 2.

5. Henry Clarke Warren, *Buddhism in Translations* (New York: Atheneum, 1970), p. 122.

6. Ibid., p. 119.

7. Ibid., pp. 120–21.

8. Edward Conze, *Buddhism: Its Essence and Development* (New York: Harper & Brothers, 1959), p. 138. In this context it may also be useful to consider the following comment by Prof. Hiriyanna: "Buddha taught only what is necessary for overcoming evil whose prevalence is, according to him, the chief characteristic of life. The principle, which guided him in his numerous discourses, is clearly shown by the following story related in one of the Suttas. Once when sitting under a śimśupa tree, Buddha took a few of its leaves in his hand and asked his disciples that had assembled there to tell him whether they were all the śimśupa leaves or whether there were more on the tree. When they replied that there were surely many more, he said: 'As surely do I know more than what I have told you.' But he did not dwell upon all that he knew, since he saw no practical utility in doing so. It would on the contrary, he thought, only make his hearers idly suspicious and delay their setting about the task of exterminating evil. 'And wherefore, my disciplines, have I not told you that? Because, my disciples, it brings you no profit, it does not conduce to progress in holiness, because it does not lead to the turning from the earthly, to the subjection of all desire, to illumination, to Nirvana; therefore have I not declared it unto you.' Deliverance from pain and evil was his one concern and he neither found time nor need to unravel metaphysical subtleties. He was thus eminently practical in his teaching, 'Philosophy purifies none,' he said, 'peace alone does.' It is sometimes maintained that Buddha was an agnostic and his silence on matters commonly referred to by other religious teachers is explained as due to a lack of certainty in his knowledge of ultimate things. But it is forgotten that to so interpret the teaching of Buddha is to throw doubt upon his spiritual sincerity. 'If he did not know the truth, he would not have considered himself to be a Buddha or the enlightened.' " *Outlines of Indian Philosophy* (London: George Allen & Unwin, 1932), pp. 137–38. The anecdote of the handful of leaves is also referred to by Walpola Sri Rahula, *What the Buddha Taught* (New York: Grove Press, 1974), p. 12.

9. Wm. Theodore de Bary et al., eds., *Sources of Chinese Tradition* (New York: Columbia University Press, 1960), 1: 29–30.

10. Ibid.

11. James Legge, *The Life and Teachings of Confucius* (London: Trübner, 1895), p. 101.

12. H. A. Giles, *History of Chinese Literature* (London: Heinemann, 1901), p. 69.

13. One must, however, as in the case of the Buddha, take another somewhat corrective view into account. As John B. Noss has remarked: "His position in matters of faith was this: whatever seemed contrary to common

sense in popular tradition, and whatever did not serve any discoverable social purpose, he regarded coldly. In his teaching, he avoided discussing such subjects as prodigies, feats of strength, crime, and the supernatural, apparently because he did not wish to spend time discussing perturbing exceptions to human and natural law. 'Absorption in the study of the supernatural is most harmful,' he said, not that he disbelieved the supernatural, but that it would not do to let the pressing concerns of human welfare suffer neglect. It is from this point of view that we should weigh two sayings of his that have perhaps received overmuch attention. His disciple Tzu-yu asked him about one's duty to the spirits of the dead. He replied: 'Before we are able to do our duty by the living, how can we do it by the spirits of the dead?' He defined what he believed was the proper attitude with great exactness thus: 'To devote oneself earnestly to one's duty to humanity, and, while respecting the spirits, to keep aloof from them, may be called wisdom.'

"Yet the effect of his desire to support whatever made for unity in the state and harmony in the home was that he went as far as he should in observing the rites and ceremonies of his time. One might even hazard the opinion with Dr. Lin Yutang, that 'Confucius would undoubtedly have been a High Churchman,' could he have been a Christian. Perhaps his interest in the stabilizing moral effect of the old inherited rituals was strengthened by his own aesthetic satisfaction in them. At any rate, at the village exorcisms he put on court dress and stood on the east steps. He took seriously the ceremonial bath before religious worship. When one of his disciples (Tzu Kung) suggested doing away with the sheep offering at the new moon, he disagreed, saying: 'Tzu you love sheep; I love the ceremony!' On going into the Great Temple he asked about everything. This once brought from a bystander the criticism that he knew shockingly little about the rites; but when he heard this, he said that asking about everything was part of the rite. In offering sacrifices to ancestors, he behaved as if they were physically present; and this was also his attitude toward the other spirits to whom sacrifices were made. He felt it his duty to participate in the sacrifice actively, saying: 'For me, to take no part in the sacrifice is the same as not sacrificing.' Asked the meaning of the Grand Sacrifice to the Imperial Ancestors, he said: 'I do not know. He who knew its meaning would find it as easy to govern the Empire as to look upon this'—pointing to his palm." *Man's Religion* (New York: Macmillan, 1980), pp. 278–79.

14. Govinda, *Psychological Attitude*, pp. 109–11.

15. De Bary et al., *Sources of Chinese Tradition*, p. 30.

16. Ibid., pp. 117–21; Zaehner, *Concise Encyclopedia*, p. 223, and passim.

17. It has been noted, though, that in the case of both of them, the absence of a metaphysical *aim* did not involve a *total* absence of a metaphysical view like belief in karma, t'ien, and so on.

18. Analects 15/28, quoted in S. Radhakrishnan and P. T. Raju, eds., *The Concepts of Man* (Lincoln, NE: Johnson Publishing Co., 1972), p. 172.

19. Quoted in Conze, *Buddhism*, p. 97.

20. Ṛg Veda 10.90.

21. Genesis 2:21–23.

22. Sometimes, perhaps even often, this differentiation results in discrimination—and in voices of protest against it. From this point of view the simultaneity of the feminist movement and the worldwide argument between the haves and the have-nots is not without significance.

23. Whereas the distinction between men and women is biologically stable (at least so one hopes), the distinction between classes is sociologically variable. Thus Dumézil speaks of three classes; the Vedas of the four *varṇas;* and the Marxists of just two—the bourgeoisie and the proletariat.

24. This differentiation, of course, may apply to a given society, or to mankind as a whole.

25. Louis Renou, ed., *Hinduism* (New York: George Braziller, 1962), p. 65.

26. Ibid.

27. Genesis 2:21–23 (Authorized Version).

28. Ibid.

29. The Puruṣasūkta also mentions the emergence of the "female counterpart of the male principle, Puruṣa" as Virāj in 10.5 but not from any part thereof. Renou, *Hinduism*, p. 64–65.

30. Michael Fishbane, "Eve," in *The Encyclopedia of Religion*, ed. Mircea Eliade (New York: Macmillan, 1987), 5: 199.

31. See Nalinaksha Dutt, *Aspects of Mahāyāna Buddhism and Its Relation to Hīnayāna* (London: Luzac & Co., 1930), pp. 96–128.

32. See A. L. Basham, *The Wonder That Was India* (New York: Hawthorn Books, 1963), p. 279.

33. T. M. P. Mahadevan, *The Philosophy of Advaita* (London: Luzac & Co., 1938), p. 195.

34. Basham, *Wonder That Was India*, p. 279.

35. Mahadevan, *Philosophy of Advaita*, p. 195. Somewhat curiously, early Western students of Vedānta seem to speak of two bodies only. "At the time of death the organs of knowledge are not supposed to be destroyed absolutely, but while there is another life before us, they are reduced to a seminal or potential form only, and though the outward organs themselves will decay, their potential or powers remain, dwelling in what is called the Sukshma-Sarira, the subtle body, the body that migrates from birth to birth and becomes again and again a Sthula-Sarira, a material body. But when real freedom has once been obtained, this Sukshma-Sarira also vanishes and there remains the Atman only, or Brahman as he was and always will be. The form assumed by the body in every new existence is determined by the deeds and thoughts during former existences: it is still, so to say, under the law of causality." F. Max Müller, *Ramakrishna: His Life and Sayings* (Bombay: Longmans, Green and Co., 1898), p. 88.

36. See Dutt, *Aspects of Mahāyāna Buddhism*, passim.

37. Wm. Theodore de Bary, ed., *Sources of Indian Tradition* (New York: Columbia University Press, 1958), p. 157.

38. Robert Lawson Slater, *World Religions and World Community* (New York: Columbia University Press, 1963), p. 254.

39. Arthur Osborne, ed., *The Teachings of Bhagavan Sri Ramana Maharshi in His Own Words* (Tiruvannamalai: Sri Ramanasramam, 1971), pp. 113–15, emphasis added.

40. Arthur Waley, *The Way and Its Power* (New York: Grove Press, 1958), p. 152.

41. Ibid., p. 173.

42. Ibid., p. 185.

43. Ibid., p. 164.

44. Witter Brynner, *Tao Te Ching—The Way of Life According to Lao Tzu* (New York: John Day, 1944).

45. Waley, *Way and Its Power*, p. 177 n. 4.

46. Ibid., n. 2.

47. Ibid., p. 177.

48. Walpola Rahula, *What the Buddha Taught* (New York: Grove Press, 1974), p. 48.

49. See Śaṅkara's commentary on Bhagavadgītā 13.12 and the opening verses of the Tao Te Ching.

50. Waley, *Way and Its Power*, p. 174. Interestingly the *ātman*, identified with Brahman in Advaita, is also called *catuṣpāt* (Māṇḍūkya Upaniṣad 2) or as consisting of four "parts."

51. *Talks with Sri Ramana Maharshi* (Tiruvannamalai: Sri Ramanasramam, 1984), p. 485. *Swaraj* = self-rule, as representing Indian aspiration for political liberty.

52. Quoted by Mervyn Sprung, trans., *Lucid Exposition of the Middle Way: The Essential Chapters of the Prasannapadā of Candrakīrti* (Boulder, CO: Prajna Press, 1979), pp. 262–83.

53. Quoted in Edward Conze, ed., *Buddhist Texts Through the Ages* (New York: Philosophical Library, 1957), p. 279.

54. Richard H. Robinson, *Early Mādhyamika in India and China* (Madison: University of Wisconsin Press, 1967), p. 153.

55. Ibid., p. 148.

56. Personal communication.

57. Personal communication.

58. Personal communication.

Chapter 12

1. Reynold A. Nicholson, *The Mystics of Islam* (London: Routledge and Kegan Paul, 1963), p. 132.

2. *Talks with Sri Ramana Maharshi* (Triuvannamalai: Sri Ramanasramam, 1984), pp. 577–78.

3. Nicholson, *Mystics of Islam*, p. 132.

4. Ibid., p. 133.

5. *Talks with Sri Ramana Maharshi*, p. 17.

6. J. G. Davies, "Christianity: The Early Church," in *The Concise Encyclopedia of Living Faiths,* ed. R. C. Zaehner (Boston: Beacon Press, 1959), p. 54.

7. I am indebted to Ian Henderson for these observations. The responsibility for their contextualization, however, is mine.

8. Edward J. Thomas, *The Life of the Buddha in Legend and History* (London: Routledge & Kegan Paul, 1949), p. 69.

9. James Legge, *The Life and Teachings of Confucius,* 3rd ed. (London: N. Trübner & Co., 1872), p. 75.

10. Ibid., emphasis added.

11. Majjhima Nikāya 1.332; see James W. Boyd, *Satan and Māra: Christian and Buddhist Symbols of Evil* (Leiden: E. J. Brill, 1975), p. 94.

12. Bimala Churn Law, *Concepts of Buddhism* (Leiden: Kern Institute, 1937), p. 93.

13. E. Conze, *Buddhism: Its Essence and Development* (New York: Harper & Brothers, 1951), p. 197–98.

14. E. J. Thomas, *Life of the Buddha,* p. 72.

15. Ibid., p. 75.

16. Ibid., p. 73. It is also worth noting here that the presence of Satan in the case of Luther plays the same role as the absence of Māra for Buddha, though their discomfiture is involved in both cases.

17. Thomas, *Life of the Buddha,* pp. 147–48.

18. Ibid., p. 146.

19. Revised Standard Version (1957).

20. Thomas, *Life of the Buddha,* pp. 68–70.

21. See M. K. Gandhi, *In Search of the Supreme,* ed. V. B. Kher (Ahmedabad: Navajivan Publishing House, 1961), 1: 121, emphasis added. For more recent work on Satan, see Elaine Pagels, *The Origin of Satan* (New York: Random House, 1995).

22. Gandhi, *In Search of the Supreme,* p. 122, emphasis added.

Chapter 13

1. R. C. Zaehner, ed., *The Concise Encyclopedia of Living Faiths* (Boston: Beacon Press, 1959), p. 16.

2. Ibid., pp. 17–18.

3. Ibid., p. 18.

4. Ibid., p. 18, emphasis added.

5. Ibid.

6. Ibid.

7. Ibid., pp. 18–19.

8. Satischandra Chatterjee and Dhirendramohan Datta, *An Introduction to Indian Philosophy* (Calcutta: University of Calcutta, 1950), p. 372.

9. Zaehner, *Concise Encyclopedia,* p. 16.

10. Satischandra Chatterjee and Dhirendramohan Datta, *Introduction to Indian Philosophy,* pp. 358–59.

11. Zaehner, *Concise Encyclopedia*, p. 17.

12. Erich Fromm, *Psychoanalysis and Religion* (New Haven, CT: Yale University Press, 1950), p. 34.

13. Ibid., p. 38.

14. Ibid., p. 45.

15. The two stories are found on ibid., pp. 38–40 and pp. 45–47.

16. Zaehner, *Concise Encyclopedia*, p. 18.

17. Ibid., p. 20.

18. Ibid.

19. A. L. Basham, *Studies in Indian History and Culture* (Calcutta: Sambodhi Publications, 1964), p. 46.

20. Namely, *The Journal of Church and State*.

21. Margaret Stutley and James Stutley, *A Dictionary of Hinduism* (London: Routledge & Kegan Paul, 1977), p. 51.

22. Ibid., p. 52 n. 2.

23. See J. Muir, *Original Sanskrit Texts* (Delhi: Oriental Publishers, 1972), pt. 1, chap. 4.

24. Kenneth K. S. Ch'en, *Buddhism: The Light of Asia* (Woodbury, NY: Barron's Educational Series, 1968), pp. 279–80.

25. Ibid., p. 144.

26. Kenneth K. S. Ch'en, *Buddhism in China: A Historical Survey* (Princeton, NJ: Princeton University Press, 1964), pp. 138–39.

27. Ibid., pp. 138–47.

28. Wm. Theodore de Bary et al., eds., *Sources of Chinese Tradition* (New York: Columbia University Press, 1960) 1: 280. Hui-yüan stated his arguments in greater detail in a treatise entitled: "A Monk Does Not Bow Down Before a King" (*Sha-men pu-ching wang-che lun*) thus: "If one examines the broad essentials of what the teachings of Buddha preach, one will see that they distinguish between those who leave the household life and those who remain in it. Those who remain within the household life and those who leave it are, in all, four kinds. In propagating the doctrine and reaching the beings their achievement is equal to that of emperors and kings, their transfiguring effect greater than that of the way of government. When it comes to affecting members and enlightening the times, there is no age that is without them. But, as chance has it, they sometimes function and sometimes conceal themselves, retiring or making their appearance as the faith diminishes or prospers. What can be discussed in words I beg to state in brief.

"Those who revere the Buddhist laws but remain in their homes are subjects who are obedient to the transforming powers (of temporal rulers). Their feelings have not changed from the customary, and their course of conduct conforms to the secular world. Therefore this way of life includes the affection of natural kinship and proprieties of obedience to authority. Decorum and reverence have their basis herein, and thus they form the basis of the doctrine. That on which they are based has its merit in the past. Thus, on the basis of intimacy it teaches love, and causes the people to appreciate natural kindness; on the basis of austerity it teaches veneration, and causes the people to understand natural respect. The achievement of these two effects derives from an invisible cause. Since the cause is not in the present, one must trace it to its source. Therefore the doctrine makes a punishment of sinful karma, causing one to be fearful and thus circumspect; it makes a reward of those heavenly places, causing one to be joyous and then to act. These are retributions that follow like shadows and echoes, and that are clearly stated in the doctrine. Thus obedience is made the common rule, and the natural way is not changed. . . .

"Hence one may not benefit by (the ruler's) virtue and neglect propriety, bask in his kindness and cast aside due respect. Therefore they who rejoice in the way of Shakya invariably first serve their parents and respect their lords. They who change their way of life and throw away their hair ornaments must always await (their parents') command, then act accordingly. If their lords and parents have doubts, then they retire, inquire of their wishes and wait until (the lords and parents) are enlightened. This, then, is how the teaching of Buddha honours life-giving and assists kingly transformation in the way of government." Ibid., pp. 280–81.

29. Ch'en. *Buddhism in China*, p. 146.

30. Harvey Cox, *The Secular City* (New York: Macmillan, 1955), p. 28.

31. R. J. Zwi Werblowsky, "Judaism, or the Religion of Israel," in Zaehner, *Concise Encyclopedia*, p. 33.

32. Ibid.

33. Ibid., p. 48.

34. H. A. R. Gibb, *Mohammedanism: An Historical Survey* (London: Oxford University Press, 1970), p. 65.

35. Ibid., p. 66.

Chapter 14

1. Though one is usually inclined to associate science with secularism rather than religion, there seems to be some room for viewing it as a "religion." See Robert Lawson Slater, *World Religions and World Community* (New York: Columbia University Press, 1963), p. 35, 240.

2. See Lynn A. de Silva, "Buddhist–Christian Dialogue" in *Inter-Religious Dialogue*, ed. Herbert Jai Singh (Bangalore: Christian Institute of Religion and Society, 1967), p. 178.

3. Ibid.

4. K. N. Jayatilleke, *The Buddhist Attitude to Other Religions* (Ceylon: Public Trustee Department, 1966), p. 23. Jayatilleke quotes the description from Anguttara Nikāya 1.227–28 and remarks: "This conception of the universe as consisting of hundreds of thousands of clusters of galactic systems containing thousands of suns and moons . . . was much in advance of the age in which it appears." Ibid. On the other hand, Lynn A. de Silva comments: "Buddhist cosmology which conceived suns as a vertical static three-dimensional universe

with thirty-one planes, is a notion derived from primitive *folklore* and is not in keeping with what astronomy knows of the universe." "Buddhist–Christian Dialogue," p. 186. However, by identifying the concept of "vertical static three-dimensional universe with thirty-one planes" as deriving from *folklore,* a way out has been provided from a Buddhist apologetic point of view, for then it is possible to argue, as Jayatelleke does, that the description of universe cited by him as early Buddhist, "in later Theravada . . . gets embedded in and confused with mythical notions about the universe." *Buddhist Attitude,* p. 23.

5. See Huston Smith, foreword to Philip Kapleau, *The Three Pillars of Zen* (Boston: Beacon Press, 1967).

6. Comparisons between Buddhism and modern science have usually been carried out in an apologetic context (see De Silva, "Buddhist–Christian Dialogue," pp. 178, 186, etc.) under the perhaps short-sighted (ibid., p. 187) impression that it is to Buddhism's credit if it is in accord with science. In this section, however, no such implication is intended.

7. Slater, *World Religions,* p. 35. Elsewhere too Slater remarks: "There is a third characteristic of the scientific spirit which is most important of all—the scientists' disciplined readiness to revise, and even abandon, cherished explanations when faced by hostile data and more adequate explanations. The word disciplined is used advisedly. It is no easier for the 'natural man' in the science laboratory than it is for the 'natural man' anywhere else to forsake opinions to which he has grown accustomed. It is only by a loyal acceptance of the stern ethic of research, and by years of scientific training that he attains sufficient strength of mind to do so." Ibid., p. 241 n. 33.

8. Wm. Theodore de Bary, ed., *Sources of Indian Tradition* (New York: Columbia University Press, 1958), 1: 100.

9. Ibid., p. 101, emphasis added.

10. Ibid., n. 3. This aspect of Buddhist relativism seems to have been somewhat overlooked in Slater, *World Religions,* chap. 4.

11. See Gunapala Dharmasiri, *A Buddhist Critique of the Christian Concept of God* (Colombo: Lake House Investments, 1974), passim.

12. I am indebted to Rev. Eric Pyle for this hypothetical comparison.

13. See Ninian Smart, *The Philosophy of Religion* (New York: Random House, 1970), p. 163.

14. Buddhism has changed, too, and will perhaps continue to do so, but these changes may be called glacial on a geological metaphor and may be contrasted with the more rapid changes of science, which may be called meteoric on an astronomical metaphor.

15. Carol S. Robb, "Liberties, Claims, Entitlements, and Trumps: Reproductive Rights and Ecological Responsibilities," *Journal of Religious Ethics* 26, no. 2 (Fall 1998): 289.

16. Ibid.

17. Ibid., p. 290.

18. Ibid.

19. Ibid., p. 291.

20. Ibid.
21. Ibid., pp. 290–91.
22. Ibid., pp. 289–90, 291.
23. Ibid., p. 291.
24. Ibid.
25. See Joseph Prabhu, "Dharma as an Alternative to Human Rights," in *Studies in Orientology: Essays in Memory of Prof. A. Basham*, ed. S. K. Maity, Upendra Thakur, and A. K. Narain (Agra, India: Y.K. Publishers, 1988), pp. 174–79.
26. Ibid., p. 176.
27. Ibid.
28. Ibid., p. 178.
29. Ibid. The two senses are explained earlier by Prabhu as follows (ibid., p. 175): "I start with the notion of human rights. The term 'right' has two different senses, one connoting righteousness or conformity to some standard as when we say, for example, that it is right that X should visit her grandmother who is ill; the second connoting entitlement, as when I say that I have a right to privacy. Now, while there may be cases where the two senses converge, such that, for example, it is both right and a matter of right to keep a contractual promise, the two concepts are by no means synonymous. Thus, if I am being mugged and you happen to be a bystander, it is right that you help me, but I have no right to your help. The same asymmetry prevails in the matter of duties and rights. In spite of the fact that rights have an essentially relational structure, such that A has a right to something with respect to other parties, the obligation created by the relationship may well conflict with what these other parties regard as their duty in the situation. The classic example here is civil disobedience."
30. Ibid., p. 179. Prabhu explains (ibid.): "It is obvious that this is a holistic and hierarchical model of life and the world, where duties, roles and functions are stressed within an overarching order of right. The whole social order exists in order to enable the attainment of liberation (*mokṣa*) or final beatitude (*parama-śreyasa*) on the part of the individual and not as an end in itself. Social ideals like freedom, justice and equality are relativized to the larger order encompassing the three worlds. And with this relativization a final contrast to the conception of human rights may be drawn. The notion of righteousness is no longer defined in purely moral or social terms, but rather in cosmic terms of harmony with the primordial order, even while acting to maintain it."
31. See Summer B. Twiss, "Moral Grounds and Plural Cultures: Interpreting Human Rights in the International Community," *Journal of Religious Ethics* 26, no. 2 (Fall 1998): 272; Robb, "Liberties, Claims," p. 286; John Witte Jr., "Law, Religion and Human Rights," *Columbia Human Rights Law Review* 28, no. 1 (Fall 1996): 13; Gregory Baum, "Human Rights: An Ethical Perspective," *Ecumenist*, May/June 1994, pp. 64–65, and passim.
32. Witte, "Law, Religion and Human Rights," p. 13.

33. Robb, "Liberties, Claims," p. 286.

34. Puruṣottama Bilimoria, "Rights and Duties: The (Modern) Indian Dilemma," in *Ethical and Political Dilemmas in Modern India*, ed. Ninian Smart and Shivesh Thakur (New York: St. Martin's Press, 1993), pp. 35–36.

35. Ibid., p. 48.

36. Robert Traer, *Faith in Human Rights* (Washington, DC: Georgetown University Press, 1991), p. 73.

37. See S. Cromwell Crawford, *Dilemmas of Life and Death: Hindu Ethics in North American Context* (Albany: State University of New York Press, 1995), pp. 162–66.

38. Louis Henkin, "Religion, Religions, and Human Rights," *Journal of Religious Ethics* 26, no. 2 (Fall 1998): 239.

39. See Kana Mitra, "Human Rights in Hinduism," in *Human Rights in Religious Traditions*, ed. Arlene Swidler (New York: Pilgrim Press, 1982), pp. 78–79.

40. See Robert Payne, *The Life and Death of Mahatma Gandhi* (New York: E. P. Dutton, 1995), pp. 460–67.

41. In this Mahatma Gandhi was opposed by some leading thinkers. Rabindranath Tagore wrote: "I believe that to wait till the moral sense of man becomes a great deal more powerful than it is now and till then to allow countless generations of children to suffer privations and untimely death for no fault of their own is a great social injustice which should not be tolerated." Cited in Crawford, *Dilemmas*, pp. 175–76.

42. William A. Young, *The World's Religions: Worldviews and Contemporary Issues* (Englewood Cliffs, NJ: Prentice-Hall, 1995), pp. 127–28.

43. Crawford, *Dilemmas*, p. 195.

44. K. Satchidananda Murty, *Vedic Hermeneutics* (Delhi: Motilal Banarsidass, 1993), pp. 62–63.

45. Ibid., pp. 62–63, emphasis added.

46. K. M. Panikkar, *Hindu Society at Cross Roads* (Bombay: Asia Publishing House, 1961), p. 68. The provision can be abused (ibid., pp. 688–89) as well as overstated (Manusmṛti 1.107–10) but it nevertheless remains valid.

47. See Hartmut Scharfe, *The State in Indian Tradition* (Leiden: E. J. Brill, 1989), p. 220 n. 125.

Chapter 15

1. W. Brede Kristensen, *The Meaning of Religion*, trans. J. B. Carman (The Hague: Martinus Nijhoff, 1960), p. 2.

2. Ibid., p. 3.

3. Ibid.

4. Ibid., emphasis added.

5. G. van der Leeuw, *Religion in Essence and Manifestation*, trans. J. E. Turner (London: George Allen & Unwin, 1963), 2: 676.

6. Kristensen, *Meaning of Religion*, p. 4.
7. Ibid., p. 3.
8. Van der Leeuw, *Religion*, 2: 672.
9. Ibid., last emphasis supplied.
10. Also compare Kristensen's use of the word *meaning* (*Meaning of Religion*, p. 6) and understanding (ibid.) with its use by van der Leeuw (*Religion*, pp. 672–73).

Chapter 16

1. Erich Fromm, *Psychoanalysis and Religion* (New Haven, CT: Yale University Press, 1950), p. 43.
2. Ibid., p. 34.
3. Ibid., p. 34–35.
4. Ibid., pp. 35–36.
5. Ibid., p. 37.
6. Ibid.
7. Ibid., pp. 37–38.
8. Walpola Rahula, *What the Buddha Taught*, rev. ed. (expanded) (New York: Grove Press, 1974), pp. 2–3.
9. Fromm, *Psychoanalysis and Religion*, pp. 45–47.
10. Ibid., p. 45.
11. Ibid., p. 44.
12. This is to be distinguished from phenomenological classification, which is typically thematic.
13. This has been the received wisdom for so long that it had found its way into general accounts of world history already even in the 1930s: "Mesopotamia produced a number of religious epics comparable to the Osiris myth in Egypt. Foremost here was the Gilgamesh epic, which tells of Creation and the first man. Scholars believe that the Hebrews obtained their biblical story of Creation and of Adam from this Babylonian source. There was another account of a great flood which destroyed all humanity save one man, the basis for the biblical legend of Noah and the ark." Harry Elmer Harnes, *A History of Western Civilization* (New York: Harcourt, Brace and Company, 1935), 1: 37.
14. William Ellery Leonard, *Gilgamesh: Epic of Old Babylonia* (New York: Viking Press, 1934), p. 67. Also see Danny P. Jackson et al., *The Epic of Gilgamesh* (Wauconda, IL: Bolchazy–Carducci Publishers, 1997), p. 82, and illustration on p. 83.
15. A. Heidel, *The Gilgamesh Epic and Old Testament Parallels* (Chicago: University of Chicago Press, 1949), p. 254.

Chapter 17

1. Quoted by Eric J. Sharpe, *Comparative Religion: A History*, 2nd ed. (London: Duckworth, 1986), p. 228.

2. W. Bede Kristensen, *The Meaning of Religion*, trans. J. B. Carman (The Hague: Martinus Nijhoff, 1960), p. 7.

3. Ibid.

4. Edward Conze, "Buddhism: The Mahāyāna," in *The Concise Encyclopedia of Living Faiths*, ed. R. C. Zaehner (Boston: Beacon Press, 1967), p. 301.

5. Ibid.

6. Ibid., p. 302.

7. Ibid., pp. 298–99. Also see Kenneth K. S. Ch'en, *Buddhism: The Light of Asia* (Woodbury, NY: Barron's Educational Series, 1968), p. 69.

8. Edward J. Thomas, *The History of Buddhist Thought* (New York: Barnes & Noble., 1971), p. 211.

9. Conze, "Buddhism," p. 301.

10. See Claude Alan Stark, *God of All* (Cape Cod, MA: Claude Stark, 1974), passim. Also see Arvind Sharma, *Ramakrishna and Vivekananda: New Perspectives* (New Delhi: Sterling Publishers, 1989).

11. Edward J. Thomas, *History of Buddhist Thought*, p. 193.

Chapter 18

1. F. Staal, *Exploring Mysticism* (Harmondsworth, UK: Penguin, 1975), p. 182.

2. Ibid., p. 17.

3. Ibid.

4. Lama Anagarika Govinda, *The Psychological Attitude of Early Buddhist Philosophy* (London: Rider & Company, 1961), p. 39.

5. Ibid., pp. 36–37.

6. Rune E. A. Johansson, *The Psychology of Nirvana* (London: George Allen & Unwin, 1969), p. 11.

7. Ibid.

8. Heinrich Zimmer, *Philosophies of India*, ed. Joseph Campbell (New York: Pantheon Books, 1951), pp. 167–69.

9. Ibid., p. 169.

10. Erich Fromm, *Psychoanalysis and Religion* (New Haven, CT: Yale University Press, 1950), pp. 39–40.

11. James P. McDermott, "Karma and Rebirth in Early Buddhism," in *Karma and Rebirth in Classical Indian Traditions*, ed. Wendy Doniger O'Flaherty (Berkeley and Los Angeles: University of California Press, 1980), p. 171.

12. Edward Conze, *Buddhist Scriptures* (Harmondsworth, UK: Penguin, 1959), pp. 231–32.

13. K. N. Jayatilleke, *The Message of the Buddha*, ed. Ninian Smart (London: George Allen & Unwin, 1975), p. 34, emphasis added.

14. Ibid.

15. Nalinaksha Dutt, *Early Monastic Buddhism* (Calcutta: Calcutta Oriental Book Agency, 1960), pp. 150–51.

16. Conze, *Buddhist Scriptures*, p. 72. It is worth speculating what Buddhaghosa might have said about the following anecdote about Confucius, which "has shocked missionaries who have made the mistake of judging Confucius as the founder of a religion rather than as a gentleman: 'Ju Pei wished to visit Confucius. Confucius excused himself, saying that he was unwell. But as Ju Pei's messenger was going out of the door, Confucius took his lute and began singing before the messenger was out of hearing' " (Analects, 17.20) Quoted in A. C. Graham "Confucianism" in *The Concise Encyclopedia of Living Faiths*, ed. R. C. Zaehner (Boston: Beacon Press, 1959), p. 371.

17. Conze, *Buddhist Scriptures*, pp. 72–73.

18. J. B. Horner, trans., *The Collection of the Middle Length Sayings* (Majjhima-Nikāya) (London: Pali Text Society, 1957), 2: 288–89.

19. G. P. Malasasekera, ed., *Encyclopedia of Buddhism* (Colombo: Government of Ceylon, 1960), 1: 627–28.

20. Zimmer, *Philosophies of India*, pp. 167–68.

21. Ibid., p. 169.

22. Fromm, *Psychoanalysis and Religion*, p. 77.

23. Ibid.

24. *Abstracts: American Academy of Religion, Society for Biblical Literature, Annual Meeting 1987* (Decatur, GA: Scholars Press, 1987), p. 133.

25. K. N. Jayatilleke, *Early Buddhist Theory of Knowledge* (London: George Allen & Unwin, 1963), p. 438.

26. Dutt, *Early Monastic Buddhism*, p. 92.

27. Jayatilleke, *Early Buddhist Theory of Knowledge*, pp. 440, 468.

28. Sigmund Freud, *An Outline of Psycho-Analysis*, trans. James Strachey (New York: W. W. Norton & Company, 1949), pp. 34–35.

29. Conze, *Buddhist Scriptures*, pp. 131–32.

30. Fromm, *Psychoanalysis and Religion*, p. 79ff.

31. See Edward Conze, I. B. Horner, David Snellgrove, and Arthur Waley, eds. *Buddhist Texts Through the Ages* (New York: Philosophical Library, 1954), pp. 77–78.

32. McDermott, "Karma and Rebirth," pp. 171–72.

33. It is interesting, given the fact that in the past the question was sometimes raised whether Buddhism should be called a religion at all, that modern alternative religions like Marxism and depth psychology both sense an affinity with Buddhism (see Zaehner, *Concise Encyclopedia*, pp. 407, 414).

Chapter 19

1. Huston Smith, "Wasson's Soma: A Review Article," *Journal of the American Academy of Religion* 40, no. 4 (1972): 481, n. 2(c).

2. Walter Huston Clark, *Chemical Ecstasy* (New York: Sheed & Ward, 1969), pp. 71–72, emphasis added.

3. R. E. L. Masters and Jean Houston, *The Varieties of Psychedelic Experience* (New York: Dell, 1966), p. 62, emphasis added.

4. Ibid., p. 9.

5. Ibid., pp. 18–25, emphasis added. The rest of the account runs as follows (ibid):

> For a period of time I had neither capacity nor wish to measure, I pondered this vision. Then, when the music had ended, I lay on my back and looked up at the ceiling where a kaleidoscope of images from ancient civilizations flickered rapidly before my eyes. Egypt and Greece, Assyria and old China sped across the ceiling. Flickering pharaohs, fluttering Parthenons and a palpitating Nebuchadnezzar—all contributed to this panoramic, historical agitation.
>
> And suddenly—destruction! The air was thick with the ammonia smell of death. Noxious vapours stung the eyes and choked the throat. The stench of the Apocalypse rose up with the opening of the graves of the new and old dead. It was the nostrils' view of the *Night on Bald Mountain*, an olfactory *Walpurgisnacht* rite. The world had become a reeking decay. Then I heard R rebuking someone with the words: "Christ, Timmy, couldn't you have used your sandbox?" Timmy was the cat and the apocalyptic smell had issued from a single turd he had deposited in the middle of the floor.
>
> I turned my attention to Timmy's tangible residues to Timmy himself. He stretched himself with infinite grace and arched his back to begin—*The Ballet*. Leaping through time and space, he hung like Nijinsky—suspended in the air for a millennium, and then, drifting languidly down to the ground, he pirouetted to a paw-licking standstill. He then stretched out one paw in a tentative movement and propelled himself into a mighty spiral, whirling into cosmic dust, then up on his toes for a bow to his creation.
>
> He was a cat no longer—but Indra, the primeval God dancing the cosmic dance in that time before time, setting up a rhythmic flux in non-being until it at last had attained to Life. The animating waves of the Dance of Creation pulsed all around me and I could no longer refuse to join in the dance. I arose to perform a *pas de deux* with the cat-Indra, but before I could allow myself more than a cursory leap into the cosmic fray a great flame erupted somewhere in the hearth and it commanded I concentrate upon it to the exclusion of all else.
>
> It was a lovely fire. Mandalas played in it and so did gods, and so did many hundreds of beings, known and unknown, rising in El Greco attenuations for one brilliant moment, only to lapse again into nothing. I fell into musing and after aeons had gone by and worlds within worlds within worlds had been explored, I looked up and said something to R. It was an attempt to define our relationship at the precise moment, and I said: "You and I, we are ships that sometimes pass one another on the seas but never meet." "Bull——!" said R—and my vast, rippling reflections were shattered.
>
> '"Let's get out of here!" I said. "Where to?" he asked, and seemed to find his question very funny. "Where to go?" he asked

again, convulsed with laughter and managed to add: "as if there were any other 'where' or 'to.' " "Where to, Brute?" he howled, and along with our guide we *headed for the second-floor apartment of a friend whose roomful of Buddhas I had planned to inspect.*

We began to descend the two flights of stairs and they never ended. Down, down, down, down, down, down, down—into the bowels of some ultimate cavern—into the centre of the earth, no doubt—or perhaps into nowhere—to descend the stairs, forever and ever. "Will they never end?" I asked, starting to panic. "Only one more flight," I was assured. And then, infinity of stair steps later, we arrived and entered the roomful of Buddhas and everything brightened.

The room was a cacophony of Buddhas! Screaming gold Gautamas seared the eye from their sunspot Satoris. Seething stone saviours revealed a Buddha-to-come in each of their granular particles. Wooden hermaphrodite Lords-of-the-East reconciled all opposites, all dualities, and all dialectics. "Yin, Yang, Jung!" I cried, and dragged R toward another room with a balcony just over the street. But the journey was long, and I felt like Alice when she had to go twice as long in order just to stay in the same place.

From the balcony the crowded street leaped up to greet us and it seemed we had only to reach out to touch the passers-by. A painted elf skipped past us and I looked after him in astonishment. "Just a fairy," R explained. "I thought it was an elf," said I—for all double meanings were lost on me. A decrepit old gargoyle tottered by. "Poor old gargoyle," said I. "He can't find his chapel." And suddenly I felt very sad, for the whole of life became explainable in terms of men losing their potentialities by default and decaying into gargoyles which could yet be happy if only they could find their proper niche—their own flying buttress, overlooking eternity.

Continuing to observe the scene below from the balcony, it seemed that my consciousness was projected downward, and with my perceptions, so that I saw the passer-by as if I were standing on the sidewalk and confronting them. *From this perspective, they became an animated waxworks*, escapees from Madame Tussaud, who bit their wax nails, clutched their wax newspapers and knit their wax brows as they thought waxen thoughts. I kept wondering how long they could keep up this charade before they melted down into puddles and oozed away along the pavement.

One strange creature approached us slowly, then yawned to reveal little stalagmite clay teeth set in a grotto of red dust. Suddenly, as if just making his decision, he turned and climbed onto a bus. I then noticed that people got on and got off of this bus. On and off. On and off. On and off. The eternal return. Primitive yet Christian. Circular but linear. And the bus plunged ahead along the route of its manifest destiny, then stopped a short distance down the street, while people kept climbing aboard at intervals to catch its life force, but only to be deposited unceremoniously along the byways of their partial, all-too-partial life segments. But where was the bus going? Toward what ultimate destination? Heaven? Fort Tryon Park? Utopia? Perhaps it was a million years away.

It seemed that a horde of people came bearing down upon us—tides of grey automata threatening to engulf us. "Don't worry," I consoled R. "I shall be Moses." And raising my arm, the crowd parted and we were free to enter the Promised Land.

People continued to stream towards us and past us. I focused on an old lady in her late seventies, a dowdy pathetic creature dressed in shabby black and carrying impossibly huge shipping bags. As she made her way heavily towards us I saw, no longer much to my astonishment, that she began to lose years. I saw her as an Italian matriarch in her sixties, then in her fifties. As she continued to bloom backwards in time, she entered her portly forties and, after that, her housewifely thirties. Her face softened, and her body grew more shapely, and still the years kept on dropping away. In her twenties she was carrying a child, and then she was a bride and carried orange blossoms. A moment later and she was a child who, in turn, shrank into a newborn baby carried by a midwife. The baby's umbilical cord was still intact and it let out a howl of awakening life. But then the process was reversed and the baby grew back into childhood, became again a bride, passed through her thirties, forties, fifties, sixties, and was the old lady in her seventies I had seen at the beginning. The old woman blinked, her eyes closed for a fraction of a second, and in that instant I clearly saw her death mask. She passed us by and had moved a little down the street when I heard from the direction she had come a baby's howl of awakening life. I turned my head, expecting to perceive afresh Our Lady of the Eternal Return, but saw instead the vortex of a crowd.

The vortex was streaming into the giant doorway of a giant building. It atomized into points of energy, radial lights and shimmering vortices converging into a single solar concentration that seethed in thermal fury to explode at last into a kaleidoscopic burst of falling jewels. Some sound had evidently come to my attention and a golden shovel crunched into a mound of opals near which was a sign that bore the incomprehensible words: DIG WE MUST FOR A GROWING NEW YORK. An ironclad tympany bruised the ears with a raucous counterpoint of digging. Construction destruction or something was in process and two protean tractors loomed before us, large and living. In their cabs these vital creatures bore little robot manikins—absurd toy trinkets, which undoubtedly they wound up every morning to mimic the motions of life. How proper it all seemed—the Man-machine playing at noblesse oblige with the machine-man. But between themselves, the living tractors maintained an uneasy truce. A crystal shelf shattered under the collective impact of their heavy, separate blows. Its sonic vibration stung the nervous system and prepared one for war. The tractors made ready for mutual assault, swinging their shovel-antennae high in the air and bellowing metallic curses at one another. Dive and attack! Attack and dive! But then their clanging vituperations acquired a primeval resonance. Voices were screaming from out of an early swamp. And I saw that the warring tractors were warring dinosaurs, their long necks diving and attacking in sinuous combat. "Too much!" I thought, and with what seemed a great effort of will I returned through the centuries to —— Street.

We continued our vigil from the terrace, but now I looked down on the scene below as if from a very high place. *I chanced to observe a particularly rough square of pavement and what I saw there caused me to cry out to R to come over and share this latest wonder. For there below us in that square of pavement lay all of Manhattan—its canyons, and skyscrapers and parks and people—laid out beneath us in miniature.* The proportions, the infinite details were perfect. We could have been in an airplane flying low over the city. But here it was in a common block of pavement—the city within the city. We could have swooped down like gods and lifted up the Empire State Building if we had so wished. But our ethics precluded that, and we left the little microcosm as it was.

And so it went—a ten thousand years'-long adventure condensed somehow into a few brief hours. It all ended very suddenly for me, when a parking meter I was watching abruptly flipped its red Time Expired flag. And I knew it was over.

The account just concluded describes quite a few of the usual phenomena of the psychedelic drug experience. The altered awareness of time is frequently mentioned and is well exemplified in the subject's description of the interminable descent down the stairs. Mood changes abruptly, often in response to awareness of some perceptual stimulus. A great many altered perceptions—visual, auditory, and olfactory—are mentioned. There are vivid eyes-closed images, the empathic experiencing of a picture, and the "projection" of consciousness to a point some distance from the body with visual perception appearing to be from that point and not from the actual physical location of the organs of sight.

Making some order out of and deriving something of value from these curious experiences and others like them will be a main concern of this book.

6. See Swami Saradananda, *Sri Ramakrishna The Great Master* trans. Swami Jagadananda (Madras: Sri Ramakrsna Math, 1952), pp. 195–97.

7. Ibid., p. 196. In this context also see Nirad C. Chaudhuri, *Hinduism: A Religion to Live By* (New York: Oxford University Press, 1979), pp. 248–54.

8. Wilhelm Halbfass, *India and Europe: An Essay in Understanding* (Albany: State University of New York Press, 1988), p. 14.

9. Heinrich Zimmer, *Myths and Symbols in Indian Art and Civilization,* ed. Joseph Campbell (New York: Harper & Row, 1946), p. 172ff.

10. Masters and Houston, *Varieties of Psychedelic Experience,* p. 315.

11. Swami Nikhilananda, trans., *The Gospel of Sri Ramakrishna* (New York: Ramakrishna-Vivekananda Center, 1952), pp. 941–42, emphasis added.

12. Also see the account of Rāmakṛṣṇa's vision of Kālī in Saradananda, *Sri Ramakrishna,* pp. 201–2.

13. Paul Brunton reports having such an experience with Ramana Maharshi; see B. V. Narasimha Swami, *Self-Realization—The Life and Teachings of Sri Ramana Maharshi* (Tiruvannamalai: Sri Ramanasramam, 1985), p. 236.

14. See Paul B. Courtright, *Gaṇeśa: Lord of Obstacles, Lord of Beginnings* (New York: Oxford University Press, 1985); Daivajna K. N. Somayaji, *Concept of Ganesa* (Bangalore: Kalpataru Research Academy, 1983); Haridas Mitra, *Ganapati* (Santiniketan: Visva-Bharati, n.d.); V. R. Mani, *Sons of Siva: A Study in the Religious Cults of Ganesa and Karttikeya* (New Delhi: Sharada Prakashan, 1990); Lakshmi Lal, *Ganesh: Beyond the Form* (Bombay: Book Quest, 1992); Alice Getty, *Gaṇeśa* (New Delhi: Munshiram Manoharlal, 1971); Robert L. Brown, ed., *Ganesh: Studies of an Asian God* (Albany: State University of New York Press, 1991).

15. Masters and Houston, *Varieties of Psychedelic Experience,* pp. 27–28.

16. Zimmer, *Myths and Symbols,* p. 70.

17. Masters and Houston, *Varieties of Psychedelic Experience,* p. 14.

18. Ibid., p. 15.

19. Saradananda, *Sri Ramakrishna,* pp. 261–62.

20. Masters and Houston, *Varieties of Psychedelic Experience,* p. 16, emphasis added.

21. Saradananda, *Sri Ramakrishna,* p. 157.

22. Ibid., p. 161 and passim.

23. Masters and Houston, *Varieties of Psychedelic Experience,* p. 14.

24. Saradananda, *Sri Ramakrishna,* pp. 261–62. The word is used here with some hesitation.

25. Ibid., pp. 383–85.

26. Masters and Houston, *Varieties of Psychedelic Experience,* p. 258.

27. Ibid., p. 237.

28. Ibid., p. 223.

29. Ibid., p. 226.

30. Ibid., p. 315. "We want to mention, too, that we hope we have established the very great importance and challenge of the eidetic images and the need to study them exhaustively both within the context of the psychedelic drug-state and outside it. Most curiously, the importance of these images has been all but overlooked by most workers, and the symbolic dramas have been ignored or barely mentioned by writers with whose work we are familiar. If these images and dramas still are but little understood, at

least we now have a much better understanding of their potential value for the psychedelic subject."

31. Ibid., p. 313.

32. Ibid., pp. 11–12.

33. Quoted in Saradananda, *Sri Ramakrishna,* p. 585.

Chapter 20

1. P. V. Kane, *History of Dharmaśāstra* (Poona: Bhandarkar Oriental Research Institute, 1974), vol. 2, pt. 2, pp. 930–31. It is not entirely clear whether, in preclassical Hinduism, the last two of the four stages of life were clearly distinguished. For a more recent work see Patrick Olivelle, *The Āśrama System: The History and Hermeneutics of a Religious Institution* (New York: Oxford University Press, 1993).

2. This sense of the word *āśrama* as a stage of life, must be clearly distinguished from its other meaning of a hermitage; see Monier Monier-Williams, *A Sanskrit-English Dictionary* (Oxford: Clarendon Press, 1970), p. 158. For its etymology see Kane, *History of Dharmaśāstra,* p. 425. For a very brief description see Kenneth W. Morgan, ed., *The Religion of the Hindus* (New York: Ronald Press Company, 1953), p. 20.

3. Kane, *History of Dharmaśāstra,* pp. 944–45.

4. Thus the people discussed in such works as David M. Miller and Dorothy C. Wertz, *Hindu Monastic Life: The Monks and Monasteries of Bhubaneswar* (Montreal: McGill-Queens University Press, 1976) are excluded.

5. Kane, *History of Dharmaśāstra,* p. 952.

6. Ibid., p. 946.

7. Benjamin Walker, *The Hindu World* (New York: Frederick A. Praeger, 1968), 1: 85, emphasis added.

8. Kane, *History of Dharmaśāstra,* p. 933.

9. The following is the minimum criterion of *sannyāsa* according to one view: "Having renounced his desire for wealth, for sons, for fear of social opprobrium, and the love of social approval, they sally back forth begging for food. This is the minimum criterion." Agehananda Bharati, *The Ochre Robe* (London: George Allen & Unwin, 1961), p. 150. See also Kane, *History of Dharmaśāstra,* p. 931.

10. T. M. P. Mahadevan, *Outlines of Hinduism* (Bombay: Chetana, 1971), pp. 147, 150, 251.

11. Henry K. Beauchamp, ed., *Hindu Manners, Customs and Ceremonies by the Abbe J. Dubois* (Oxford: Clarendon Press, 1928), p. 527. Also see Olivelle, *Āśrama System,* p. 176 n. 34.

12. This statement is made on the basis of the author's own contact with numerous *sannyāsins* in India.

13. Bharati, *Ochre Robe,* p. 158–59, 167.

14. Ibid., p. 158

15. On Nārāyaṇa see Manusmṛti 1.10. Also see Walker, *Hindu World,* 1: 123–24.

16. Kane, *History of Dharmaśāstra,* p. 957 n. 2189, mentions the expression *brahmabhājana* occurring in the texts, wherein it could mean the bowl of alms or the body of the ascetic.

17. For another attempt to apply Durkheimian analysis to *sannyāsa,* see Louis Dumont, *Homo Hierarchicus: The Caste System and Its Implications* (Chicago: University of Chicago Press, 1980), pp. 51–52.

18. Emile Durkheim, *The Elementary Forms of the Religious Life,* trans. Joseph Ward Swain (London: George Allen & Unwin, 1925), p. 10.

19. S. G. F. Brandon et al., *A Dictionary of Comparative Religion* (New York: Charles Scribner's Sons, 1973), p. 583.

20. J. T. F. Jordens, *Dayānanda Sarasvatī: His Life and Ideas* (Delhi: Oxford University Press, 1978), p. 20, emphasis added.

21. R. C. Majumdar, *Svami Vivekananda: A Historical Review* (Calcutta: General Printers and Publishers, 1965), p. 21.

22. Ibid., p. 22.

23. Sailendra Nath Dhar, *A Comprehensive Biography of Swami Vivekananda* (Madras: Vivekananda Prakashan Kendra, 1975), pt. 1, p. 248.

24. Ibid.

25. Veena Das, *Structure and Cognition: Aspects of Hindu Caste and Ritual,* 2nd ed. (Delhi: Oxford University Press, 1982), p. 117.

26. Durkheim, *Elementary Forms,* p. 444. In his conclusion he writes: "In summing up, then, we must say that society is not all the illogical or a-logical, incoherent and fantastic being which it has too been considered. Quite on the contrary, the collective consciousness is the highest form of the physical life, since it is the consciousness of the consciousness. Being placed outside of and above individual and local contingencies, it sees things only in their permanent and essential aspects, which it crystallizes into communicable ideas. At the same time that it sees from above, it sees farther; at every moment in time, it embraces all known reality; that is why it alone can furnish the mind with the moulds which are applicable to the totality of things and which make it possible to think of them. It does not create these moulds artificially; it finds them within itself; it does nothing but become conscious of them. They translate the ways of being which are found in all the stages of reality but which appear in their full clarity only at the summit, because the extreme complexity of the psychic life which passes there necessitates a greater development of consciousness."

27. Dhar, *Comprehensive Biography,* p. 352.

28. Paramhansa Yogananda, *Autobiography of a Yogi* (Los Angeles: Self-Realization Fellowship, 1956), chap. 2.

29. Milton Singer, ed., *Krishna: Myths, Rites, Attitudes* (Honolulu: East-West Center Press, 1966), pp. 103, 112, 208; Benjamin Walker, *The Hindu World* (New York: Frederick A. Praeger, 1968), 1: 561; and Surinder Mohan Bhardwaj, *Hindu Places of Pilgrimage in India* (Berkeley and Los Angeles: University of California Press, 1973), pp. 81, 88.

30. Madadev Haribhai Desai, *Mahatma Gandhi: The Story of My Experiments with Truth*, trans. Pyarelal Nair, parts 4–5 (Ahmedabad: Navajivan Press, 1929), p. 27.

31. Ved Mehta, *Gandhi and His Apostles* (New York: Viking Press, 1976), pp. 59–65.

32. As he was affectionately called.

33. Troy Wilson Organ, *Hinduism: Its Historical Developments* (Woodbury, NY: Barron's Educational Series, 1974), p. 366.

Chapter 21

1. W. Montgomery Watt, *Bell's Introduction to the Qur'ān* (Edinburgh: Edinburgh University Press, 1977), p. 158.

2. Qur'ān 5.116: "O Jesus, son of Mary! Didst thou say unto mankind: Take me and my mother for two Gods beside Allah?" (M. Pickthall's translation.) Also see Qur'ān 5.17.

3. A similar situation can be seen in relation to Hinduism when the roles of both virgins and mothers are glorified, though one cannot become a mother normally without ceasing to be a virgin.

4. This seems to be the implication of Qur'ān 5.17.

5. Hans Küng, "Christianity and World Religions: Dialogue with Islam," in *Toward a Universal Theology of Religion*, ed. Leonard Swidler (Maryknoll, NY: Orbis Books, 1987), pp. 202–3. I will also pass over his suggestion here that Muḥammad may have gained his information about Christianity from sources representing Jewish Christianity. Ibid., 205–6.

6. J. G. Davis, "Christianity: The Early Church," in *The Concise Encyclopedia of Living Faiths*, ed. R. C. Zaehner (Boston: Beacon Press, 1959), pp. 54–55.

7. R. J. Zwi Werblowsky, "Eschatology: An Overview," in *The Encyclopedia of Religion*, ed. Mircea Eliade (New York: Macmillan, 1987), 5: 150.

8. A. L. Basham, *The Wonder That Was India* (London: Sidgwick & Jackson, 1988), p. 321.

9. Ibid., p. 307.

Conclusion

1. Kimberley C. Patton and Benjamin C. Ray, eds., *A Magic Still Dwells: Comparative Religion in the Postmodern Age* (Berkeley and Los Angeles: University of California Press, 2000), p. 1.

2. Benson Saler, *Conceptualizing Religion: Immanent Anthropologists, Transcendent Natives, and Unbounded Categories* (Leiden: E. J. Brill, 1993).

3. Ibid., p. 225.

4. Ibid., p. 208. The prototypicality of these religions themselves is also duly recognized (ibid., p. 217).

5. Ibid., p. 223.
6. Ibid., p. 221.
7. Ibid., p. 223.
8. Ibid., p. 200.
9. Jonathan Z. Smith, "The 'End' of Comparison: Redescription and Rectification," in Patton and Ray, *Magic Still Dwells*, p. 237.
10. Ibid., p. 239.
11. Robert Cummings Neville, *Religious Truth: A Volume in the Comparative Religious Ideas Project* (Albany: State University of New York Press, 2001), p. xiii.
12. Ninian Smart, *Dimensions of the Sacred* (Berkeley and Los Angeles: University of California Press, 1996), p. 5.
13. Ibid., p. 13.
14. Ibid., pp. 10–11.
15. Ibid., pp. 7–8.
16. Ibid., p. 8.
17. Ibid., p. 6.
18. William E. Paden, *Religious Worlds: The Comparative Study of Religion* (Boston: Beacon Press, 1988).
19. Wesley J. Wildham, "Annotated Bibliography: Theories of Comparison," in *Ultimate Realities: A Volume in the Comparative Religious Ideas Project*, ed. Robert Cummings Neville (Albany: State University of New York Press, 2001), p. 335.
20. Dale Cannon, *Six Ways of Being Religious: A Framework for Comparative Studies of Religion* (Belmont, CA: Wadsworth Publishing Co., 1996).
21. Ibid., pp. 11, 71.
22. Ibid., p. 9.
23. Ibid., chap. 15.

Author Index

Subject Index